The Hip Hop Reader

TITLES IN THE LONGMAN TOPICS READER SERIES

A LONGMAN TOPICS READER

The Hip Hop Reader

TIM STRODE
Nassau Community College

TIM WOOD
Nassau Community College

PEARSON

Longman

New York   San Francisco   Boston
London   Toronto   Sydney   Tokyo   Singapore   Madrid
Mexico City   Munich   Paris   Cape Town   Hong Kong   Montreal

Senior Sponsoring Editor: Virginia L. Blanford
Senior Supplements Editor: Donna Campion
Senior Marketing Manager: Sandra McGuire
Project Coordination, Text Design, and Electronic Page Makeup:
  Carlisle Publishing Services
Production Manager: Bob Ginsberg
Cover Design Manager: Wendy Ann Fredericks
Cover Photo: © Image100/Age Fotostock
Manufacturing Manager: Mary Fischer
Printer and Binder: RR Donnelley & Sons Company, Harrisonburg
Cover Printer: Phoenix Color Corporation

For permission to use copyrighted material, grateful acknowledgment is made to the copyright holders on pp. 237–239, which are hereby made part of this copyright page.

Library of Congress Cataloging-in-Publication Data
Strode, Timothy Francis.
    The hip hop reader/[edited by] Tim Strode, Tim Wood.
      p.   cm.—(Longman topics reader; 49)
    Includes bibliographical references.
    ISBN 0-321-38512-8
  1. Rap (Music)—History and criticism. 2. Rap (Music)—Social
  aspects. I. Wood, Tim.
    ML3531. H58 2008
    782. 421649—dc22   2006052726

Copyright © 2008 by Pearson Education, Inc.

Visit us at www.ablongman.com

ISBN-13: 978-0-321-38512-3
ISBN-10:   0-321-38512-8

345678910—DOH—10 09 08

CONTENTS

ABOUT HIP HOP

On the album *Let's Get Free*, Dead Prez spit fire, addressing an oppressive school system in the song titled "They Schools." The song's title shows the disconnect between the students whom Dead Prez speaks for and the teachers and administrators whom they address. The grammar of the title "They Schools" flouts institutional standards of English, opting for an alternative standard, the grammar of the street. Note how *they* is simultaneously pronominal and possessive. This linguistic decision concisely dramatizes the ways in which many students, especially those from the inner city are disempowered and even dispossessed by the school system. In the song, Dead Prez tell a first-person narrative about a history class. The speaker is a student who eagerly tries to counter the dominant culture's narrative that reduces a black individual to being three-fifths of a human being while it celebrates the achievements of the colonizing white Europeans. Relating the school system to the prison system, a military compound, and a twelve-step rehabilitation program, the song views school as an institution of power for the dominant culture, turning its captive population into passive recipients of the stultifying myths of the ruling classes.

Critics might argue that the foregoing complaints about America's education system are simply a product of youthful angst. But Dead Prez represent experientially and in raw terms what Michel Foucault identifies as the main function of the classroom in *Discipline and Punish:* against the threat of masses of people acting in concert, schools play a pacifying and atomizing function, creating docile subjects, not thinking beings. Dead Prez are not merely being angry or reactionary. Dead Prez make clear that the problem isn't with education per se. They insist in the song that they love education. Implicit in "They Schools" is a radical pedagogy reminiscent of the revolutionary ideas of Paulo Freire: education, as its etymology implies, should attempt to "draw out" the best in students rather than alienate students from themselves.

Of course, identifying the problem is easier than offering solutions. But Dead Prez do both. After their critique of the school system, Dead Prez offer their own version of education in a song aptly titled "Hip Hop." "Hip Hop" is both an answer and a palliative to "They Schools." As the title of this song states, it is "Hip

Hop" that can remedy the injustices and inadequacies in the school system. It does so by giving students a voice and, through that voice, a means of self-empowerment and access to political power.

In the song and the remix of the same song near the end of the album, Dead Prez set out to define what hip hop is and what it is not. "Hip Hop" argues that "true" hip hop—unlike its commodified counterpart that serves to degrade hip hop and make its participants economic slaves—is a powerful vehicle for conveying potent ideas. In the first song, *hip hop* is defined by being a "fighter," a "flame-igniter," and a "crowd-exciter" as opposed to a "wolf-crier" or an "agent wit' a wire." In this pointedly poetic and concrete way, Dead Prez show how hip hop is inherently *rhetorical* and fundamentally concerned with composition: hip hop is obsessed with the efficacy and power of language to incite and excite.

In the remix they go further, saying that hip hop is not about "pimps and hoes" and is "bigger than bling bling." Dead Prez flout these common misconceptions about hip hop, insisting that the music and the culture are about what is "really real," which means being able to speak eloquently and forcefully, truthfully and poetically. Against the mindless mantra of "keeping it real," a phrase endlessly repeated but rarely probed in rap circles, Dead Prez advocate a lyrical stance that penetrates the superficial dazzle of commodified reality to a deeper, "realer" real. Dead Prez's critical realism can help inspire in student readers and writers a similarly suspicious attitude toward the texts of political and consumer cultures.

The power, efficacy, use, and complexity of expression in hip hop through graffiti, b-boying, style of dress, and rap show the power of artistic expression to respond to and change culture by negotiating power, constructing identity, and re-imagining personal and social relationships, spaces, and communities. As the linguistic expression of hip hop culture, rap has particular relevance for a book focused on hip hop and composition. So while our book addresses hip hop as a cultural whole, we emphasize its oral manifestation: rap. We privilege rap music in order to show the power of language to articulate personal experience and political arguments; to see things as they are and imagine them as they should be; and to make the connection between authority and authorship, idea, and identity.

From its earliest days to its more recent expressions, hip hop has possessed political and rhetorical force. Consider "The Message" by Grandmaster Flash and the Furious Five or "Juicy" by The Notorious B.I.G.: in both songs, we hear powerful personal narratives conveyed through effective and artful writing. Although "The Message" was written in the early 80s and "Juicy" in the early 90s, both songs still feel immediate and real because of the hard and harsh details of street life eloquently described in each song. Hip hop's clear specific description arrests the senses. Its detail and powerful imagery show, not tell. Moreover, via their art, these songs instruct and exemplify: they have something to say. Again, consider the title: "The Message."

It is not just vivid language and detailed narratives that connect hip hop with composition. Within hip hop, you will find examples not only of the personal essay but of all common rhetorical modes. You will find *description*, of course. Gritty urban textures and scenes populate songs by artists such as Common, Black Star, and Nas. Common's "The Corner"—each verse of which is built around a single dominant sound—brilliantly captures the living detail of this urban crossroad. Black Star's "Respiration" personifies the city, bringing us in contact with an almost living and breathing being. Nas's "Represent" not only describes the city, but also enables meditation on the concept of artistic representation. Songs like Public Enemy's "Night of the Living Baseheads" or "Ebonics" by Big L show the possibilities of a *definition* essay by exploring the complex meanings of a word and by showing how to use that definition to come to terms with personal experience or social realities. Such songs make palpable the importance of diction or word choice. In "Crack Music," Kanye West insists on the particular power and significance of hip hop's "dark diction" not only for rappers but for American culture as a whole. As the introductions to the race and gender chapters in this text reveal, many songs and many artists take up key and controversial words and work to transform them through their songs.

Hip hop delights in the habitations and errant itineraries of words. Reveling in the pure plasticity of language, hip hop exemplifies to student writers the pleasures that exist in verbal dexterity and writerly performance.

What hip hop also demonstrates is the considerable risk that a writer needs to take to say something interesting and true, whether it is exploring personal crisis as in Jay-Z's "Song Cry" or a social crisis as in Goodie Mobb's "Cell Therapy." The vitality of hip hop captures that elusive quality of writing that makes it leap off the page, makes it both salient and relevant. Hip hop as a culture shows writing—and, for that matter, music, painting, and dancing—as more than an academic exercise, as more than just a way to get a grade in a class. Murs, for example, in his album

The End of the Beginning, insists that he did not begin rapping to become famous or make a lot of money, as is often said or thought. Instead, he wanted to create, communicate, and get a response—fundamental impulses behind composition. Murs even discovers that the ideas of fame and money, the fundamental values of the rap industry, get in the way of that desire.

The impulses behind hip hop are distinct from its commodified image. The great freestyler Supernatural reading the dictionary every day and rapping "off the dome," the cover of Eminem's album *The Marshall Mathers LP* showing him writing his thoughts madly in a notebook, the stories of Jay-Z as a little boy banging on the kitchen table while he spits out rhymes—all reveal writing and literacy to be fundamental ways of being in the world. Our book celebrates hip hop's profound immersion in writing and culture. Our greatest desire is that the book, building on the enormous popularity and potency of hip hop music and culture, will bring more students to writing in a more engaged and enthusiastic way.

ABOUT THIS BOOK

The Hip Hop Reader is an anthology of essays on hip hop directed toward the composition student and the composition class. As a result, this is not intended to be a comprehensive text, although it addresses many of the most important issues in hip hop in a substantive way. While there are probably better places to go for a grand overview of hip hop, *The Hip Hop Reader* can quite competently serve as an introduction to hip hop. However, the book directs its inquiry toward the art of writing. This reader is devoted to the way that hip hop uses language to reflect, critique, and create the reality in which we all live.

The essays themselves are not only topical but also demonstrate a range of effective ways to write about hip hop. In this book you will find scholars and journalists as well as students and cultural critics who produce essays in various styles and modes. The authors represented in the book include some of the most eloquent and best known writers at work today: bell hooks, Michael Eric Dyson, Tricia Rose, and Mark Anthony Neal, to name just a few. Also present is the work of some of the best up-and-coming talent in the world of hip hop writing: Imani Perry, Marcyliena Morgan, and Kiese Laymon. Two student writers, Shana Kent and Ayanna Parris, undergraduates at Vassar College when they wrote their essays, have contributed two very fine and very different pieces: Kent examines the transcendent lyricism of Nas's *Illmatic* and Parris shares with us a fascinating, firsthand encounter with Tanzanian hip hop. Both student pieces beautifully demonstrate hip hop's potential to inspire first-rate student work. This book's wonderful writing will take students through composition's styles and subgenres: they will find reviews, historical analysis, scholarly criticism, personal narrative, editorials, and many others.

In addition to its stylistic diversity, *The Hip Hop Reader* grapples with many of the key issues and debates confronting not only hip hop but American culture as a whole. Besides broad categories such as race, gender, and identity, the book examines key cultural and political conflicts: freedom of expression vs. censorship; cultural imperialism vs. the integrity of local cultures; corporate culture vs. artistic freedom; and many others. Readers will discover that the book's local topic—hip hop—opens doors to innumerable global concerns. Hip hop's enormous popularity naturally draws students into writing and thinking about issues of central concern to all disciplines within the humanities and social sciences.

Each chapter of *The Hip Hop Reader* begins with an introduction intended to raise issues more fully explored in the readings that follow. It is important that we point out that the introductions are not to be construed as general overviews of the topic at hand. We have tried to avoid commentary on the chapters and let the essays speak for themselves. Our introductions model some ways to write about hip hop. They exemplify and demonstrate a focused response to the topic and issues raised by the chapter's individual readings. Because the introductions mean to instruct as well as introduce, they can be used by students and instructors as models of essay writing and close reading. We have kept the introductions concise so that they might correspond to what a student could easily produce in a composition course devoted in whole or in part to hip hop.

We would like to thank the following reviewers for their helpful comments: Laura Apfelbeck, University of Wisconsin–Manitowoc; Kermit Campbell, Colgate University; Kiese Laymon, Vassar College; Andrew J. Ryan, George Mason University; Jeff Rice, Wayne State University.

Let's go!

TIM STRODE
TIM WOOD

CHAPTER 1

Back in the Day: Origins and Definitions of Hip Hop

Little of beauty has America given the world save the rude grandeur God himself stamped on her bosom; the human spirit in this new world has expressed itself in vigor and inge- nuity rather than in beauty. And so by fateful chance the Ne- gro folksong—the rhythmic cry of the slave—stands today not simply as the sole American music, but as the most beautiful expression of human experience born this side the seas. It has been neglected, it has been, and is, half despised, and above all it has been persistently mistaken and misunderstood; but notwithstanding, it still remains as the singular spiritual her- itage of the nation and the greatest gift of the Negro people.
— W. E. B. DU BOIS, "Souls of Black Folk"

Hip hop has many origins. The rapper's penchant for narrative can be traced back to the *griot* [ghree-o] or storyteller in tradi- tional African societies. The music and the DJ continue traditions of the blues born, as Du Bois says, from "the rhythmic cry of the slave." Hip hop has precursors in the Black Arts Movement, poets like Amiri Baraka, Nikki Giovanni, and The Last Poets; novelists like Donald Goines and Iceberg Slim; and musicians like Gil Scott-Heron, all of whom write out of and respond to the late 20th- century urban black American experience. And then there are hip hop's originators themselves: the Jamaican-born Kool Herc, who would wire turntables to lampposts and then pass a needle between two records, rhythmically repeating phrases and beats that would blast into the night; Grandmaster Flash, an electrician who figured out how to toggle between two records and invented scratching; and many, many others, too many to name. Finally, there are the songs that preserve in the most concrete terms the history and the music of hip hop. "Rapper's Delight" is particularly interesting not because it is considered hip hop's first hit, but rather because it coined the term *hip hop* along with its sometime synonym *rap*, a word whose etymology will offer us yet another kind of history, especially when thinking about hip hop as composition.

The rise of the MC, hip hop's poet and orator, is perhaps an unexpected result of the success of "Rapper's Delight," a song that privileged words over music in order to make a record. "Rapper's Delight" codified the genre and the term *hip hop* with its catchy chorus. "Rapper's Delight" would also allow rappers access to the airwaves at a time when post-Civil Rights era segregation in the music industry was at its worst. For example, the path "Rapper's Delight" chartered would allow Grandmaster Flash to produce "The Message." Recorded in 1982, "The Message" ushered in an era of politically potent hip hop that would anticipate seminal groups such as Public Enemy and NWA. While "Rapper's Delight" may still be considered hip hop's anthem, it is "The Message" that embodies its prophetic aspirations.

As hip hop became centered on the MC, its music was most often referred to as "rap." Indeed, the chorus of "Rapper's Delight" talks about "hip hop," but its title and its delight are reserved for the rapper. Although fuzzy distinctions between hip hop and rap are constantly being made—with *rap* usually carrying a slightly derogatory tone and *hip hop* usually connoting something pure or true—the terms are, in fact, integrally related. And while rap has literally gotten a bad rap, the tradition of rapping and the etymology of the word are instructive. Following Geneva Smitherman, who traces the evolution of the word *rap* in her essay "The Chain Remain the Same: Communicative Practices in the Hip Hop Nation," rapping as a mode of storytelling connects hip hop to the African *griot*. In the 20th century, at least within African-American communities, *rap* referred to seductive or romantic talk.

This etymology may not only help explain why sex (and sexual tropes such as pimping) is so deeply ingrained in the music, but also highlights hip hop's interest in the seductiveness of language in general. It also highlights an important and related paradox. While hip hop often promotes misogyny and the record industry seems to reify a patriarchal system, the person responsible for transforming, and popularizing hip hop (by producing "Rapper's Delight") was a woman, Sylvia Robinson. It is generally true that the hip hop industry is run by men and often excludes women, but the exceptions to this rule are so extraordinary that they are not just notable but even call such perceptions into question.

So without ever entirely losing its sexual connotation, the word *rap* eventually evolved and, generalized by its use in mainstream speech, came to refer to any powerful or persuasive speech. This definition is most fitting when considering rap music as composition. At its root, the word *rap* both connotes and denotes a complex conception of language use. As an onomatopoetic word, *rap* conceives of language as a forceful sound. Moreover, "to strike with a quick, smart blow; to utter suddenly and forcibly; to deliver with a bang" is not only descriptive of what we often hear when listening to rap songs, but also may be a particularly useful way to envision what language becomes when it is most potent and effective. As composition, rap highlights the ingredients in most good writing: it is poetic and rhetorically forceful; it incites pleasure and surprise while, at the same time, it sends a meaningful message; it transforms language into action by either moving people (both emotionally and physically) or offering an alternative way to perceive and live in the world. The history of hip hop is exquisite for its social and historical complexity, but it is crucial to remember that the history of hip hop relies on personal and artistic expression, especially through innovative use of language.

The Roots and Stylistic Foundations of the Rap Music Tradition
CHERYL L. KEYES

An Associate Professor of Ethnomusicology at UCLA, Cheryl L. Keyes has conducted fieldwork on hip hop culture in London, Los Angeles, Detroit, New York City, and Mali. She has published work in many leading journals, including Ethnomusicology, Folklore Forum, Journal of American Folklore, *and* The World of Music. *The following selection is an excerpt from her book* Rap Music and Street Consciousness *(2002).*

———————— ✦ ————————

THE AFRICAN NEXUS

Most critics and scholars concur that rap music is a confluence of African American and Caribbean cultural expressions, such as sermons, blues, game songs, and toasts and toasting—all of which are recited in a chanted rhyme or poetic fashion. As Paul

Gilroy observes, hip-hop culture grew out of the cross-fertilization of African American vernacular cultures with their Caribbean equivalents rather than springing fully formed from the entrails of the blues (1993:103). While rap artists forthrightly confirm an African American and Caribbean nexus by regarding rap as having a close resemblance to the Jamaican toast or "Jamaican rhymes," they also view their music through a historical lens by which (West) Africa is primarily perceived as the place of origin for the rap music tradition.

When I asked about the origins of rap, several veteran rap artists pointed to Africa as a reference for its performance practices. Hip-hop's proclaimed godfather Afrika Bambaataa indicated, "although it [rap] has been in the Bronx, it goes back to Africa because you had chanting style of rappin" (Bambaataa interview). Elaborating further, Lumumba "Professor X" Carson refers to an African context out of which he believes a style of rap was born: "Once upon a time ago, a long long time ago, every Friday of the month, it was the duty of the grandfather in a tribe to sit down and bring all of the immediate children around him to rap. One of the instruments that was played while grandfather rapped his father's existence was a guy playing the drum. I guess that's why we are so into rap today" (Carson interview). When I occasionally mentioned to academics how rappers would locate Africa as the foundation of the rappin style, some of them immediately marveled at this while simultaneously wondering, "Who told them that?"[1] Despite some queries by academicians about artists' knowledge of the rap music–African nexus, Bambaataa and Carson's statements suggest, nonetheless, that rappin is similar to the West African bardic tradition.

Beyond whatever traditions and history may have been passed down to African Americans through the oral traditions of their families and communities, the impact of a particular book published in the 1970s gave those who did have access to oral history a new means by which to understand their contemporary culture and practices through examining their heritage. The considerable contributions of this book may underlie the strong assertions that rhymin MCs make about the bard-rap continuum. The comparative literature scholar Thomas A. Hale notes that the West African bard's rise in popularity in the United States can be attributed to the 1976 publication of Alex Haley's *Roots: The Saga of an American Family*. The televised version of *Roots*, which was produced as a miniseries in 1977, "drew the largest audience in the history of U.S. television" (Hale 1998:2). The series retold the story of Haley's African ancestor, Kunte Kinte, who is said to have come from the

Gambia. *Roots* also stimulated African Americans' interest in genealogy. *Roots* was followed by its miniseries sequel, *Roots: The Next Generations* (1979). An autobiographical sketch of Haley's life as a journalist and novelist, the sequel revealed how he embarked upon his research on Kunte Kinte. In the last episode, Haley, played by the actor James Earl Jones, travels to the Gambia where he is directed by the Ministry of Culture officials to a keeper of oral history, a *griot*, who would probably know the story of Kunte Kinte. Undoubtedly *Roots* informed viewers about the role African bards played as purveyors of the past, recorders and guardians of history, and scholars of African culture. Thomas A. Hale best summarizes the impact of *Roots*: "thanks to the continuing impact of *Roots*, West African griots have dramatically expanded their performance contexts. They have appeared on the stages of university auditoriums, in churches, and in television and recording studios in Paris, London, New York, and Tokyo" (1998:2). It would not be farfetched to presume that among the audiences of these performances were rappers, who recognized rap's strong link to an old African practice, a practice whose influence they may have unconsciously adopted from their families, churches, and cultures. To understand why rappers identify with the role of the African bard, we must examine its historical context.

In traditional African societies, the bard is a storyteller-singer and above all a historian who chronicles the nation's history and transmits cultural traditions and mores through performance. Early accounts of the bard can be found in the writings of the Syrian scholar al-'Umari and the memoirs of the Moroccan traveler Ibn Battūta during the fourteenth century. Both al-'Umari's work *Masālik al-absār fimamālik al amsār* (1337) and Ibn Battūta's chronicle (1355) describe a praise singer poet who serves as an intermediary and interpreter among a host of court poets. Al-'Umari cites the following about a sultan in Mali named Sulaymān, the brother of the sultan Mansā Mūsa: "In front of him there stands a man to attend him, who is the executioner . . . and another, called shā'ir, 'poet,' who is his intermediary (safir) between him and the people. Around all these are people with drums in their hands, which they beat" (al-'Umari in Levtzion and Hopkins 2000:265).

Several years following al-'Umari's visit, Ibn Battūta witnessed the following: "I arrived at the town of Mālī, the seat of the king of the Sūdān. . . . I met the interpreter Dūghā . . . one of the respected and important Sūdān. . . . I spoke with Dūghā the interpreter, who said: 'Speak with him, and I will express what you want to say in the proper fashion' " (Battūta in Levtzion and Hopkins 2000: 5

288–89). Ibn Battūta noticed the importance of music affiliated with the interpreter and poets during council meetings and festivities associated with the sultan's court.

> Inside the council-place beneath the arches a man is standing. Anyone who wishes to address the sultan addresses Dūghā and Dūghā addresses that man standing and that man addresses the sultan. . . . The sultan comes out of a door in the corner of the palace with his bow in his hand and his quiver between his shoulders. . . . The singers come out in front of him with gold and silver stringed instruments (qunburī) in their hands. . . . As he sits the drums are beaten and the trumpets are sounded. . . . at the two festivals of the Sacrifice and the Breaking of the Fast . . . [a] seat is set up for Dūghā and he sits on it and plays the instrument which is made of reed with little gourds under it, and sings poetry in which he praises the sultan and commemorates his expeditions and exploits and the women and the slave girls sing with him and perform with bows. On the feast day, when Dūghā has finished his performance, the poets come. They are called julā, of which the singular is jāli. (291–93)[2]

In traditional West African society, the bard is a member of a caste of artisans (i.e. blacksmiths, leather workers, etc.) known among the Mande as *nyamakala*. It is believed that whenever a bard utters a word or any member of the nyamakala performs a task within their respective profession, a powerful force called *nyama* is released. Westerners have often translated *nyama* as "malevolent force," which is partially correct. But as the linguist and Mande scholar Charles Bird puts it,

> Nyama is essentially associated with action, acts and the individual's capacity to act. For this reason, I prefer to translate it as the energy of action. Whatever the act, the individual requires a certain amount of energy to perform it and the performance of the act itself releases a certain amount of energy. From the point of view of equilibrium, the energy of action is dangerous, since, if it is not appropriately controlled, it will lead to disequilibrium and upheaval. . . .
> Speech itself is considered to contain this energy as denotes the expression *Nyama be kuma la* [or] The energy of action is in speech. (1976:98)

When nyama is operative, a bard's utterance can transform chaos into peace or "transmute things and man himself" (Anyanwu 1976:576).

The words of bards abound in several quasi-song forms from epics—long narrative poems centered around a legendary hero, for example, Sunjata, a celebrated epic about the founder of the Mali Empire—to praise songs or poetry exalting a patron's namesake. While performing, a bard makes use of formulaic expressions, poetic abstractions, and rhythmic speech—all recited in a chantlike fashion that prefigures rap.

The effectiveness of a bard's performance is achieved through the use of the imagery that is created through the bard's words. As described by Leopold Senghor: " 'African-Negro imagery is therefore not imagery-equation but imagery-analogy, surrealist imagery. . . . The elephant is force, the spider, prudence; horns are the moon and the moon is fecundity. Any representation is imagery, and imagery, I repeat, is not equation but symbol, ideogram.'" (quoted in Taylor 1977:25). Senghor's picturesque statement sheds light on the African aesthetic of verbal performance, that is, to paint pictures with words through the use of metaphors and symbols. Because of the masterful use of words, a bard is revered and highly respected in a community, a role claimed later in the diaspora by the most adept MCs.

A bard's performance is further advanced through the use of musical accompaniment. Most storyteller-singers are accompanied by a harp-lute (e.g. kora) or percussion instrument, whose repetitive beat interlocks with the bard's voice. A bard may also be accompanied by an apprentice, the *naamu-sayer*, who responds by singing "naamu" in affirmation of the bard's words, adding an active interchange between the bard and naamu-sayer, who represents the voice of the listener.

Although the bard seemingly gives credence to the historical   10
roots of rap's poetic performance, this aspect is not confined to the African continent alone but is rather idiosyncratic to oral traditions throughout the African World, diaspora, or what Paul Gilroy refers to as "The Black Atlantic" (1993).[3] During the trans-Atlantic slave trade, many Africans, including bards, were transplanted to the Western world. In the New World, Africans were enslaved and forced to learn a culture and language different from their own. In the face of this alien context, blacks transformed the new culture and language of the Western world through an African prism. The way in which they modified, reshaped, and transformed African systems of thought resonates in contemporary culture. For example, many rap music performance practices represent what I call cultural reversioning: the foregrounding (consciously and unconsciously) of African-centered concepts. While rap music is considered an art form indigenous to the United States, it is important to

discuss its roots in this context, which I trace to early African
American expressive culture. I contend, however, that the convergence of African American and Caribbean expressive culture and
the influence of the latter on the former in the making of rap music occurred in a more discernible manner during the 1970s. The
following section discusses African American antecedents of rap
music and the basis for some of rap's verbal performance practices. The Caribbean impact on rap and hip-hop will be addressed
more fully in chapter 2 and subsequent chapters.

THE CULTURAL REVERSION OF AFRICAN
CULTURE IN THE UNITED STATES

Poetic speech remained paramount to African peoples in the New
World, circumscribing their everyday experience. Essentially, "the
communication system that evolved among the Africans [in
America] stemmed from their creativity and their will to survive.
Language quickly became not only a means of communication but
also a device for personal presentation, verbal artistry, and commentary on life's circumstances. In effect the slave was . . . a poet
and his language was poetic" (Baber 1987:78). Enslaved Africans
devised ways by which to encode messages about their condition.

Black poetic speech is fluid and predicated on what communication scholars call *nommo*, "the power of the word," a concept derived from the Dogon of Mali.[4] Nommo permeates speech and oral
performance throughout the African diaspora. In discussing the efficacy of nommo, Ceola Baber opines that it "generates the energy
needed to deal with life's twists and turns; sustains our spirits in the
face of insurmountable odds [and] transforms psychological suffering into external denouncements . . . and [into] verbal recognition of
self-worth and personal attributes" (1987:83). These concepts will become important as we look to place rap music in a historical context.

Poetic language of African peoples eventually flourished in the
New World as testimony of enslavement. Under the strictures of
institutionalized slavery, blacks were forced into human bondage.
Out of such conditions came black vernacular expressions that
documented one's existence, hopes, and desires.

Slavery existed in varying degrees throughout the United
States. The population of black enslaved persons in the North was
relatively small compared to that in the South. Owing to the
shorter summer months and growing antislavery sentiments,
"there was no desire for slaves" (Franklin and Moss 1994:65).

In the North, slavery has been described as "relatively mild, with slaves receiving fairly humane treatment and many considerations as to their personal rights" (63). A smattering of slave insurrections during the 1740s in areas like New York, however, resulted in statutes sometimes sanctioning severe punishments. Africanisms did thrive in the North, as documented with the reinterpretation of European-derived (Dutch) holiday celebrations such as Pinkster Day and the slave community's 'Lection Day.[5] But by the 1790s slavery in the North was rapidly dwindling. "The decline of slavery in the region is revealed by the fact that by 1790 there were approximately 14,000 free blacks, comprising about 28 percent of the total black population" (85). Such demographics fueled the antislavery debates in the North.

The South rose to become an economic empire on the backs of enslaved blacks. The historians John Hope Franklin and Alfred A. Moss Jr. note that when the indentured status of blacks expired between the 1640s and 1650s, southern colonists began to notice how they "fell behind in satisfying the labor need of the colony with Indians." After carefully scrutinizing the success of black slavery in the Caribbean, "it was then that the colonists began to give serious thought to the 'perpetual servitude' of blacks" (1994:56). By the 1660s slavery was institutionalized throughout the South, establishing the region as a growing reservoir of Africanisms as compared to the North. In many areas of the south, blacks outnumbered whites. As Franklin and Moss note,

> In 1790 Virginia had already taken the lead in black population, which it was to hold during the entire slave period. Virginia's 304,000 blacks were almost three times the number in South Carolina, Virginia's nearest rival. Most of the states in that region, however, presented a picture of an abundant black population. . . . By the last census before the Civil War, the slave population had grown to 3,953,760! The states of the cotton kingdom had taken the lead, with 1,998,000 slaves within their borders. Virginia was still ahead in the number of slaves in a single state, but Alabama and Mississippi were rapidly gaining ground. (1994:84, 123)

Enslaved blacks lived primarily on plantations in separate quarters from whites, with occasional interaction. Within this context evolved what the historian John W. Blassingame terms "slave culture." The plantation or slave quarter, densely populated by blacks, comprised the "primary environment" of this culture, while blacks living in contact or close confines with whites made up the "secondary environment" (see Blassingame 1979:105–6). The former environment fostered the maintenance, reinforcement, and continuation of African-derived practices in music making, oral narratives, material culture, philosophy, and belief systems. When unsupervised by whites, blacks retreated to their traditions in such contexts as the "invisible church," secluded places in the woods aptly termed "brush harbors" or makeshift religious structures called "praise houses, and secular celebrations."[6] While it is obvious that the art of preaching or sermonizing took precedent in black religious contexts, expressions that emerged out of secular or recreational pastimes included storytelling and song forms such as field hollers and work songs, precursors to the blues. Although the institution of slavery ended officially with the ratification of the Thirteenth Amendment in 1865, African-derived locution, phraseology, and musical forms forged in the crucible of bondage continued to survive and evolve into newer modes of expression. The southern-based expressions that provided a foundation for rap are storytelling, ritualized games (i.e. "the dozens" and signifyin), blues songs, and preaching.

Stories told in rhyme have been collected throughout the rural South for many years. One storytelling tradition that provides a structural model for rap music is the toast. The toast is a long narrative poem composed in rhymed couplets and recited in a humorous manner. Its text centers around the feats and foes of a trickster, for example, the Signifying Monkey and the character Shine, or a badman hero type, such as Mr. Lion or Stackolee.[7] These stories are performed in secular contexts merely for amusement. Salient features of the toast include the use of exaggerated language, metaphor, expletives, boasting, repetition, formulaic expressions, and mimicry. Several verbal forms are also structurally interwoven in the body of toast tales, such as the dozens and signifyin. The dozens (also known in contemporary culture as "snaps") is described as "the oldest term for the game of exchanging insults" (Labov 1972:274). This game involves an interplay or a verbal duel between two opponents in which one makes a direct statement about the other's family member, especially the mama, in rhymed couplets such as, "I saw yo' mama yesterday on the welfare line/Lookin like she done drank some turpentine," or "Talk about one thing, talk about another/But ef you talk about me, I'm gwain talk about your mother" (Keyes 1982; Oliver 1968:236).

Signifyin occurs when one makes an indirect statement about a situation or another person; the meaning is often allusive and, in some cases, indeterminate. I recall from my southern background an incident involving a married man's attempt to flirt with an unmarried woman. Aware of his marital status, the unmarried woman reminds the man, through indirection, that he is married. Her response places the man in an indeterminate position as to continue or cease from flirting.

MARRIED MAN: Hey mama, you sho' look good to me today.
UNMARRIED WOMAN: Oh, by the way, how's yo' wife?

One popular version of the traditional "Signifying Monkey" clearly illustrates features and verbal forms—the dozens and signifyin—common to the toast tradition:

> Way down in the jungle deep,
> The baddass lion stepped on the signifying monkey's feet.
> The monkey said, "Muthafucka can't you see,
> Why you're standin' on my goddamn feet."
> The lion said, "I ain't heard a word you said. . . .
> If you say three more, I'll be stepping on yo' muthafuckin'
>   head."
> And the monkey hid in the jungle in an old oak tree.
> Bullshittin' the lion everyday in the week.
> Everyday befo' the sun go down,
> The lion would kick his ass all through the jungle town.
> But the monkey got wise and start using his wit.
> Said "I'm gon' put a stop to this old ass kickin' shit."
> So he ran upon the lion the very next day.
> Said, "Oh Mr. Lion, there's a big bad muthafucka comin'
>   yo' way. . . .
> He's somebody that you don't know,
> 'Cuz he just broke a loose from Ringling Brothers show.
> Said, Baby he talked about yo' people in a helluva way.
> He talked about yo' people 'til my hair turned gray.
> He said, 'Yo' daddy's a freak, and yo' moma's a whore,'
> Said he spotted you runnin through the jungle sellin' . . .
>   from door to door. . . ."[8]

As a rule, the effectiveness of the toast lies in its style of delivery rather than in content. Nonverbal gestures, such as facial expressions or hand movements, further enhance effective delivery of a toast. While the dozens, signifyin, metaphor, expletives, boasting, and mimicry are stylistic features of the toast, the structural unit remains the rhyming couplet. The rhyming couplet structure and the aforementioned verbal forms of the toast remain present in rap music.

Rhyme is integral to several African American expressive traditions. In the blues tradition, for example, verses are structured in an AAB rhyme scheme: "(A) I don't know where my baby done gone/(A) I don't know where my baby done gone/(B) All I can do is sing a sad sad tone." The blues singer Furry Lewis says, "If you don't rhyme it up, you don't understand nothing and you ain't getting nowhere" (Titon 1994:47).

20   Rhyme is a stylistic and structural device in other African American contexts as well. For example, in the black traditional church, preachers occasionally interject rhyming verses in their sermons: "Giving honor to God, Christ Jesus, pulpit associates, members and friends. I'm glad to be here today, just to say that God is the way . . ." (Smitherman 1986:146). Rhyme also serves as a structural device in the African-derived dance-song, called "the hambone." Derived from an antebellum dance called the "juba," the hambone is executed by the patting and clapping of one's thighs, chests, and hands to rhyming verses. The hambone is commonly performed by males as a courtship game, for instance, "Hambone, hambone, ham in the shoulder/Gimme a pretty woman and I'll show you how to hold her" (Milton Lowe, personal communication, Baton Rouge, La., December 22, 1988).

Though rhyme is not germane to every African American oral expression, tonal inflections are important to the proper interpretation of an expression. Black vernacular speech utterances depend heavily on tonal contouring to convey meaning. Tonal aspects employed in the English language by African American speakers are clear evidence of African tonal language retention. The anthropologist Melville Herskovits, in his monumental study, *The Myth of the Negro Past* (1958), discusses the tonal element or "'musical' quality . . . prominent in Negro-English" (1958:291). Such vocal inflections are particularly employed in performance. For example, the preacher's most proven stylistic feature is the use of musical tone or chant in preaching (Jackson 1981:213). Blues singers talk-sing their melodies as well. Thus, it is not surprising that hip-hop MCs describe their verbal performances as "a melody in itself [or] . . . like talking" (Melle Mel interview).

While tonal inflections help the performer to convey the meaning of an utterance, call and response creates a sense of cohesion between performer and auditor. Call and response is ubiquitous to the African American aesthetic in that it synchronizes speakers and listeners within a performance event, but more importantly, it is the life force of black communication. Without this interchange, black communication is lifeless. African American preachers, for example, commonly admonish their congregation that they cannot "preach to no dead church," a church in which the presence of the spirit is not made manifest by active vocal response to "the Word" as conveyed in the preached sermon (Davis 1985:27). In addition, African American artists thrive on audience response to the extent that the success of a performance is measured by the active interplay between the performer and the audience. The concept of call and response is also crucial to the status of rap artists to the extent that rappers are considered worthless by others if they do not have an entourage. For this reason, some rap artists re-create in their records a sense of liveliness by incorporating audience cheers and responses.

Rap music predominantly utilizes the artifice and art characteristic of other black oral performances. The philosopher Cornel West asserts that " 'the rap artist combines the potent tradition in black culture: the preacher and singer, [who] appeals to the rhetorical practices eloquently honed in African American religious practices' " (quoted in Dyson 1993:12). While it is perhaps more apparent how rap resembles Christian preaching, its nexus in African religions is less pronounced and more subtle. Among the corpus of texts analyzed for this study there were occasional references to the West/Central African concept known as "crossroads." Crossroads represent "the juncture of the spiritual realm and the phenomenal world" (Drewal 1992:205). The art historian Robert Farris Thompson elaborates: "the points of literal intersection [are] where one might go to offer sacrifice or prayer to ancestors. . . . The crossroads, also, function as a powerful symbol in African American folklore . . . as legends of black musicians going to crossroads and trading their guitars with spirits to confirm or enhance their talents" (1990:153, 154).

The crossroads concept is not alien to black folksong traditions like the blues. For example, Robert Johnson's "Cross Road Blues" remains the most well-known of crossroads songs. Legend has it that Johnson sold his soul to the devil in exchange for his musical success. But after realizing his mistake, Johnson supposedly wrote "Cross Road Blues" as a repentant plea to God for forgiveness. The following is an excerpt from that song: "I went to the crossroad fell down on my knees/I went to the crossroad fell down on my knees/Asked the Lord above 'Have mercy, now save poor Bob, if you please' " (Thompson 1990:154). The crossroads concept is more abstract in rap than in the blues. In "To the Crossroads" (1990) Isis and Professor X of X-Clan rap about the creation of the world and humankind as evident through their deification of the ancient Kemetic (Egyptian) deities—Isis "Divine Woman/Mother" (of Horus, Son of Osiris) and Ra (Professor X), the Sun deity. Isis raps: "The I in my own song. Isis deeper and beneath those who ain't strong./ The radiant rising sun, the bright light in the world of none/ . . . we'll take a walk with the black and the bold./ I'll take you there and let us meet at the crossroad." Professor X intones, "I am Ra from whom time begins./ Rising away, severing the wind, turning. /I am the hub of a wheel, a daystar hovering over in the sea./ I am not the harvest. I am the seed. Off to the crossroad we go!" The concept of crossroads is used here in a traditional African cosmic sense, meaning the place where all spiritual forces or creations are activated. In a sense, Ra, positioned at the "hub of the wheel," parallels the deity Esu-Elegba, who in the Yoruba tradition is the guardian of the crossroads.

25   In another X-Clan song, "Funkin Lesson" (1990), Professor X alludes to the crossroads as a place where one goes to get in touch with spiritual forces—the ancestors—in order to empower oneself for the future. Professor X orates: "Out of the darkness, in panther's skin comes doctors, driving pink caddys, bearing the remedy of your existence. Yes, it gets blacker. With a Nat Turneric, Martin, Adam, Malcolm, Huey; there's a party at the crossroads." " 'Driving pink caddys,' " explains Professor X, is a metaphor for a " 'travelling time machine.' " He adds, " 'the year of that particular pink caddy is significant. It's a '59 [Cadillac]. That was another turning point of black men's existence in America. . . . The pink caddy is significant in what Detroit Red went through to become Malcolm X' " (quoted in Romain 1992:35). Professor X's teaching as a modern-day bard illuminates the continuous history of the crossroads from its place in ancient African lore to the diaspora. Today the crossroads includes not only deities and ancient ancestors but African American leaders such as Nat Turner, Martin Luther King Jr., Adam Clayton Powell, Malcolm X, and Huey Newton, who have made indelible marks on America. In referring to what "Detroit Red went through to become Malcolm X" and later El-Hadjj Malik El-Shabazz, Professor X also clearly invokes the crossroads as the place black mortals continue to visit in contemporary times to seek guidance in preparation for change—physically, mentally, and spiritually—from the old self to the new self. References to the crossroads as an ancestral or spiritual gathering place are also made in "Tha Crossroads" (1998) by Bone Thugs-N-Harmony.

The African bardic tradition and its retention in southern-based oral expressions are antecedents of the rap music tradition. However, it was in the context of the urban North that rap was first introduced as a street style of speaking. It was also in this environment that rap, as a speech style, developed into a distinct musical genre. The evolution of rap from a speech style to a musical form occurred during and after the migrations of southern blacks to northern urban centers.

Notes

1. Such a conversation happened after my initial field research in 1986. While attending the Society for Ethnomusicology's annual meeting at the Rochester School of Music in 1986, a prominent sociolinguist poked fun at a similar discussion he had with a rap artist. He said condescendingly that he felt the artist was told or had read about rap's African connection and could not have drawn this connection without having done so. This conversation recalled the "African retention" and "Origins of the Negro Spirituals" debates of the mid-twentieth century.

2. Eric Charry makes a distinction between *jeli* and *jail*, the Mande words equivalent to English "bard." Both words come from the Mande people's language of the "Upper Niger River roughly between Bamako in southwestern Mali and Kouroussa in northeastern Guinea" (2000:1). *Jeli* (pl. *jelilu*) is the Mande word for "bard" as used by those from the Maninka society situated in Mali and Guinea, whereas *jali* or *jalo* (pl. *jalolu*) is the Mande word for bard as used by those from the Mandinka society of Senegal, the Gambia, and Guinea-Bissau. Charry also notes other common uses of the word *Mandinka* as "Mandingo in British writing," and he traces the first use of *griot*, a seventeenth-century word for "bard," to the writings of French travelers (1).

Charry also notes that the *jeli* art (*jeliya*) is not confined to Mande culture but has other counterparts or terms. "Jelis have their analogue in the Wolof *gewel*, Fulbe *gaulo* (*gawlo*), Moorish *iggio* (*iggiw*), and Soninke *jaare*, all of whom come from societies that have had close contact with the Ghana and Mali Empires" (91).

3. Paul Gilroy's employment of "The Black Atlantic" raises excellent points, for the African experience outside of Africa or the "African World" (Clarke 1991) or "diaspora" is not limited to African Americans or African Caribbeans, as is commonly believed, but includes those who live in Europe as well. Throughout this book, I will use the term "black" to refer to those of Africa and the diaspora (Europe, Latin America, the Caribbean, and the United States) and "African American" to refer to blacks in the United States.

4. *Nommo* is a term used among the Dogon of Mali, West Africa, as suggested by the French ethnographer Marcel Griaule. In *Dieu d'eau: entretiens avec Ogotemmeli* (1948) and *Conversations with Ogotemmeli* (1970), Griaule reveals the origins of nommo. According to an interview he conducted with the blind elderly informant Ogotemmeli, the elder translated *nommo* (spelled *Nummo* in the text) as a set of twins created by God and of His divine nature. They were "conceived without untoward incidents and developed normally in the womb of the earth. The Pair were born perfect and complete; they had eight members, and their number was eight, which is the symbol of speech. The *Nummo* is water and heat, the life-force, which is the bearer of the Word, which is the Word"

(1970:18,138). The Africanists and philosophers Janheinz Jahn (1961) and Paul Carter Harrison (1972) find that the essence of nommo permeates both literature and spoken word produced by Africans and those within the African world (diaspora).

5. For further information about early African American celebrations and holidays see Raboteau (1978), Wiggins (1987), and Southern (1997:52–55).

6. Although slavery was abolished in the North much earlier than in the South, northern blacks still experienced racial segregation from whites. Blacks established their own secular and sacred organizations that, in turn, assisted in the maintenance and continuum of African-derived practices (see Raboteau 1978). Among these organizations were the Free African Society, spearheaded by Richard Allen and Absalom Jones, the Grand Lodge (black Masons), founded by Prince Hall, and religious sects such as the African Methodist Episcopal Church, established by Richard Allen, and the First African Baptist Church, organized by Thomas Paul.

7. The latter type is "peculiar to African Americans and collected most frequently in jails" (Dance 1978:225) and in urban areas. See also Bruce Jackson (1974).

8. "The Signifying Monkey" version I often heard while growing up in Louisiana also appears in Daryl Dance's collection of folk narratives, *Shuckin' and Jivin': Folklore from Contemporary Black Americans* (1978), and a similar rendition of this toast is performed by the comedian Rudy Ray Moore on his album *This Pussy Belongs to Me* (1972).

Questions for Discussion and Topics for Writing

1. Keyes points out that rap music derives from what she refers to as the "West African bardic tradition." What is this tradition? What is the role of the *griot* in this tradition? What parallels do you see between the *griot* and a hip hop MC (the rapper, often the main writer of lyrics for a group)?

2. What does the term *nyama* mean? Why does Keyes focus on this word? Note: You may need to make an inference to answer this second question. Try to answer the question in light of Keyes's argumentative purpose here: to forge a connection between West African oral traditions and hip hop culture.

3. A key section of the Keyes reading involves her use and application of the term *cultural reversion*. Define this term. How does Keyes apply this term to her analysis of the transition of African oral cultures to American soil following slavery? Finally, make a list of the key oral traditions that developed in the American South that Keyes sees as being particularly important to the development of rap music.

4. Write an essay in which you reflect on Keyes's discussion of the West African bardic tradition. In your essay, show how the bardic tradition helps us understand the role of the hip hop artist in her or his community.

5. Use two key terms from Keyes's essay—*nyama* and *nommo*—to examine hip hop in terms of its power to move or persuade. Note: The particular influence of the language of hip hop need not necessarily be positive.

Rap Music
TRICIA ROSE

Tricia Rose is Professor of American Studies at the University of California, Santa Cruz. A pioneering scholar in the field of hip hop culture, Rose has written and edited numerous articles and books, including Longing to Tell: Black Women Talk About Sexuality and Intimacy, Black Noise: Rap Music and Black Culture in Contemporary America, *and* Microphone Fiends: Youth Music and Culture *(1994). The following piece is taken from the second chapter of Rose's seminal 1994 work,* Black Noise.

———————— ✦ ————————

Rapping, the last element to emerge in hip hop, has become its most prominent facet. In the earliest stages, DJs were the central figures in hip hop; they supplied the break beats for breakdancers and the soundtrack for graffiti crew socializing. Early DJs would connect their turntables and speakers to any available electrical source, including street lights, turning public parks and streets into impromptu parties and community centers.

Although makeshift stereo outfits in public settings are not unique to rap, two innovations that have been credited to Jamaican immigrant DJ Kool Herc separated rap music from other popular music and set the stage for further innovation. Kool Herc was known for his massive stereo system speakers (which he named the Herculords) and his practice of extending obscure instrumental breaks that created an endless collage of peak dance beats named b-beats or break-beats. This collage of break-beats stood in sharp contrast to Eurodisco's unbroken dance beat that dominated the dance scene in the mid- to late 1970s. Kool Herc's range of sampled b-beats was as diverse as contemporary rap music, drawing on, among others, New Orleans jazz, Isaac Hayes, Bob James, and Rare Earth. Within a few years, Afrika Bambaataa, DJ and founder of the Zulu Nation, would also use beats from European disco bands such as Kraftwerk, rock, and soul in his performances. I emphasize the significance of rap's earliest DJs' use of rock, because popular press on rap music has often referred to Run DMC's use of samples from rock band Aerosmith's "Walk This Way" in 1986 as a crossover strategy and a departure from earlier sample selections among rap DJs. The bulk of the press coverage on Run DMC regarding their "forays into rock" also suggested that by using rock music, rap was maturing (e.g., moving beyond the "ghetto") and expanding its repertoire. To the contrary, the success of Run DMC's "Walk This Way" brought these strategies of inter-textuality into the commercial spotlight and into the hands of white teen consumers. Not only had rock samples always been reimbed-ded in rap music, but also Run DMC recorded live rock guitar on *King of Rock* several years earlier.[1] Beats selected by hip hop pro-ducers and DJs have always come from and continue to come from an extraordinary range of musics. As Prince Be Softly of P.M. Dawn says, "my music is based in hip-hop, but I pull everything from dance-hall to country to rock together. I can take a Led Zeppelin drum loop, put a Lou Donaldson horn on it, add a Joni Mitchell gui-tar, then get a Crosby Stills and Nash vocal riff."[2]

Kool Herc's Herculords, modeled after the Jamaican sound systems that produced dub and dance-hall music, were more pow-erful than the average DJ's speakers and were surprisingly free of distortion, even when played outdoors.[3] They produced powerful bass frequencies and also played clear treble tones. Herc's break-beats, played on the Herculords, inspired breakdancers' freestyle moves and sparked a new generation of hip hop DJs. While work-ing the turntables, Kool Herc also began reciting prison-style rhymes (much like those found on The Last Poet's *Hustler's Convention*), using an echo chamber for added effect. Herc's rhymes also drew heavily from the style of black radio personali-ties, the latest and most significant being DJ Hollywood, a mid-1970s disco DJ who had developed a substantial word-of-mouth following around the club scene in New York and eventually in other cities via homemade cassettes.

Like the graffiti and breakdance crews, DJs battled for territo-ries. Four main Bronx DJs emerged: Kool Herc's territory was the west Bronx, Afrika Bambaataa dominated the Bronx River East, DJ Breakout's territory was the northernmost section of the Bronx, and Grandmaster Flash controlled the southern and central sec-tions.[4] These territories were established by local DJ battles, club gigs, and the circulation of live performance tapes. DJs' perform-ances, recorded by the DJ himself and audience members, were copied, traded, and played on large portable stereo cassette play-ers (or "ghetto blasters"), disseminating the DJ's sounds. These tapes traveled far beyond the Bronx; Black and Puerto Rican army recruits sold and traded these tapes in military stations around the country and around the world.[5]

5   Grandmaster Flash is credited with perfecting and making fa-mous the third critical rap music innovation: scratching. Although

Grand Wizard Theodore (only 13 years old at the time) is considered its inventor, Theodore did not sustain a substantial enough following to advance and perfect scratching. Scratching is a turntable technique that involves playing the record back and forth with your hand by scratching the needle against and then with the groove. Using two turntables, one record is scratched in rhythm or against the rhythm of another record while the second record played. This innovation extended Kool Herc's use of the turntables as talking instruments, and exposed the cultural rather than structural parameters of accepted turntable use.

Flash also developed the backspin and extended Kool Herc's use of break beats.[6] Backspinning allows the DJ to "repeat phrases and beats from a record by rapidly spinning it backwards." Employing exquisite timing, these phrases could be repeated in varying rhythmic patterns, creating the effect of a record skipping irregularly or a controlled stutter effect, building intense crowd anticipation. Break beats were particularly good for building new compositions. Making the transition to recordings and anticipating the range of sounds and complexity of collage now associated with sampling technology, Flash's 1981 "The Adventures of Grandmaster Flash on the Wheels of Steel" lays the ground-work for the explosive and swirling effects created by Public Enemy producers, the Bomb Squad, seven years later. In an attempt to capture the virtuosity of Flash's techniques and the vast range of his carefully selected samples, I have included a lengthy and poetic description of his performance of the "The Adventures of Grandmaster Flash on the Wheels of Steel." Nelson George describes the Grandmaster's wizardry:

> It begins with "you say one for the trouble," the opening phrase of Spoonie Gee's "Monster Jam," broken down to "you say" repeated seven times, setting the tone for a record that uses the music and vocals of Queen's "Another One Bites the Dust," the Sugar Hill Gang's "8th Wonder," and Chic's "Good Times" as musical pawns that Flash manipulates at whim. He repeats "Flash is bad" from Blondie's "Rapture" three times, turning singer Deborah Harry's dispassion into total adoration. While playing "Another One Bites the Dust," Flash places a record on the second turntable, then shoves the needle and the record against each other. The result is a rumbling, gruff imitation of the song's bass line. As the guitar feedback on "Dust" builds, so does Flash's rumble, until we're grooving on "Good Times." Next, "Freedom" explodes between pauses in Chic's "Good Times" bass line. His

bass thumps, and then the Furious Five chant, "Grandmaster cuts faster." Bass. "Grandmaster." Bass. "Cut." Bass. "Cuts . . . cuts . . . faster." But the cold crusher comes toward the end when, during "8th Wonder" Flash places a wheezing sound of needle on vinyl in the spaces separating a series of claps.[7]

Using multiple samples as dialogue, commentary, percussive rhythms, and counterpoint, Flash achieved a level of musical collage and climax with two turntables that remains difficult to attain on advanced sampling equipment ten years later.

The new style of DJ performance attracted large excited crowds, but it also began to draw the crowd's attention away from dancing and toward watching the DJ perform.[8] It is at this point that rappers were added to the DJs' shows to redirect the crowd's attention. Flash asked two friends, Cowboy and Melle Mel (both would later become lead rappers along with Kid Creole for Flash and the Furious Five) to perform some boasts during one of his shows. Soon thereafter, Flash began to attach an open mike to his equipment inspiring spontaneous audience member participation. Steve Hager's description of their intertextuality, fluidity, and rhythmic complexity indicates a wide range of verbal skills not generally associated with early rappers: "Relying on an inventive use of slang, the percussive effect of short words, and unexpected internal rhymes, Mel and Creole began composing elaborate rap routines, intricately weaving their voices through a musical track mixed by Flash. They would trade solos, chant, and sing harmony. It was a vocal style that effectively merged the aggressive rhythms of James Brown with the language and imagery of *Hustler's Convention*."[9] Many early rappers were inspired by the intensity of Melle Mel's voice and his conviction. Kid, from rap group Kid-N-Play, attributed some of this intensity to the fact that Mel was rapping for a living rather than a hobby: "For Melle Mel, rapping was his job. Melle Mel made a living rapping each weekend at a party or whatever. So he's rapping to survive. As such, his subject matter is gonna reflect that. I go on record as saying Melle Mel is king of all rappers. He's the reason I became a rapper and I think he's the reason a lot of people became rappers. That's how pervasive his influence was."[10] Melle Mel's gritty dark voice was immortalized on Flash and Furious Five's 1982 "The Message," voted best pop song of 1982. The power of rappers' voices and their role as storytellers ensured that rapping would become the central expression in hip hop culture.

The rappers who could fix the crowd's attention had impressive verbal dexterity and performance skills. They spoke with authority, conviction, confidence, and power, shouting playful ditties reminiscent of 1950s black radio disc jockeys. The most frequent style of rap was a variation on the toast, a boastful, bragging, form of oral storytelling sometimes explicitly political and often aggressive, violent, and sexist in content. Musical and oral predecessors to rap music encompass a variety of vernacular artists including the Last Poets, a group of late 1960s to early 1970s black militant storytellers whose poetry was accompanied by conga drum rhythms, poet, and singer Gil Scott Heron, Malcolm X, the Black Panthers, the 1950s radio jocks, particularly Douglas "Jocko" Henderson, soul rapper Millie Jackson, the classic Blues women, and countless other performers. "Blaxsploitation" films such as Melvin Van Peebles' *Sweet Sweetback's Baadasss Song*, Donald Goines's gangsta fiction, and "pimp narratives" that explore the ins and outs of ghetto red-light districts are also especially important in rap. Regardless of thematics, pleasure and mastery in toasting and rapping are matters of control over the language, the capacity to outdo competition, the craft of the story, mastery of rhythm, and the ability to rivet the crowd's attention.[11]

Rap relies heavily on oral performance, but it is equally dependent on technology and its effects on the sound and quality of vocal reproduction. A rapper's delivery is dependent on the use and mastery of technology. The iconic focus of the rapper is the microphone; rappers are dependent on advanced technology to amplify their voices, so that they can be heard over the massive beats that surround the lyrics. Eric B. & Rakim's "Microphone Fiend" describes the centrality of the microphone in rap performance:

> I was a microphone fiend before I became a teen.
> I melted microphones instead of cones of ice cream
> Music-oriented so when hip hop was originated
> Fitted like pieces of puzzles, complicated.[12]

As rapping moved center stage, rappers and DJs began to form neighborhood crews who hosted block parties, school dances, and social clubs. Like breakdance crew competitions, rappers and DJs battled for local supremacy in intense verbal and musical duels. These early duels were not merely a matter of encouraging crowd reaction with simple ditties such as "Yell, ho!" and "Somebody Scream." (Although these ditties have important sentimental value.) These parties and competitions lasted for several hours and required that the performers had a well-stocked arsenal of rhymes and stories, physical stamina, and expertise. Local independent record producers realized that these battles began to draw consistently huge crowds and approached the rappers and DJs about producing records. While a number of small releases were under way, Sylvia Robinson of Sugar Hill records created the Sugar Hill Gang whose 1979 debut single "Rapper's Delight" brought rap into the commercial spotlight. By early 1980, "Rapper's Delight" had sold several million copies and rose to the top of the pop charts.[13]

10   "Rapper's Delight" changed everything; most important, it solidified rap's commercial status. DJs had been charging fees for parties and relying on records and equipment for performance, but the commercial potential at which "Rapper's Delight" only hinted significantly raised the economic stakes. Like rock 'n' roll's transition into mainstream commercial markets, rap was fueled by small independent labels and a system of exploitation in which artists had no choice but to submit to draconian contracts that turned almost all creative rights and profits over to the record company if they wanted their music to be widely available. Black-owned and white-owned labels alike paid small flat fees to rappers, demanded rigid and lengthy production contracts (such as five completed records in seven years), made unreasonable demands, and received almost all of the money. Salt from the female rap group Salt 'N' Pepa said that before they signed with Next Plateau Records they were paid $20 apiece per show. When she challenged her manager about their arrangement he threatened her and eventually beat her up for asking too many business questions.[14]

"Rapper's Delight" has also been cited by rappers from all over the country as their first encounter with hip hop's sound and style. In fact, the commercial success of "Rapper's Delight" had the contradictory effect of sustaining and spawning new facets of rap music in New York and elsewhere and at the same time reorienting rap toward more elaborate and restraining commercial needs and expectations. Within the next three years Kurtis Blow's "The Breaks," Spoonie Gee's "Love Rap," The Treacherous Three's "Feel The Heartbeat," Afrika Bambaataa and the Soul Sonic Force's "Planet Rock," Sequence's "Funk You Up," and Grandmaster Flash and the Furious Five's "The Message" were commercially marketed and successful rap singles that made and continue to make more money for Sugar Hill records and other small labels than they do for the artists.[15]

Although Salt 'N' Pepa have been cited as the first major female rapers, some of the earliest rap groups, such as the Funky Four Plus One More had female members, and there were a few all-female groups, such as Sequence. In keeping with young women's experiences in graffiti and breaking, strong social sanctions against their participation limited female ranks. Those who pushed through found that "answer records," (rap battles between the sexes records) were the most likely to get airplay and club response. The first "queen of rap," Roxanne Shante, wrote and recorded a scathing rap in response to UTFO's "Roxanne Roxanne," a rap that accused a girl named Roxanne of being conceited for spurning sexual advances made by UTFO. Roxanne Shante's "Roxanne's Revenge" was a caustic and frustrated response that struck a responsive chord among b-girls and b-boys.[16] Rapped in a sassy high-pitched girl's voice (Shante was 13 years old at the time), Shante told UTFO: "Like corn on the cob you're always trying to rob / You need to be out there lookin' for a job." And the chorus, "Why you have make a record 'bout me? The R/O/X/A/N/N/E?" has become a classic line in hip hop.[17]

Although black and Latino women have been a small but integral presence in graffiti, rapping, and breaking, with the exception of Sha Rock, who was one of the innovators of the beat box, they have been virtually absent from the area of music production. Although there have been female DJs and producers, such as Jazzy Joyce, Gail 'sky' King, and Spindarella, they are not major players in the use of sampling technology nor have they made a significant impact in rap music production and engineering. There are several factors that I believe have contributed to this. First, women in general are not encouraged in and often actively discouraged from learning about and using mechanical equipment. This takes place informally in socialization and formally in gender-segregated vocational tracking in public school curriculum. Given rap music's early reliance on stereo equipment, participating in rap music production requires mechanical and technical skills that women are much less likely to have developed.

Second, because rap music's approaches to sound reproduction developed informally, the primary means for gathering information is shared local knowledge. As Red Alert explained to me, his pre-hip hop interest and familiarity with electronic equipment were sustained by access to his neighbor Otis who owned elaborate stereo equipment configurations. Red Alert says that he spent almost all of his free time at Otis's house, listening, learning, and asking questions. For social, sexual and cultural reasons young women would be much less likely to be permitted or feel comfortable spending such extended time in a male neighbor's home.

Even under less intimate circumstances, young women were not especially welcome in male social spaces where technological knowledge is shared. Today's studios are extremely male-dominated spaces where technological discourse merges with a culture of male

15

bonding that inordinately problematizes female apprenticeship. Both of these factors have had a serious impact on the contributions of women in contemporary rap music production. Keep in mind, though, that the exclusion of women from musical production in rap is not to be understood as specific to rap or contemporary music, it is instead the continuation of the pervasive marginalization of women from music throughout European and American history.

One of the ways around these deterrents is to create female-centered studio spaces. I have always imagined that rap's most financially successful female rappers would build a rap music production studio that hired and trained female technicians and interns, a space in which young women of color would have the kind of cultural and social access to technology and musical equipment that has, for the most part, been a male dominion. It would also quickly become a profitable and creative space for a wide range of musicians committed to supporting women's musical creativity and forging new collaborative environments.

Unlike breakdancing and graffiti, rap music had and continues to have a much more expansive institutional context within which to operate. Music is more easily commodified than graffiti, and music can be consumed away from the performance context. This is not to suggest that rap's incorporation has been less contradictory or complicated. Quite to the contrary; because of rap music's commercial power, the sanctions against as well as the defenses for rap have been more intense, and thus resistance has been more contradictory.

Throughout the late 1980s, rap music's commercial status increased dramatically, rappers began exploring more themes with greater intertextual references and complexity, and hip hop crews from urban ghettos in several major cities began telling stories that spoke not only of the specifics of life in Houston's fifth ward for example but also of the general bridges between the fifth ward and Miami's Overtown or Boston's Roxbury. In the same time period, Run DMC's mid- to late 1980s popularity among white teens prompted the *New York Times* to declare that rap had finally reached the mainstream.[18] At the same time, Eric B. & Rakim, Public Enemy, KRS One, L.L. Cool J., MC Lyte and De La Soul also emerged as major figures in rap's directional shifts.[19]

During the late 1980s Los Angeles rappers from Compton and Watts, two areas severely paralyzed by the postindustrial economic redistribution developed a West Coast style of rap that narrates experiences and fantasies specific to life as a poor young, black, male subject in Los Angeles. Ice Cube, Dr. Dre, Ice-T, Ezy-E, Compton's Most Wanted, W.C. and the MAAD Circle, Snoop Doggy Dog, South

Central Cartel, and others have defined the gangsta rap style. The Los Angeles school of gangsta rap has spawned other regionally specific hardcore rappers, such as New Jersey's Naughty by Nature, Bronx-based Tim Dog, Onyx and Redman, and a new group of female gangsta rappers, such as Boss (two black women from Detroit), New York-based Puerto Rican rapper Hurrican Gloria, and Nikki D.

Mexican, Cuban, and other Spanish-speaking rappers, such as Kid Frost, Mellow Man Ace and El General, began developing bilingual raps and made lyrical bridges between Chicano and black styles. Such groups as Los Angeles-based Cypress Hill, which has black and Hispanic members, serve as an explicit bridge between black and Hispanic communities that builds on long-standing hybrids produced by blacks and Puerto Ricans in New York. Since 1990, in addition to gangsta raps, sexual boasting, Afrocentric and protest raps, rap music features groups that explore the southern black experience, that specialize in the explicit recontextualization of jazz samples, live instrumentation in rap performance and recording, introspective raps, raps that combine acoustic folk guitar with rap's traditional dance beats and even New Age/Soul rap fusions.[20]

These transformations and hybrids reflect the initial spirit of rap and hip hop as an experimental and collective space where contemporary issues and ancestral forces are worked through simultaneously. Hybrids in rap's subject matter, not unlike its use of musical collage, and the influx of new, regional, and ethnic styles have not yet displaced the three points of stylistic continuity to which I referred much earlier: approaches to flow, ruptures in line and layering can still be found in the vast majority of rap's lyrical and music construction. The same is true of the critiques of the postindustrial urban America context and the cultural and social conditions that it has produced. Today, the South Bronx and South Central are poorer and more economically marginalized than they were ten years ago.

Hip hop emerges from complex cultural exchanges and larger social and political conditions of disillusionment and alienation. Graffiti and rap were especially aggressive public displays of counterpresence and voice. Each asserted the right to write[21]—to inscribe one's identity on an environment that seemed Teflon resistant to its young people of color; an environment that made legitimate avenues for material and social participation inaccessible. In this context, hip hop produced a number of double effects. First, themes in rap and graffiti articulated free play and unchecked public displays; yet, the settings for these expressions always suggested existing confinement.[22] Second, like the consciousness-raising sessions in the early stages of the women's rights movement and black power movement of the 1960s and 1970s, hip hop produced internal and external dialogues that affirmed the experiences and identities of the participants and at the same time offered critiques of larger society that were directed to both the hip hop community and society in general.

Out of a broader discursive climate in which the perspectives and experiences of younger Hispanic, Afro-Caribbeans and African-Americans had been provided little social space, hip hop developed as part of a cross-cultural communication network. Trains carried graffiti tags through the five boroughs; flyers posted in black and Hispanic neighborhoods brought teenagers from all over New York to parks and clubs in the Bronx and eventually to events throughout the metropolitan area. And, characteristic of communication in the age of high-tech telecommunications, stories with cultural and narrative resonance continued to spread at a rapid pace. It was not long before similarly marginalized black and Hispanic communities in other cities picked up on the tenor and energy in New York hip hop. Within a decade, Los Angeles County (especially Compton), Oakland, Detroit, Chicago, Houston, Atlanta, Miami, Newark and Trenton, Roxbury, and Philadelphia, have developed local hip hop scenes that link various regional postindustrial urban experiences of alienation, unemployment, police harassment, social, and economic isolation to their local and specific experience via hip hop's language, style, and attitude.[23] Regional differentiation in hip hop has been solidifying and will continue to do so. In some cases these differences are established by references to local streets and events, neighborhoods and leisure activities; in other cases regional differences can be discerned by their preferences for dance steps, clothing, musical samples, and vocal accents. Like Chicago and Mississippi blues, these emerging regional identities in hip hop affirm the specificity and local character of cultural forms, as well as the larger forces that define hip hop and Afrodiasporic cultures. In every region, hip hop articulates a sense of entitlement and takes pleasure in aggressive insubordination.

Few answers to questions as broadly defined as, "what motivated the emergence of hip hop" could comprehensively account for all the factors that contribute to the multiple, related, and sometimes coincidental events that bring cultural forms into being. Keeping this in mind, this exploration has been organized around limited aspects of the relationship between cultural forms and the contexts within which they emerge. More specifically, it has attended to the ways in which artistic practice is shaped by cultural traditions, related current and previous practice, *and* by the ways in which practice is shaped by technology, economic forces, and race, gender, and class relations. These relationships between form, context, and cultural priority demonstrate that hip hop shares a number of traits with, and yet revises, long-standing Afrodiasporic practices; that male dominance in hip hop is, in part, a by-product of sexism and the active process of women's marginalization in cultural production; that hip hop's form is fundamentally linked to technological changes and social, urban space parameters; that hip hop's anger is produced by contemporary racism, gender, and class oppression; and finally, that a great deal of pleasure in hip hop is derived from subverting these forces and affirming Afrodiasporic histories and identities.

Developing a style nobody can deal with—a style that cannot be easily understood or erased, a style that has the reflexivity to create counterdominant narratives against a mobile and shifting enemy—may be one of the most effective ways to fortify communities of resistance and *simultaneously* reserve the right to communal pleasure. With few economic assets and abundant cultural and aesthetic resources, Afrodiasporic youth have designated the street as the arena for competition, and style as the prestige-awarding event. In the postindustrial urban context of dwindling low-income housing, a trickle of meaningless jobs for young people, mounting police brutality, and increasingly draconian depictions of young inner city residents, hip hop style *is* black urban renewal.

Notes

1. See Peter Watrous, "It's Official: Rap Music Is in the Mainstream," *New York Times*, 16 May 1988, p. C11; After expressing frustration over the coverage of "Walk This Way" as a crossover strategy, Run describes his motivation: "I made that record because I used to rap over it when I was twelve. There were lots of hip-hoppers rapping over rock when I was a kid." Ed Kierch, "Beating the Rap," *Rolling Stone*, 4 December 1986, pp. 59–104.

2. Cited in Jon Young, "P.M. Dawn Sample Reality," *Musician*, June 1993, p. 23.

3. According to Hager, the Hurculords were two Shure brand speaker columns aided by a Macintosh amplifier. Hager, *Hip Hop*, p.33. It is also interesting to note that, even though the equipment and Herc's style were heavily influenced by Jamaican sound systems and dub, Herc claims that he could not get the crowd to respond to Jamaican music. This is one of many interesting points of diasporic hybridity in which the influences move bidirectionally.

4. MTV, *Rapumentary* (1990).

5. Interview with Red Alert, 8 May 1990.

6. Not long after his rise to local fame, Kool Herc was stabbed multiple times during one of his shows. After this incident, he dropped out of the hip hop scene.

7. George et al., *Fresh*, pp. 6–7. I explore the technical and artistic practices in rap music production in Chapter 3.

8. According to Flash and Red Alert, a still crowd seemed to be more prone to fighting and confrontations.

9. Hager, *Hip Hop*, p. 48. *Hustler's Convention* is the 1973 album written and performed by Jalal Uridin, leader of the black militant ex-convicts, The Last Poets. *Hustler's Convention* (and the related blaxsploitation genres of the late 1960s and early 1970s) are clear predecessors to contemporary gangsta rap's thematic and stylistic preference for violence, drugs, sex, and sexism. The critical formal difference is rap's emphasis on danceable beats and its musical complexity.

10. Interview with Kid, from Kid-N-Play, 11 January 1990.

11. Rap's roots in black oral practices are extensive, and research on black oral practices is equally so. Some major texts that explore the history of black oral practices are listed here: Houston Baker, *Long Black Song: Essays in Black American Literature and Culture* (London: University Press of Virginia, 1972, 1990); Gates, *The Signifying Monkey*; Dennis Wepman, Ronald Newman, and Murry Binderman, *The Life The Lore and Folk Poetry of the Black Hustler* (Philadelphia: University of Philadelphia Press, 1976); Dundes, ed., *Mother Wit from the Laughing Barrel*; Daniel Crowley, *African Folklore in the New World* (Austin: University of Texas Press, 1977); Lawrence Levine, *Black Culture and Black Consciousness: Afro-American Folk Thought from Slavery to Freedom* (New York: Oxford University Press, 1977); Roger D. Abrahms, *Deep Down in the Jungle: Negro Narrative Folklore from the Streets of Philadelphia* (Chicago: Aldine, 1970); Geneva Smitherman, *Talkin' and Testifyin': The Language of Black America* (Boston: Houghton Mifflin, 1977).

12. Eric B. & Rakim, "Microphone Fiend," in *Follow the Leader* (Uni Records, 1988). In Chapter 3 I explore the relationship between technology and orality in rap in much greater depth.

13. There is a great deal of controversy regarding the Sugar Hill Gang's sudden, albeit short-lived success. According to a number of rappers and DJs from this period, the three members of Sugar Hill Gang were not local performers. One of the members, Hank was a doorman/bouncer at a rap club in New York and had access to bootleg tapes that he played back in northern New Jersey, an area that at this point had no local rap scene. Sylvia Robinson heard one of Hank's tapes and approached him about recording a rap single. According to Hager's *Hip Hop*, Hank borrowed Grandmaster Caz's rhyme book and used his rhymes in "Rapper's Delight." Kool Moe Dee, Red Alert, and others explained to me that when they heard the record, they were shocked. Not only had they never heard of the Sugar Hill Gang, but they could not believe that a rap record (even one that they thought was so elemental) could become commercially successful.

14. Rose interview with Salt, 22 May 1990.

15. "Rapper's Delight" sold over two million copies in the United States, and "The Breaks" sold over 500,000 copies. These record sales were primarily the result of word of mouth and hip hop club play.

16. Shante's single "Roxanne's Revenge" (Pop Art Records, 1984) sold over two million copies.

17. Women rappers are the subject of Chapter 5, in which their contributions and an analysis of rap's sexual politics are explored in greater depth.

18. Watrous, "Rap Music in the Mainstream."

19. The purpose of this chapter is not to give a chronological history of all the developments in hip hop. As stated, I have focused on the context for creativity and hip hop's links to Afrodiasporic styles and practices. For more background on hip hop artists and commercial developments, see Havelock Nelson and Michael A. Gonzales, *Bring the Noise: A Guide to Rap Music and Hip Hop Culture* (New York: Crown, 1991); Joseph D. Eurie and James G. Spady, *Nation Conscious Rap: The Hip Hop Version* (New York: PC International, 1991); David Toop, *Rap Attack 2* (Boston: Consortium Press, 1992); Bill Adler, *Tougher Than Leather: Run DMC* (New York: Penguin, 1987); Bill Adler, *Rap: Portraits and Lyrics of a Generation of Black Rockers* (New York: St. Martin's Press, 1991). For a sobering look at how independent labels (where almost all rappers contracts are negotiated) have been maneuvered into a subcontractor's position in relation to the large music companies, see Frederic Dannen, *Hit Men: Powerbrokers and Fast Money inside the Music Business* (New York: Random House, 1990), especially Chapter 17.

20. For examples, see Gang Starr, *Step in the Arena* (Chrysalis, 1990); Guru *Jazzamatazz* (Chrysalis, 1993); MTV, *Rap Unplugged* (Spring 1991); Basehead *Play with Toys* (Image, 1992); Disposable Heroes of Hiphoprisy, *Disposable Heroes of Hiphoprisy* (Island, 1992); P.M. Dawn, *Of the Heart, Of the Soul and Of the Cross* (Island, 1991); and Me Phi Me, *One* (RCA, 1992); Arrested Development. *3 Years, 5 Months and 2 Days in the Life Of* (Chrysalis, 1992).

21. See Duncan Smith, "The Truth of Graffiti," *Art & Text*, no. 17, 84–95, April 1985.

22. For example, Kurtis Blow's "The Breaks" (1980) was both about the seeming inevitability and hardships of unemployment and mounting financial debt and the sheer pleasure of "breaking it up and down," of dancing and breaking free of social and psychological constrictions. Regardless of subject matter, elaborate graffiti tags on train facades always suggested that the power and presence of the image was possible only if the writer had escaped capture.

23. See Bob Mack, "Hip-Hop Map of America," *Spin*, June 1990.

Questions for Discussion and Topics for Writing

1. At the end of the essay, Rose talks about the relationship between cultural forms and contexts. Identify a few cultural forms and their contexts and discuss how this shaped what came to be called hip hop. What effect do you think changing either one or more of these cultural forms or altering the specific contexts would have on hip hop?

2. Rose argues that women "are not major players in the use of sampling technology nor have they made a significant impact in rap music production." List some of the reasons why Rose makes this claim. Does Rose provide evidence that counters or complicates her argument? In other words, how have

women been, despite being clearly marginalized, essential to the development and production of hip hop?

3. Rose discusses how the popularity of the DJ ironically led to the rise of the MC and emphasizes how both graffiti and rap "asserted the right to write." How does the evolution of hip hop make writing a centrally important act and how can the act of writing become of particular importance in the age of "high-tech telecommunications" and for "emerging regional identities"? How can hip hop affect your understanding of composition?

4. In her conclusion, Rose writes that "developing a style nobody can deal with—a style that cannot be easily understood or erased, a style that has the reflexivity to create counter dominant narratives against a mobile and shifting enemy—may be one of the most effective ways to fortify communities of resistance and *simultaneously* reserve the right to communal pleasure." As an exercise and by way of demonstrating what you think Rose means here, write a brief essay that embodies such a style. While content is relevant, in this exercise emphasize *how* you write over *what* you write. Try to make the way you write and express yourself an essential part of what you mean to say. (Along with a myriad of hip hop lyrics, you might look at Kiese Laymon's essay "Hip-Hop Stole My Black Boy" as an example of what such a style might look like.)

Puerto Rican and Proud, Boyee!
Rap, Roots and Amnesia
JUAN FLORES

Director of the Center for Puerto Rican Studies at Hunter College, Juan Flores has authored many books in the fields of Puerto Rican studies and cultural studies, including Divided Arrival, Divided Borders: Essays on Puerto Rican Identity, *and* From Bomba to Hip Hop: Puerto Rican Culture and Latino Identity. *The following essay is excerpted from* Microphone Fiends: Youth Music and Culture *(1994).*

———————— ✦ ————————

MC KT (Tony Boston) of Latin Empire commented recently on a television special:

There's a lot of Puerto Ricans out there that don't speak Spanish and aren't into the Spanish music, a lot of them, and they're still proud to be Puerto Rican. But if you don't know nothing about it, if you don't try to learn about it, then you're gonna be lost in the sauce.[1]

Writing and performing for a wide range of audiences while projecting "a Puerto Rican perspective" has keyed Latin Empire, the best-known Nuyorican rap group, into the dynamics of cultural identity. Many of their own raps are about who they are and where they come from, and their experience as rappers, both in the streets and in the "business," has been a constant struggle to uphold that self-representation in the face of strong pressures to re-do their act so that it fits into more familiar, preestablished categories.

In his brief comment, KT is actually setting forth a view of culture and identity. First he disengages cultural belonging and pride from any necessary attachment to the recognized markers or traditions of the culture, thus freeing the young Puerto Ricans raised here from the weight of having to "prove themselves" and compensate for their remove from familiar roots and life-ways. But leaving them room does not mean letting them off the hook: addressing his fellow Nuyoricans directly. KT reminds them that if one pitfall is the strait-jacket of fixed codes and canons, the other is "the sauce," the undifferentiated hodgepodge of contemporary cultural blending under the sway of the commercial media and pluralist ideology.

If you want to draw lines and mark yourself off, you have to be willing to reconnect; if you want to celebrate borders, you have to learn how to build bridges and know about the alternatives. Culture as a source of identity does need to be understood as a flexible, open-ended process grounded in lived experience; but it is also a process in the sense that it is constituted by people on the basis of action and choice, KT and Puerto Rock (Rick Rodríguez), his cousin and partner in Latin Empire, like to tell about how they used to reject, or at least not relate to, the boleros and plenas and Puerto Rican Spanish they were surrounded by growing up, and how exposure to the larger public has taught them to appreciate this background, and incorporate it into their rhymes and beats. The challenges of cultural expression and representation have amounted not so much to a professional "career," as to a process of growth and learning, a shift in their sense of cultural inheritance, from something imposed and exclusionary to a force of self-assertion and historical contestation.

The experience of Puerto Ricans in rap has been the story of 5 intense cultural negotiation, of jostling for a place within an ever-broadening field of expressive practices, without relinquishing the particularities of their own community and heritage. It is a story of special interest to the study of contemporary youth culture because of its unmatched historical depth: Puerto Ricans have been involved in hip hop since the beginning, since it first emerged in the streets of Harlem and the South Bronx nearly twenty years ago.[2] Along with their African-American counterparts, "Puerto Rocks" (as Puerto Rican hip-hoppers came to be called) were an intrinsic part of the forging of expressive styles which have become the hallmark of an entire generation, and have diffused throughout the country and worldwide. While the relation of other cultural groups to rap has been one of adoption and rearticulation, Puerto Ricans have been present as initiators and co-creators, such that their recent history as a community can be tracked by way of reference to their participation in the trajectory of the genre.

It is necessary to emphasize this point of historical origination, because the dominant construction of rap in the media and most narrative accounts has tended systematically, or at least symptomatically, to elide precisely the Puerto Rican role and dimension in staking out this preeminent field of contemporary youth sensibility. For, in terms of ethnic composition, that construction has proceeded in three main directions, all of which have had the effect of omitting the many Puerto Rican breakers, rappers and graffiti writers who were such a conspicuous part of the hip hop scene when it was still in the streets and schoolyards, and as it began to find exposure among a broader public. According to the prevalent images and definitions, rap is either particularized as a "black thing," generalized as a multicultural "youth thing," or variegated into a set of subcategories ("gangsta rap," "message rap," "female rap," and so on) which in the last few years has come to include "Latino rap." None of these versions allows for a reconstruction of rap which would account for its formation and original social function.

Of course rap has traveled far and wide since back in the days, and there is no particular gain to be had from privileging origins or some presumed authenticity as a means of stemming the levelling, deracinating impact of commercial mediation. The reinstatement of Puerto Ricans onto the historical map of hip hop need not be nostalgic or retrospective in this way, nor compensatory in aiming at granting a people just recognition for services rendered. But with all the renovations and reinventions of rap that have constituted its most familiar trajectory, the fact is that the past does not just go away, and traces of its initial articulation continue to resonate, explicitly or covertly, at every twist and turn of the historical course. The practice of sampling and the continual recycling of old-school fashion provide ample space for this kind of percolating influence, which is expressed thematically as a recurrent reference to cultural community and historical memory.

The point, then, is not that "it's a Puerto Rican thing too," or even, "yo, we were here from jump," though contentions for turf or pieces of the pie are integral to the conventional grammar of toasting and boasting, and obviously germane to any geography of rap as public discourse. The revision called for, rather than merely additive, is actually conjunctive, such that the emergence of rap may be seen as testimony to the cultural interaction between the black and Puerto Rican communities, especially as evident among the young people. Of course it is possible to identify specifically Puerto Rican ingredients that went into the original brew of hip hop, that formative contribution being even more apparent in breakdance and graffiti than in rap. But this line of analysis usually leads to the notion of the "tinge," or the touches of salsa thrown in to add zest to the recipe. The beginnings of rap are connective not so much because they link black traditions and Puerto Rican traditions, but because they mark off one more step in a long and intricate black-and-Puerto-Rican tradition of popular culture, based primarily in the long-standing black-and-Puerto-Rican neighborhoods of New York City.

Seen in this way, rap and hip hop can be understood to have not only identifiable social origins, but a prehistory as well. For long before there was any talk of rap as a mode of public performance, or for that matter of cultural "fusions," "crossovers" or "hybridization," blacks and Puerto Ricans were already busy jamming, partying, struggling or just hanging together in all aspects of everyday life, all the while building a new cultural tradition which is more and different from the sum of its component parts. Latin jazz, doo-wop, the Last Poets and the Third World Revelationists, bugalú, Latin soul and many other movements and styles are all examples of this meshing and increasingly seamless tradition. This emergent tradition attests at an artistic level to the African foundations of both cultural backgrounds, and to the close confines of their common social placement—shared tenement buildings, shared workplaces and welfare lines, shared classrooms and playgrounds, shared and coalescing political causes. And it is this joining of expressive forces, this construction of a new cultural memory in common, that comprises the most immediate source of hip hop.

Early Puerto Rican participation in graffiti has been noted all along, since the insightful writings of Craig Castleman, in his book *Getting Up*, and of Herbert Kohl.[3] Such recognition is all but obligatory in the case of breakdance, what with the overwhelmingly Puerto Rican composition of Rock Steady Crew and its obvious choreographic reliance on rumba, mambo and Latin hustle movements. Pioneering hip hop films like *Wild Style* and *Style Wars* would be unthinkable without the preponderant casting and underlying social experience of New York Puerto Ricans. By comparison, rap is generally regarded as the most uniformly African-American form within hip hop, the main "outside" influence being not Puerto Rican but West Indian, as when writers like David Toop and Dick Hebdige accent the importance of the dub and reggae backgrounds of founding practitioners like Kool Herc and Grand Master Flash.[4] Though much can be made of this Jamaican link to Caribbean models and sources, the tendency of this kind of emphasis is to lend the story a decidedly "African roots" inflection, an image which has been fueled in more recent constructions with the infusion of dancehall and neo-Rasta modalities. Without denying the catalytic and enduring presence of West Indians in Harlem and other African-American communities, or the lively interplay between rhythm and blues and reggae traditions, it is Puerto Ricans who most directly shared with young African-Americans the demographic base and creative stage of hip hop in its origins.

The Puerto Rican participation in rap falls into three main periods or historical constellations: the formative years, through the later 1970s and early 1980s, prior to and including the first recordings; the breakthrough, since about 1984, when rap first achieved its immense popularity and commercial success; and the period of "Latino rap," beginning at the end of the 1980s. To this sequence we might add the "prehistory" already mentioned, those many antecedents of rap in the gathering black-and-Puerto-Rican tradition of the preceding decades, and a coda or fourth stage of the past few years, as rap has arrived and taken hold among popular music styles in Puerto Rico. A brief overview of this history, with all of its uniqueness to the Puerto Rican case, suggests a cultural dynamic of a more general kind, a process of exclusion, negotiation and reassertion that has to do with larger social determinations than those most directly impinging on the Nuyorican hip hoppers themselves. The net effect of the process, that there has still not been one Nuyorican rap superstar or best-selling record, is of course astounding, but should not blind us to the changes and, indeed, the progress toward recognition and the projection of a distinctive voice.

Rap in the early days was "a street thing." That is the consensus phrase which emerges from conversations with some of the Puerto Rican participants of that time, "veterans" (now in their early thirties) like Charlie Chase of the Cold Crush Brothers, Rubie Dee of the Fearless Four, TNT (Tomás Robles) and KMX Assault (Jenaro Diaz).[5] When it was still in the streets, rap was marked off not so much racially but in terms of class, geography age and, though they tend to make little reference to it, of course gender. The original B-boys were inner-city teenagers from the poorest neighborhoods, which in New York means overwhelmingly black and Puerto Rican. Going beyond rap's embryonic forms of stylized talking and improvised drumbeats, the first crews and performance groups grew out of the prevailing gang structures. The turn to rhyming and music served, consciously in the case of Afrikka Bambaataa's Zulu Nation, to channel youth energy and anger away from the internecine street violence running rampant in the South Bronx neighborhoods.

This story of the brewing of rap discourse is already a familiar one, and there is no sense going back over ground adequately covered, with some sociological attention, by chroniclers like Steven Hager and Peter Toop.[6] But though they make mention of the presence of Puerto Ricans on the scene, nowhere do these accounts nearly approximate the magnitude of that involvement, much less probe the perspective of the Puerto Rocks themselves. For one thing, as in graffiti and breakdancing, Puerto Ricans were everywhere in rap, and in substantial numbers—a large, integral part of practicing groups, security and set-up crews, supportive sidekicks and, of course, audiences. As for what it was like for the young Puerto Ricans involved, testimonial recollections describe an abiding sense of community, of inclusiveness and familiarity sometimes bordering on the familial. The word tribe suggests itself, and were it not for its primitivist overtones, the cultural progeny of Zulu Nation might be considered to evidence a "tribal" degree of organic bonding. In everyday street life and in the heat of rap practice, black and Puerto Rican B-boys and B-girls were virtually interchangeable; whether you were one or the other or, as was often the case, some combination of the two, was for practical purposes a matter of relative indifference.

But within this framework of cohesion and mutuality there were of course differences, just as there are always those areas of contention and distrust among groups of different backgrounds sharing the bottom. The overriding, ideologically buttressed attitudes of white racism and hostility toward foreigners, especially immigrants from the colonial backwaters, inevitably get played out among and between the most direct victims, sometimes with a tragic vengeance. Among young blacks and Puerto Ricans, hip hop has generally been a mortar of remarkable intensity, probably unmatched in the interracial war zone of contemporary U.S. society; its unifying potential has certainly been one of its strongest legacies and sources of appeal among youth in countless settings around the world. But another attraction of hip hop, equally a part of its underlying ethos, is that it shows how to draw boundaries, mark off terrain, face up to differences and call them by their name. Here again the interaction of black and Puerto Rican youth in the incubation of rap sets the stage for the momentous act to follow.

15   As Charlie Chase and many others recall, Puerto Rican rappers always knew that they were operating in a "black world." However "down" they felt and were made to feel with the homies, however much they loved the music, the angry question: What the fuck are you doing here, Porto Rican? still resonates in their memory. Charlie tells vividly of the times when he barely escaped an ass-kicking if he dared venture behind the ropes at the early jams, and when the black rappers and fans simply would not believe that he was actually responsible for the sounds and rhythms he came up with as DJ with Cold Crush. "No way, it can't be, you're not even black, you're Porto Rican." At the same time, a lot of the early Puerto Rocks remember how in the privacy of the family they were warned to stay away from "los morenos," or at least to watch out for them, words which were often accompanied by the silent grimace of racial prejudice. Whatever their "tribal" solidarity with the brothers and sisters, the Puerto Rocks could not be deaf to such influences, as some of their accounts betray, and as is evident in the strong "Spanish" and "Indian" inflections they sometimes give to their ancestral lineage. Cultural baggage and black-white racial antinomies in the U.S. thus conspire to perpetuate a construction of Puerto Rican identity as non-black.

As a result of these conflicting pressures, the situation of Puerto Ricans in early rap contexts was typically one of camouflage. Belonging and not belonging, owning and not owning this cultural domain, Puerto Ricans had to test the waters with due caution, and know how far they could tread. Timing was of the essence, as Charlie Chase stresses when asked about the use of Spanish in rhymes or the splicing of Latin rhythms into the more accepted registers. At a musical level it was a fascinating kind of intercultural poaching, with the mostly black audiences usually not even knowing where the samples were coming from, but loving them. As for self-presentation, while not directly denying that they were Puerto Rican, they could never be obtrusive about it, and would predictably brandish all the trappings of street blackness. This adaptation has long been obvious in Puerto Ricans' English speech practices, and became paramount when it came to taking on rap nomenclature. Individuals, groups and song lyrics carefully avoided all suggestions of Spanish usage or references to anything Puerto Rican. How Charlie Chase arrived at his name is a particularly rich example:

> I made up my name because of Grand Master Flash. Flash is a friend of mine. I first saw Flash doing this, cutting and all of this, and I says, aw, man, I can do this. I'll rock this, you know. And I practiced, I broke turntables, needles, everything. Now Chase came because I'm like, damn, you need a good name, man. And Flash was on top and I'm down here. So I was chasing that nigger. I wanted to be up where he was. So I said, let's go with Charlie Chase.[7]

As interesting as it is, Carlos Mandes's choice of a new name was anything but unique: Who ever knew Rubie D., TNT or Prince Whipple Whip by their "Spanish" names, anyway?

Once rap began to be recorded for commercial distribution the scramble was on, and proprietary considerations at many levels served only to reinforce the patrols over language and musical taste. An early exception, but indicative of the rules, was the record *Disco Dream* by the Mean Machine, which came out in 1981. Often referred to by later, bilingual rappers like Mellow Man Ace and Latin Empire as an inspiration, *Disco Dream* did dare to include rhymes in Puerto Rican Spanish; but as they are quick to point out, it was limited to a few unobtrusive party exhortations that nobody even noticed, and besides, neither *Disco Dream* nor the Mean Machine ever got anywhere. When rap went big-time around the mid-1980s any signs of Puerto Rican presence were all but erased. Of course they were there, even in high-profile groups like the Fat Boys and Master Don and the Def Committee, but their invisibility and anonymity as Puerto Ricans were complete; nobody, that is only a fraction of the public, had any idea of their background. Needless to say, they were still very much there in the streets, and continued to contribute to the history of the genre under its rapidly changing conditions. But in the public eye, trained as it was on commercial film, video and concert fare, they were hidden in the woodwork, their historical role as cocreators totally occluded.

As mentioned, the effect of mass distribution on the ethnic and racial image of rap moved in two directions: it was simultaneously particularized as "African" and generalized as "multicultural" both versions the rather transparent result of marketing and ideological strategies. In neither, of course, was there any place for Puerto Ricans, much less for any sense of their intricate cultural conjunction with African-Americans in the very formation of rap. It was either a "black thing," which you could only "understand" by mimicking or diluting it, or it was an all-purpose thing, of equal utility and relevance to anyone, anywhere, as long as you're "with it." The disappearing of Puerto Ricans from the public representation of rap was thus part of a larger process aimed at its disengagement from the concrete social context in which it arose. The fatalities of this process were of course many, having as much to do with gender, class and regional considerations as with ethnic and racial interaction. But it is the Puerto Ricans, as a group and as co-creators of new forms of cultural expression, whose reality was most manifestly elided.

20   Then, when "Latino rap" burst onto the scene in 1990, the whole situation changed, or so it seemed. Mellow Man Ace went gold with "Mentirosa" in the summer of that year. Kid Frost's debut album *Hispanic Causing Panic* became the rap anthem of La Raza. Gerardo ("Rico Suave") took his place as the inevitable Latin rap sex symbol, and El General established the immense popularity of Spanish-language reggae-rap in barrios here and all over Latin America and the Caribbean. Suddenly Spanish and the "Latin" sound were "in," and it wasn't long before high-profile performers like Queen Latifah and Nice & Smooth began sprinkling in some salsa and Spanglish. The door opened in the other direction, too, as Latin groups as diverse as El Gran Combo, Wilfredo Vargas, Manny Oquendo's Libre and Los Pleneros de la 21 started to let their guard down and add a rap number or two into their acts. The breakthrough was so intense and so far-reaching that, by late 1991, the Village Voice was already referring to Latino rap as the "Next Big Thing," marking off "a defining moment in the creation of a nationwide Latino/Americano hip hop aesthetic."[8]

Such hyperbole aside, the pop emergence of bilingual rap has signalled a major opening, as the "multicultural" generalization of rap's reference and idiom finally extended to the Latino population. Rap thus goes on record as the first major style of popular music to have effected this musical and especially linguistic crossover, even more extensively than the Latin jazz and Latin R & B fusions of earlier generations. And coming as it did in times of loud public alarm over "America's fastest growing minority" and a burgeoning "English Only Movement," Latino rap assumes a crucial political role as well. Not only does bilingual usage become common practice in rap vocabulary, but Spanglish rhyming and the interlingual encounter have even become a theme in some of the best-known rap lyrics, like Kid Frost's "Ya estuvo," Cypress Hill's "Funky Bi-lingo" and Latin Empire's "Palabras."

For the Puerto Rocks, though, for whom hip hop had long been a way of life, this victory has turned out to be Pyrrhic at best. Most obviously, none of the Latino rap superstars are Puerto Ricans from New York: Mellow Man was born in Cuba and raised in Los Angeles. Kid Frost is a Chicano from East L.A., Gerardo is from Ecuador, El General is Panamanian, and Vico C and Lisa M are Puerto Ricans from the Island. What Puerto Ricans there are, even in breakthrough Latino acts like those in the Latin Alliance, are still backgrounding their Puerto Rican identity in deference to some larger, more diluted ethnic construction. Cypress Hill, which gives the impression of Puerto Rican participation, is actually a combination of Cuban, Mexican and Italian in its ethnic composition.[9] One thing that KT of Latin Empire is seeing a lot of these days is—to expand on his own phrase—that when you don't get lost in the sauce you can still get lost in the "salsa."

Notes

1. *The Americans*, part 10 of *Americas*, produced by Peter Bull and Joseph Tavares for WGBH Boston, 1993. For an introduction to Latin Empire see my interview, "Latin Empire: Puerto Rap." *Centro* (Bulletin of the Center for Puerto Rican Studies) III:2 (Spring 1991), pp. 77–85.

2. For an earlier look at the role of Puerto Ricans in the beginnings of hip hop, see my "Rappin', Writin' and Breakin': Black and Puerto Rican Street Culture in New York City," *Centro* II:3 (Spring 1988). pp. 34–41.

3. Craig Castleman, *Getting Up: Subway Graffiti in New York* (Cambridge: MIT Press, 1982); Herbert Kohl, *Golden Boy as Anthony Cool: A Photo Essay on Naming and Graffiti* (New York: Dial, 1972).

4. David Toop. *The Rap Attack: African Jive to New York Hip Hop* (Boston: South End, 1984): Dick Hebdige, *Cut 'n' Mix: Culture. Identity and Caribbean Music* (London: Routledge, 1987).

5. For a closer look at the experiences of the early Puerto Rican rappers, see my interview with Charlie Chase. "It's a Street Thing!" *Callaloo* 15:4 (1992), pp. 999–1021. See also my essays "Rappin', Writin' and Breakin'"; and "Puerto Rocks: New York Ricans Stake Their Claim," in *Droppin' Science: Critical Essays on Rap Music and Hip Hop Culture*, Eric Perkins, ed., (Philadelphia: Temple University Press, forthcoming 1994), and the interview with KMX Assault. *Centro* 5:1 (Winter, 1992–93), pp. 40–51.

6. Toop, *The Rap Attack*; Hager, *Hip Hop: The Illustrated History of Break Dancing, Rap Music and Graffiti* (New York: St. Martin's, 1984).

7. See "It's a Street Thing!"

8. Ed Morales, "How Ya Like Nosotros Now?" *Village Voice*, (November 26, 1991), p. 91.

9. In his article "The Cypress Hill Experience" in *The Source* (July 1993), Michael Gonzales mentions that Sen (Mellow Man Ace's brother) is Cuban and Muggs is Italian, but does not identify B-Real's background. It was in a friendly follow-up phone conversation that Gonzales informed me that B-Real is part Cuban, part Mexican.

Questions for Discussion and Topics for Writing

1. How does understanding Puerto Ricans' role in hip hop change your sense of the music's origins?

2. Flores gives several factors that contributed to the occlusion of Puerto Ricans from the mythic origins of hip hop. What are some of the reasons that Flores gives for this erasure? What is at stake in recovering Puerto Rican participation in the invention of hip hop?

3. How has Latin hip hop in particular both utilized and elided the Puerto Rican roots of hip hop? How has it affected Puerto Rican identity within hip hop? Do you believe this is something that is inevitable or something that needs to be rectified?

4. How does understanding the Puerto Rican roots of hip hop allow us to understand the importance of boundaries, turf, and difference within hip hop? How is this an important consideration for understanding hip hop's cultural power and its ability to form and reform social identities?

Ghost's World
A Wu Tang Clan Member's New Album
SASHA FRERE-JONES

Sasha Frere-Jones is the pop music critic for The New Yorker. *His pieces have appeared in many publications, including* Slate, LA Weekly, The Village Voice, *and* The New York Times. *The following article appeared in* The New Yorker *on March 20, 2006.*

———————— ✦ ————————

I own only one piece of art depicting a musician. It's a photograph of an m.c. known as Ghostface Killah. He is smoking a cigarette and singing into an old-fashioned ribbon microphone. In his knit cap and sunglasses, he looks a bit like Frank Sinatra crossed with a jewel thief. *Fishscale*, Ghostface's new album, is his fifth, and it is the most exciting record I've heard recently. This is more than a little surprising, because Ghostface is thirty-five, and rappers seldom have long careers, let alone ones in which the quality of the work steadily improves.

Ghostface, who was born Dennis Coles, is one of the nine (or ten, depending whom you count) members of the Wu-Tang Clan, a hip-hop group from Staten Island that for the past fifteen years has been one of the genre's most unpredictable and respected collectives. The band's début record, *Enter the Wu-Tang (36 Chambers)*, was released in 1993, and though none of the group's four albums—or the thirty solo albums released by its members—have sold more than two million copies, the Wu-Tang Clan has accrued cultural capital rare in hip-hop. (Perhaps only the Notorious B.I.G., Jay-Z, and Tupa can claim equally august status.) The Wu-Tang style is sui generis, and seems especially so now, in the context of more popular hip-hop, which tends toward clean electronic sounds and simple, repetitive choruses.

Wu-Tang music sounds dirty—not just profane but unclean. The songs are overstuffed with cryptic slang and complex stories. A typical track contains a looped sample of an old soul record overlaid with squeals, beeps, echoes, and virtuosic rhyming that goes and goes, then simply stops. The group borrow words and images from kung-fu movies—the source of Wu-Tang and Shaolin, an alias for Staten Island—and each member has several, not necessarily intelligible, nicknames. Last year, one of the group's founders and its main producer, The RZA, co-authored a book called *The Wu-Tang Manual*, an attempt to explain the band's use of Buddhism and martial arts, pop-culture references, and weird nomenclature. The name Ghostface Killah, for instance, is derived from a 1979 movie called *The Mystery of Chess Boxing*. Not many hip-hop groups need a reader's guide.

The group has not released an album since 2001, and its live appearances are limited to occasional reunion shows, the most recent in New York being an entertaining but ragged performance in February at Hammerstein Ballroom. In 2004, Ol' Dirty Bastard, one of the band's bawdiest and most popular members, died of a drug overdose. The RZA has lately been scoring Hollywood movies—Jim Jarmusch's *Ghost Dog* and Quentin Tarantino's *Kill Bill* epic—and the Wu-Tang's first breakout star, Method Man, has been acting in films. He appeared in *Soul Plane* and *How High* and on a short-lived television sitcom called *Method & Red*.

5   Ghostface Killah, though, has stuck to recording and has become the de-facto Wu-Tang standard-bear (He is also the only member of the group to have had a doll produced in his likeness: a limited-edition five-hundred-dollar action figure that comes with a paisley print robe and a tiny gold chalice studded with Swarovski crystals.) Ghostface embodies the Wu-Tang dualism—the tension between the accessible and the esoteric. Some songs, including one of his highest-charting hits, "Cherchez la Ghos" from 2000, incorporate long samples of familiar old songs (in this case, Dr. Buzzard's Original Savannah Band's 1976 hit "Cherchez la Femme"); others are larded with dissonant machine noises. Both styles complement his lyrics, which alternate between candid autobiographical vignettes and delightful non sequiturs. His voice is a gorgeous instrument, mellifluous even when he's yelling, which he does an awful lot.

His 1996 single "All That I Got Is You" was a tearjerker about growing up poor: "Seven o'clock, pluckin' roaches out the cereal box, some shared the same spoon, watchin' Saturday cartoons. Sugar water was our thing, every meal was no thrill; in the summer, free lunch held us down like steel." By contrast, "Nutmeg," the lead track on his 2000 album, *Supreme Clientele*, contains so many unrelated images, laid over a silky 1977 soul record by Eddie Holman called *It's Over*, that what you take away is mostly Ghostface's joy in the sonorous possibilities of the English language: "Swing the John McEnroe, rap rock n'roll, Ty-D-Bol, gung-ho pro, Starsky with the gumsole. Hit the rump slow, parole kids, live Rapunzel but Ton' stizzy really high, the vivid laser eye guy."

Few hip-hop artists can squeeze as many words onto an album as Ghostface, and on *Fishscale* he charges into every track, including the romantic numbers, with harried force. His lyrics sound unedited and unrehearsed—he frequently changes his mind or corrects himself from one verse to the next—but the songs aren't rushed or sloppy. He has an ear for prosaic details (what time it was when the police busted in, what show was on TV) that bring freshness to hip-hop's often rote tales of drugs, guns, and girls. "Barbershop," for example, begins with Ghostface complaining to his barber—over a female chorus crooning "You better believe it"—"Didn't I tell you don't touch the sides? I'm going bald on top!" His griping is interrupted when the police raid the shop. The customers scatter, and Ghostface raps: "And out of breath, I tossed the burgundy Tec in the bushes where it landed on the side of the 'jects. I hope the pigs don't find it; it will fuck up my rep."

The point of the song isn't what happens but that nothing much does. In "Run," a duet with the gravel-voiced New York rapper Jadakiss, which appears on *The Pretty Toney Album* (2004), the police also show up, and Jadakiss and Ghostface take off, though Ghostface isn't sure why they're fleeing: "Running through the pissy stairwells, I ain't hear nothing, bugging. Only thing I remember was a bullshit summons." (In an aside of the kind that makes Ghostface's songs great, Jadakiss adds, "I'm asthmatic, so I'm lookin' for somewhere to hide at.") Like "Barbershop," "Run" evokes a sense of permanent environmental instability.

That anxiety permeates *Fishscale*. The first song, "Shakey Dog," suggests the gory opening scene of *Pulp Fiction*, in double time. With an accomplice named Frank, Ghostface enters an apartment building, where he smells plantains and rice; Frank proceeds to shoot a pit bull and "put two holes in the door man's Sassoon." In "Kilo," Ghostface describes the process of producing crack cocaine in brilliantly casual dialogue, backed by the sound of a spoon stirring something in a bowl: "Yo, Sharifa, go to the store for me. I need some razors and a fresh box of baggies, the ones with the tint in them. Yo, son, turn that water down a little bit, just a little bit. Thank you. I need two waters, a Dutch, and a cranberry Snapple."

His reactions to his violent surroundings are as unexpected as   10
his observations. In "Whip You with a Strap," an uneasy song built from a long sample of Luther Ingram's "To the Other Man," he tells of being beaten as a child by his mother. "Mama shake me real hard, then get the big gat—that's called the belt. 'Help me,' as I yelled, I'm in the room like 'huh, huh, huh' with mad welts. Ragged out, bad belt, yes, her presence was felt." And yet Ghostface apparently approves of corporal punishment: "She was famous for her slaps, and to this day she's on it. But when I was a little dude, her son was a little rude. . . . Nowadays kids don't get beat, they get big treats—fresh pairs of sneaks, punishment's like 'Have a seat.' "

And what to make of "Underwater," a lighthearted and goofy song produced by the rapper and producer MF Doom, who is responsible for four of the album's twenty-three tracks? The sound is odd and noisy, reminiscent of early Wu-Tang songs produced by the RZA. Flutes swoop around the beat and gurgling water punctuates Ghostface's ungangsterlike reverie of being "lost underwater": "Amazed that I'm not drowning, butterflies took control when I arrived. I opened the door—No, I knocked first." (Ghostface likes to interrupt himself.) He swims past fish, ogles "pearls on the mermaid girls, Gucci belts that they rock for no reason, from a different world," and sees SpongeBob SquarePants sitting "in the Bentley coupe," listening to the Isley Brothers. It's not exactly a song for kids—a more commercially minded rapper might have made it less weird—but Ghostface doesn't seem to care about tailoring his music to the market.

Last fall, in the middle of a riveting show at B.B. King's Ghostface asked a member of the stage crew to turn on a blue light. The d.j. put on "My Ebony Princess," a 1977 single by Jimmy Briscoe & the Little Beavers, and Ghostface began to sing along: "Your eyes are dark as the night." He stopped, listened to the record for a few seconds, and began talking about how his parents had conceived him while listening to this kind of soul music. Then he told the d.j. to stop the music. "For those that don't have no soul, y'all wouldn't really understand or know where the fuck I'm coming from when I play shit like that," he said. "See—I was born in 1970, yo. You know what, I'm a seventies man, a Taurus and shit, and I love, like, shit like that. I'd rather write to shit like that than hip-hop any day."

Questions for Discussion and Topics for Writing

1. What composition strategy does Frere-Jones use to begin his review of Ghostface Killah's album? What name would you give to this strategy? Assuming this strategy works, why do you think it is effective?
2. After the introduction to his essay, how does Ghostface write with an awareness of his audience (in the next two or three paragraphs)? Does knowing that this article originally appeared in *The New Yorker* make a difference in answering this question? How so?
3. What does Frere-Jones like about Ghostface's writing? In other words, what qualities in the rapper's lyrics (a) make them good writing and (b) make them stand out from many hip hop lyrics?
4. Frere-Jones's essay is an album review. How might it be different from your idea of what a review should do? To answer this question, look at how the author writes about the album. What does he emphasize?

Illmatic
A Journey into Nas's State of Mind
SHANA KENT

Shana Kent, the author of the student essay that follows, is a 2006 graduate of Vassar College. In the fall of 2006, Shana will enter the Ph.D. program in American Studies at the University of Maryland, where she plans to continue her study of film and music as evidence of American multicultural experience.

✦

I wasn't into rap much when Nas's first album, *Illmatic*, was released, but it's said that many true "hip-hop heads" were surprised at the way the cover of the album looked. Somehow it wasn't what they were expecting; maybe they were looking for something "harder," like a picture of "Nasty Nas" all grown up with an angry, threatening look on his face. But after listening to *Illmatic* enough times, I can't imagine a cover more representative of the album's contents. The whole image appears faded into countless shades of brown, worn down and having seen some tough times. Project buildings appear from either side, surrounding Nas's head, and continue into a vanishing point centered right between his eyes. On one side of his street, everything looks to be completely still, and on the other a car is in rapid motion, rushing to leave the frame altogether. And in the middle of it all is young, nappy-headed, squinty-eyed Nas, watching and searching, creating almost a hologram-type effect. Looking once, it seems like Nas is concentrating on the landscape in front of him, observing its every move. Look again, and Nas is emerging right out of its vanishing point, looking past the buildings straight at us with a wise, guarded distrust that is far beyond his years.

At the end of the first track on the album, "The Genesis," Nas prophetically proclaims to AZ and Cormega, "it's illmatic." *What is* "illmatic"? And why "ill, plus matic"? If "it" were "ill" alone, the genius (or illness) in Nas's creation would be remarkable, yes, but also finite, static. The term "illmatic" implies continuity; it modifies not a motionless object, but a complex entity with constant activity—a function, or even a state of mind. As the face of *Illmatic*, the cover's stationary and moving halves become a unified whole.

The truth is, *Illmatic* is the previously intangible vanishing point, the center at which the two halves meet, where everything in Nas's physical, imaginary, and spiritual landscapes collides and flows in and out of itself freely and masterfully, magnified and visible at last. Through constant conversation with the music and rhythms behind him, the vivid characters and scenes he creates and recreates, and his listeners, Nas blurs his physical reality with his dreams, his revelations, and his imagination. A graceful collision is created with thoughtful wordplay and loaded metaphors, and Nas steadily stirs his concoction—brimming with dichotomies of young and old, time and timelessness, dangerous and endangered, the factual and the hypothetical, the personal and the collective—into one cohesive sensibility.

The first full song, "NY State of Mind," sets the theme of collision and blurred lines for the rest of *Illmatic*, and the contents of the

song embody not only its title, but the overall spirit and meaning of
the album. It begins with a steady rhythm and a heavy, menacing,
descending bass line that enters right before Nas announces his
emergence right out of the "dungeons of rap," establishing the dangerous, threatening tone of the bass line that remains throughout
the rest of the song. A few bars later, the bass line is met with a high-
pitched, slightly dissonant piano chord that continues in response
to the bass line, constantly contrasting the thudding bass with a
ring of instability and alarm. The resulting collision is translated
and extended in Nas's verses, beginning with the declaration that
he is a "musician, inflictin' composition." In this first verse he portrays himself as a criminal, "inflicting" pain through threatening
narrative rather than physical aggression, and using "the pen" as
his "M-16." He seamlessly slips into a rampage provoked by his
"thoughts of an assassin," until he reaches a building lobby and
finds that it is "filled with children" armed with guns. This is one of
two points in the song where several components of Nas's composition come to a collision. Up until this point, Nas was a proclaimed
"assassin," a danger to his "foes," but just as the piano meets the
bass with alarm, Nas himself becomes threatened by the realization that "the game ain't the same." The younger generation has become a sudden threat to the older, established people of power.

5   In local terms, Nas is discovering that the guns in his Queensbridge, New York streets have fallen into the hands of younger hustlers, threatening the power of older men like himself—a
description that in itself complicates Nas's relationship with time,
as he is both old and "high," and part of the same young generation in question. Figuratively, Nas is also speaking from the position of older members of the rap game reacting to Nas's youthful
invasion, realizing that he is "bringing fame to [his] name" on this
very album by pulling the trigger on his pen. At the end of the
verse, Nas blurs the line between actual criminal "inside information" involving real characters (much like the "baseheads" selling
"broken amps") and the information gathered in his lyrics, which
also blurs the point where his own narrative ends and the characters' narratives begin. His reference to the "walls of intelligence"
situates him within the realm of contradiction, and also "beyond"
the point where his own mental intelligence is hindered by the
physical walls and obstacles of his surroundings. This complex,
personal and communal perspective is Nas's proclaimed definition
of the complete "N.Y. State of Mind."

The following song, "Life's A Bitch (featuring AZ)," not only
focuses on Nas's distinction between his physical reality and his

metaphysical, heightened state, but simultaneously captures Nas and AZ's surroundings and later renders them timeless. It begins with AZ's verse, which is rooted in physical observations and experiences, and revolves around sin and the moment of death. His lyrical journey culminates with the realization that "somehow we all gotta go" and leads into the song's hook and principal phrase, "life's a bitch and then you die." AZ's verse is concise, very literal and composed from a consciously mortal perspective, especially in comparison to Nas's verse, which begins after the chorus. By claiming that he "woke up early" the day he was born, Nas implies that he is a superhuman, godly entity who existed and lived before he was even born, a "blessing" by definition. In the lines that follow, he depicts himself as reborn immediately following the end of his adolescence, now "fresh in [his] physical frame" which is distinguished as only one part of his entire existence as a "godly like thing." Nas then creates a double meaning in the next two lines, specifically with the term *made* that establishes the co-existence of his physical and "godly" states. His "physical frame is celebrated" because he "made it" (survived one quarter of the human life span), and his physical frame is celebrated by others because he himself, in his godly form, created or "made it." Towards the end of his verse he refers to time as "*illmatic* keep static like wool fabric," a phrase that proves his ability to experience time at a standstill while others (like AZ) are living in anticipation of death, literally the end of their time. While Nas is able to exist with one foot in the mortal and immortal realms, this entire song spotlights his "godlier" side. The placement of his verse after AZ's verse as a human "sinner" establishes his words in comparison as heightened revelation, scripture coming from the "street's disciple."

Nas's proclamations of godliness transition smoothly into other, more complex metaphors on "Memory Lane." Not only does he remind us that his "duration's infinite," his "rap [is] divine" and his intellect hangs from a "cross with nails," but he also begins to blur the line more between his words in written form and the life experiences they depict. In his first verse on the song, he refers to a sentence that begins "indented . . . with formality," making it impossible to know whether he is speaking of a jail sentence or an "indented" written sentence, both entirely capable of "formality." Later in the same verse, while recalling an old friend who was murdered for his coat, Nas remarks that the "childhood lesson" forced him to watch the man "drop" in Nas's "weed smoke"—an observation which not only describes the physical details of his experience, but suggests a correlation between his "weed smoke" and his lyrics, as he is also making us visualize his friend dropping to the ground in his words. Both techniques blend his creative expressions of imagination with his detailed observations of reality into one continuous flow.

Tensions between the contents of his lyrics and reality are furthered in "One Love," a song that speaks directly to people close to him who are in prison. This song marks the point in the album and in Nas's narrative where his understanding of reality and acceptance of the present grapple with unresolved thoughts of the past and the future through nostalgia and regret, as well as musings on imagined possibilities. This constant tension is expressed musically after the very beginning of the song, which starts off with a dialogue between several inmates. During their conversation, we can hear hints of subtle melody being played behind them along with heavy drums, but the two chords supporting the melody do not directly converse with each other until Nas begins rapping. As he begins with the first two lines of his verse, sympathizing with his incarcerated friend and wishing he had taken cover from the cops in Nas's home, the bass and vibraphone dance around a single minor piano chord that expresses Nas's unsettled reflection on possibilities of the past. Then just as the instruments follow a new, murkier chord and descend into lower notes, he too changes his tone, admits there is "no time for looking back," and congratulates his friend on the birth of his son, suddenly shifting his perspective into forced acceptance and optimism of the present. The sentiments of these two complex chords are placed directly next to each other again at several other points throughout the song, one example being the end of the first verse, where Nas mentions money he has left in his friend's commissary (thus giving his friend hope for the future), and then returns immediately to their past, reminiscing that Nas's friend had his back when "push came to shove." By ending his expressions of the present and the past with "one love," Nas is defining the song's title as the collision of these two heavy, seemingly opposing perspectives into a love that welcomes, and even necessitates this opposition in order to exist and survive.

The construction of the narrative in "One Love" also involves the metaphor of his microphone as a joint or an "L," a current that runs persistently throughout *Illmatic*. In "Life's A Bitch," Nas introduces this concept with imagery of "loading up" his mic, puffing on it, and exhaling smoke clouded with the complexities of his imagination. The image is sharpened in "One Love," during a scene where he sits with a younger boy on a bench and smokes weed with him. After "talkin' mad shit," the boy passes the blunt to Nas, who only warns him to "take heed" and "make the right man bleed" after he has taken the "L." The bulk of Nas's rhyme scheme in this section rests primarily on the final words of each line. In the context of the scene, this sonic pattern might function as a cautionary mechanism that emphasizes the potential for fatality in his message to the younger generation—and in a larger sense, Nas's generation. The fact that Nas only begins responding to the young boy after he is passed the "L" suggests that the blunt functions as a microphone shared between them, amplifying their words. Nas provides words of wisdom once again in hypothetical terms, but here his lyrics express ideas for the future prevention of mistakes, rather than regret of the past and rumination on what could have been. Further, he positions himself physically within the scene but also in a place of transcendence. As he rises, "wiping the blunt's ash from [his] clothes" he shows his ability to cleanse himself of the chaos in a way that his younger, inexperienced friend does not, or cannot. After stopping to "blow smoke through [his] nose," he declares that he has planted "some jewels in the skull," suggesting that the "words of wisdom" were passed on through the smoke he exhaled, in hopes that his listener can "rise up above" just as he has.

In the scheme of things, this scene is one of many "snapshots" 10 that together compose the bigger picture. From looking at this complex image we can see that the vanishing point of *Illmatic* exists, but one must travel before reaching that point, and the entire album is structured to reflect that journey. It begins with a first song that defines the "state of mind" necessary to embark on the journey, and progresses with spiritual revelations that must be realized between the physical and metaphysical states; reflections bouncing between composed art and reality that must be seen; and tensions between the hypothetical and the factual, the metaphorical and the literal, that must be successfully understood and balanced in order to arrive at our destination.

Naturally the last song, "It Ain't Hard To Tell," is a celebration of this journey. With blazing, triumphant horns, heavy drums and harmonized voices singing and hollering, the song carefully brings together many aspects of *Illmatic* to create a sense of experienced survival and accomplishment. By calling his mic check "life or death," Nas constructs the microphone as a weapon with violent potential, but more importantly with the potential for "life." Through this metaphor he inspires listeners to now use microphones the way he has used his, as a figurative tool for artistic respiration and a guide for taking "righteous steps" to their next destination. He later triumphantly declares that in his "physical" self, he can "express through song" and "delete stress" after he has given Medusa "shotguns in hell" from his spliff, a journey presumably taken while in his godly form. With his technique, he is able to express himself musically in his physical state and use "song" to alleviate stress for the people around him, but he can also travel to hell in his godly state and pass on "shotguns" of knowledge through his "L" to even the most condemned and hopeless of spirits, as he does in "One Love."

And Nas is right. By the end of the album, it ain't hard to tell that he has created a masterpiece of an album: a tangible embodiment of the point where every dichotomy in Nas's personal and communal consciousness collides, converses, and becomes one. As the image on the album cover shows, Nas is physically young, but behind his eyes is the constant crafting of collision into intricate, elaborate music that transcends space and time altogether. *Illmatic* is the amplification of Nas's timeless, self-proclaimed enlightened journey from the depths of Queensbridge Projects to the vanishing point in his eyes where every shade of brown, every moment of fast motion and reflective stillness, every tough time and consequent revelation together becomes supernatural, organized chaos—a state of mind.

Questions for Discussion and Topics for Writing

1. At several points, Kent points out Nas's use of an extended metaphor between street violence and composition. How does this metaphor imagine the act of writing? Do you think this metaphor works to deflect or encourage actual violence?

2. Kent explores the function of time in Nas's album. How does time work, according to Kent? What is significant about Nas's view of time for the meaning of the album? Does this sense of time relate to your own?

3. Kent devotes her introduction to a description of Nas's album cover. Choose an album cover that you find provocative and use it to set up your essay. Describe the album cover as a way of leading into an argument about the album's content.

4. Kent shows how a series of songs can be linked together to tell a story. Select an album and listen to the songs. Then write an essay about the story the songs tell when taken together. Remember that it is not only what the songs say but also their order on the album that create the narrative.

Making Connections

1. Watch Alex Haley's *Roots*. Can you identify themes in the movie that reverberate with hip hop and its origins?
2. Consider the song "Rapper's Delight." How does this song or other songs use traditional poetic devices such as toasting, boasting, playing the dozens, and call and response? Do you see formulaic expressions? Can you find in the song what Leopold Senghor calls "imagery-analogies"?
3. Listen to Ice Cube's "You Ain't Gonna Take My Life" (and perhaps read the introduction to "Gangsta Rap"). In the last stanza, Ice Cube alludes to Petey Wheatstraw. Who is this character and what is he doing in the song? How does this situate hip hop in a larger music or literary tradition?
4. Watch the video "Walk This Way." Do you think the video represents "a biracial and musical fusion"? Or is it merely an instance where rap is made palatable to white audiences by the appropriation of rock 'n' roll beats?

CHAPTER 2

Crossing the Color Line: Hip Hop Negotiates the Complexities of Race

A significant reason for hip hop's often infamous position within popular culture is its provocative deployment of culturally explosive words. None is more incendiary than the racially charged epithet *nigga*. A version of *nigger*, which has roots in sixteenth-century Spanish colonization, *nigga* retains offensive, derogatory, oppressive, and racist connotations. Yet, many have argued that in the context of hip hop, *nigga* is an example of "flippin' the script": the term does not repeat but *signifies* on the word *nigger*; that is, it is a way of saying one thing and meaning another, a way of reversing the positions of power implied by the word. As such, *nigga* is a means of empowerment, a means of silencing the white oppressor by appropriating the word's use for identification within the black community where it becomes a means of acknowledging a shared history of oppression and a shared struggle to overcome its continued effects in the present.

Within hip hop, then, *nigga* has been used not only to empower black communities, but to make distinctions between those in the ghetto and those middle-class black Americans who may have more in common with the white dominant culture. As many hip hop critics insist, most notably Robin D. G. Kelly, *nigga* is not synonymous with *black*. Rather it signifies the specific and collective experience of those who live in poverty within the urban blight of the projects that exist as the epicenter of ghettos. While such a definition goes a long way to clarifying the term by saying precisely whom it identifies and in what specific circumstances, this definition also privileges a class distinction rather than a racial one. While this shift may be useful in some contexts, it has had some unpredictable and—at least for some—troubling effects. Muting the distinct racial history of the word has allowed youth of all races to appropriate the word as a way of announcing their fealty to hip hop culture even if they themselves do not come from the projects or the 'hood. As a result, it is possible for an Asian kid to approach a Hispanic friend and, without irony, greet him by saying, "What up, my nigga?" Weirdly, in this instance of appropriation, the term suddenly becomes racially inclusive even without entirely losing its racial connotations.

Perhaps more disturbing than this appropriation itself, the use of the word outside the context of the ghetto codifies middle- and upper-middle-class youth's aspirations to take on the mantle of what Tupac popularized as the "thug life." Conflating what are otherwise mutually exclusive terms, the good life becomes the same as ghetto life through a perverse fantasy of a life born of poverty and oppression imagined from a position of privilege that can evacuate the experience of any real violence or racism. Appropriated this way, *nigga* connotes not an identity of resistance and struggle, but rather a caricature based on a series of superficial yet provocative tropes. Within hip hop, of course, the word is used both ways: it acknowledges and resists both institutional racism and ideologies of hate and, conversely, evokes images intended to titillate and thereby sell records.

No matter how racially generic the term becomes within hip hop and among youth, there remains resistance to white kids using the word, as the term relies on this fundamental racial distinction for its meaning. In fact, as Imani Perry points out in *Prophets of the Hood*, hip hop has not really given any new meaning to or invented any new use for the word, but rather has made it possible for a word once limited to use within the black community to be spoken if not by white people then, at least, in their presence. Among other things, this erases the distinct uses of the word within the black community and within a white one—a volatile situation, indeed, when the definition of the word relies on the context within which it is uttered.

When there is no distinction between the black linguistic world and the white, the word with an -*er* and the word with an -*a*, meant to demarcate these discreet contexts, becomes for many a superficial matter of spelling. But the obvious need to maintain a distinction between the two words has led to other variations, like a derivation of *nigga* that applies to Caucasians who identify with hip hop: *wigga*. But *wigga*, even within the hip hop community, clearly does not have the same social consequences and force as the word *nigga;* rather, it is generally regarded as dismissive and distancing.

As a white rapper Eminem contends with the word and uses it to flip an already flipped script and critique these kinds of racial distinctions. In the song "The Way I Am," Eminem critiques his fans who make the mistake of seeing Marshal Mathers, the individual, as indistinguishable from Eminem, the performer. In a song whose chorus asserts that the rapper's identity is whatever his audience wants it to be, this is no simple complaint, as Eminem acknowledges that his identity as well as his fame is constructed by his audience. This exploration and critique of identity climaxes at the end of the song, when Eminem addresses the subject of his race. He spoofs those who call him black, exposing the slippery interstices between race, culture, and class that he occupies. He then goes on to deflate the racialized criticism that he is a "wigga." By recognizing the word *wig* inside of *wig*ga, he shows race to be not only constructed but no different from other kinds of "wardrobes" (a pun occurring earlier in the song in reference to buying a wardrobe in response to a law*suit*.) But even if race is a "wig," it is one that can't easily be taken off. At the end of the song, Eminem finds himself pulling out his own hair in frustration.

As Eminem dramatizes, rappers have not resolved the debate around *nigga* and its derivations. Rather, the word has become an essential dialectic within hip hop. For example, in the song "Sucka Nigga," A Tribe Called Quest venerates the word. Q-Tip, an emcee in the group, first gives a cursory history of a word in the song. He acknowledges its explicit racial use in the Deep South, how the world tumbled from the white man's *dome*, a word that signified that the African-American race would never grow. Q-Tip, demonstrating a sense of the term's plasticity, then indicates how black youth use the word *nigga* as a term of endearment and as a way to manage adversity. Q-Tip thus redefines the word, but clearly remains uneasy about this transformation: using the word causes him to "flinch," even as he is seduced into using the term because of its transgressive cultural power.

In contrast, The Coup, in their song "I Ain't the Nigga," critiques the use of the word. Boots Riley, the group's principle lyricist, begins the song reflecting on the etymology of *nigga*. He points out that the word didn't always refer to skin color, but that it was used in reference to a machine, the cotton gin. In giving his own history of the word, Boots reveals it to be derogatory, objectifying, and heinously offensive when applied to a person. In the next stanza, E-Roc, a second emcee in the group, follows up by making clear that there is no real distinction between the word with an -*er* or with an -*a*. E-Roc strongly opposes those who argue that the meaning is different if an *a* is used: such an argument, he notes, makes him itch and twitch. Just as Q-Tip flinches as he finds himself seduced into using *nigga*, E-Roc twitches at attempts to justify a word that he considers "mental trash."

The tension evident in the different reactions to the term *nigga* in the music of The Coup and A Tribe Called Quest should suggest that hip hop is much more representative of the complexities of mainstream culture than some would like it to be. In the song "Mr. Nigga," Mos Def complicates the diametrically opposed positions sketched above. He does so in part by critiquing the tolerant view of *nigga* taken in "Sucka Nigga" by signifying upon its chorus. Where the chorus of "Sucka Nigga" repeats the song's title, Mos Def quotes and signifies on it by substituting *Mistah* for *Sucka* in the chorus to his own song, exhuming the subservience and the empty, double-edged politeness in the word's historical usage. His gesture, therefore, is simultaneously an indication of kinship and critique. Mos Def's song itself is a long, intricate narrative about Mos Def's experiences as a famous black artist and his specific and almost ubiquitous confrontations with institutional racism. Through his stories, the rapper demonstrates how ideological ghosts—as related to the word's original repressive use by white supremacists—haunt it even as it undergoes transformation within the black community.

As one example from the song, Mos Def tells about being in first class on a flight. Startled to see a young black male in first class, the flight attendant doesn't believe he is in the right place. Noting his boarding pass, she attempts to apologize for her initial incredulity by giving him an extra bit of lime in his drink, and later, asking him for his autograph. For Mos Def, the scene demonstrates how the flight attendant maintains a view of him as a second-class citizen despite his wealth and his fame. Her suggestion that he is in the wrong place reveals her assumption that he belongs at the back of the plane, an assumption that painfully resonates with Southern white expectations before the Civil Rights Movement that blacks dwell separately but "equally" at the back of the bus. Her embarrassment can be seen as an acknowledgment of her mistake, although it is evident that, despite the extra lime and the request for an autograph, there has been no fundamental change in her attitude.

Despite signifyin' on the chorus of "Sucka Nigga," Mos Def does not necessarily critique Q-Tip's use of the word, and it remains uncertain whether he would side with The Coup in their criticism of its use within the black community. Rather, what Mos Def shows is that even if the definition of the word *nigga* changes among black people, its highly pejorative meaning remains within the dominant culture. Even more problematic, the word has become internalized so that the racist attitudes that the word connotes remain even when it goes unsaid.

This last observation leads us to one further consideration. Even if rappers succeed in redefining *nigga* for the white as well as the black linguistic world, the potential overuse of the word within hip hop may desensitize the user and the auditor to its meaning rather than intentionally remind users of slavery and continued social oppression as a way of encouraging social change. By the same token, even if the word is seen to have no redemptive value, there is a danger in making the word unspeakable. Enforcing a kind of indirect censorship may be a kind of desensitizatation by other means, since expunging the word from the lexicon of hip hop runs the risk of obfuscating a sociohistorical reality that so many—from Frederick Douglass and W. E. B. Dubois to Martin Luther King and Malcom X—have struggled to change by identifying the very racial divide that *nigga* identifies. Whatever position one takes in the end, the word pervades hip hop and provides a context where the merits and abuses of the word can be kept in play, allowing for a continuing and evolving discussion about race and its social, historical, and political impact.

Guarding the Borders of the Hip-Hop Nation

N.R. KLEINFIELD

N.R. Kleinfield covers metropolitan news for The New York Times. *Kleinfield contributed articles for two* Times *series that won Pulitzer Prizes: "How Race Is Lived in America" and "A Nation Challenged," a series documenting life in post-September 11, 2001 America. His most recent notable contribution to the* Times *was a 2006 series chronicling an epidemic of diabetes in New York City. The following article, part of the Pulitzer-winning series mentioned earlier, appeared in* The New York Times, *July 6, 2000.*

---------------------- ✦ ----------------------

He waited until the bus was ready to leave before squeezing up front to address the passengers. The Greyhound was going from Chicago to Indiana. It was winter. The sky was suffused with gray.

He surveyed the bunched rows of seats. There were only 19 passengers, most of them young, most of them black. Billy Wimsatt was white. It was an audience that made him especially comfortable.

He held aloft a slender book. "I wrote this book," he said over the chitter of talk. "It's pretty good. It normally sells for $12. On this bus, I'll sell it for $5, and you can read it along the way free."

It was called "No More Prisons," and was about incarceration and philanthropy and hip-hop, always hip-hop, for hip-hop was the everlasting undertone to his life. He was a writer and activist, and over the years his work had made him something of a minor cult figure in the hip-hop world, a white man with unusual credibility among blacks deeply protective of their culture. He was an unbudgeable optimist, convinced he could better the world by getting whites and people of other races to talk together and work together. He spent most of his time on the road, on a yearlong tour of several dozen college campuses, preaching his message. Now the bus was taking him to Earlham College in eastern Indiana.

Some passengers gave grudging looks of curiosity. What gives with this guy? Six people beckoned for copies. One woman gave hers back after 15 minutes, opting for sleep. A man behind her bought one. A woman said she'd take one, too. "Cool," Mr. Wimsatt said. He gave her a big smile and a hug.

Billy Wimsatt was 27, still clinging to the hip-hop life. He didn't look terribly hip-hop, and not because he was white. He was balding and brainy-looking, with an average build and an exuberant nature.

He was born as rap music was being invented by blacks and Latinos in the South Bronx. What began as party music became their cry of ghetto pain and ultimately their great hope for a way out. And as hip-hop—not just rap music but fashion, break-dancing, graffiti and the magazines that chronicle it all—blossomed into the radiant center of youth culture, Billy Wimsatt and lots of white kids found in it a way to flee their own orderly world by discovering a sexier, more provocative one.

Like many young hip-hop heads, he regarded hip-hop, with its appeal to whites and blacks, as a bold modern hope to ease some of the abrasiveness between the races. Hip-hop, as he saw it, endowed him with cultural elasticity, allowed him to shed the privilege of whiteness, to be as down with blacks as with whites. For a long time, he felt black in every respect but skin color, he says, which was why he had been able to get away with that much-noticed article seven years ago in *The Source,* a magazine considered one of the bibles of hip-hop.

It was a withering critique of "wiggers," whites who try too hard to be black so they will be accepted. Soon, he argued, "the rap audience may be as white as tables in a jazz club." In the last paragraph, which *The Source* cut from the final version, he warned black artists that the next time they invented something, they had better find a way to control it financially, because whites were going to steal hip-hop.

10 "And since it's the 90's," he concluded, "you won't even get to hear us say, 'Thanks, niggers.' "

Yes, Billy Wimsatt seemed about as authentically hip-hop as a white guy could get. But as he slid into the complexities of adulthood, he said, he often found himself wondering if that was enough, unsure which culture was truly his. He had drifted a long way from his black hip-hop roots. Now, on these unsettled grounds, he was far from certain he could stay true to his ideas.

A BELIEVER ON THE BRINK

On a clangorous Manhattan sidewalk, Elliott Wilson stopped to study the bootleg rap tapes splayed on a street vendor's blanket. Music emanated from a portable stereo.

"Some dope stuff here," Mr. Wilson, a gangly, light-skinned young black man with inquisitive eyes and a contagious laugh, said approvingly. The bargains got him pumped up. He peeled off a five-dollar bill and bought "Opposite of H2O" by Drag-On.

Elliott Wilson had never met Billy Wimsatt, but their lives had traced similar trajectories across the hip-hop landscape. As a writer and editor, he too had spent much of his adult life thinking about hip-hop. And not just hip-hop, but race and hip-hop. Race was unavoidable in hip-hop—what with all those black rappers idolized by white teenagers—and like Billy Wimsatt, Elliott Wilson was preoccupied with that conjunction and what it meant in his own life.

Which culture was his was not Elliott Wilson's worry. Hip-hop 15 had inspired him to believe that, precisely because he was black, he could achieve what whites simply assumed was theirs by birthright—a gainful life over which he asserted control.

When he read Mr. Wimsatt's "wigger" article, he and a black friend were beginning their own hip-hop publication, Ego Trip. They saw it as a brash challenge to the established, white-owned magazines like *The Source*. Bubbling with assurance, Mr. Wilson had judged the "wigger" article amusing; for all its ridicule of whites, he had still considered it "a white boy's perspective on hip-hop." He certainly hadn't seen it as a prophecy of personal doom.

Now, he sometimes had to wonder. He was closing in on 30, trying to hold fast to his own idea of the hip-hop life. He had watched with anger and growing pessimism as Ego Trip folded and whites asserted ever-greater control over the hip-hop industry. Recently, he had become editor of a promising hip-hop magazine, *XXL*. It was white-owned. And so he wondered if he was selling out, if he would ever become what he wanted on his own terms. Was hip-hop his story, the black man's story, after all? Did hip-hop unite the races or push them further apart?

A WHITE BOY CONFINED IN HIS SKIN

Growing up in Chicago, Billy Wimsatt remembers, he believed the only way he could have a good life was to be black.

His own life felt proscribed. He was an only child. There was rarely music in the house, just the droning news stations. He saw an awful lot of "Nova" on PBS. He was to avoid the unsavory black neighborhoods.

Yet, he recalls, black children seemed to roam freely. They 20 seemed to grow up faster. In fourth grade, his teacher asked if anyone baby-sat. A black girl's hand shot up. Incredible. Black girls were mature enough to baby-sit. He says he longed to live in the projects.

Where he lived was the integrated neighborhood of Hyde Park, in a perfectly diverse six-flat: two white families, two black, two mixed. His father taught philosophy of science at the University of Chicago. His mother was sort of a perpetual student.

At his mostly white private school, he was not especially popular. He imagined becoming a computer programmer, a scientist, an astronaut. Then, in sixth grade, a black kid told him to listen to a rap song, "Jam On It." "It was like a message from another world," he said.

Increasingly, he disconnected from a white culture that he equated with false desires. He had jumped out of his container, he said, "like spilled milk." After sixth grade, he persuaded his parents to transfer him to a largely black public school. The cool kids, he noticed, wore fat sneaker laces, favored gold jewelry, did graffiti. He began shoplifting fat laces, fake gold jewelry and markers and selling them to hip-hop heads.

He started break-dancing on the streets. And at 13, he began sneaking out at night and riding the trains with black and Latino friends, bombing the city with spray paint. Upski was his chosen tag. From then on, little Billy Wimsatt became Upski, one of Chicago's most prolific graffiti artists.

25   His frazzled mother, dogged by insomnia, would discover him gone at 2 a.m. She barred his graffiti crew from the house (one of them even burglarized the place), sent him to a psychiatrist, threatened military school. When he persisted, his parents plunked him back in private school. But he barely associated with white classmates, he says. Hip-hop had cloaked him in a new identity.

Astonishingly, and much to the dismay of many older people who abhorred its defiant attitude, its frequent misogyny, violence and vulgarity, hip-hop culture was becoming a great sugar rush for young people of all races. Before long, rap would eclipse country and rock to become America's top-selling pop-music format. And whites would be the ones buying most of those rap albums—a full 70 percent.

For many, even most, young whites, hip-hop was ultimately a hobby, to be grown out of in good time. For Upski, it became a cause, especially as the late 80's gave rise to politically conscious rappers like Public Enemy, with its peppery blend of black nationalism and rebellion. "Once it became a pretty full critique of American life—race, politics and political hypocrisy—that's when it really registered with me," he said.

A BLACK 'LEADER OF THE NERDS'

Elliott Wilson grew up in the Woodside Houses project in Queens, the oldest of three brothers. His mother was of Greek and Ecuadorean roots; his father, a printer from Georgia, was black. Elliott was very light-skinned, and his hair was different from the black kids'. When it came to skin color, he picked up some mixed messages.

He was 5 when his father told him: "You're going to be judged by who your father is. I'm black. So you're black. Accept it before you get hurt." And he did, he said: "I felt like the black man from the jump."

He also spent a lot of time with his father's mother. She was 30 tough, and she had friends of all races. She called white people crackers, but told Elliott, "Never trust a black person darker than you."

Attending predominantly white schools, self-conscious about his looks, he never really fit in, he says, recalling that time now. The black and white students didn't mix much, and while the black football players were cool, he was no football player. Instead, he befriended the outcasts.

"I wanted to be a cool kid and I wasn't," he said. "But I didn't want to sacrifice who I was to fit into the system. I'd rather create my own system. I wasn't going to be a fake. So I was the leader of the nerds."

His parents sheltered him from the influence of the streets. He watched a lot of television. He loved *Happy Days* and *Good Times*, admired Howard Cosell and imagined becoming a sportscaster. In high school, he says, he increasingly felt himself an outsider. His grades, always good, fell.

But there was hip-hop. Hip-hop was cool, and his growing love of it made him begin to feel cool. His parents bought him a set of Technics 1200 turntables and a mixer. On weekend nights, while classmates were out on dates, he would be home taping the hip-hop shows off the radio.

When he listened to Public Enemy, he began to shake his head 35 knowingly. For young Elliott Wilson, unaware of so much, the group's powerful lyrics of oppression and rage, especially the album "It Takes a Nation of Millions to Hold Us Back," were an awakening to what it meant to be black in America. He got a Public Enemy jacket, with the group's logo on the back: a black man in the cross hairs of a gun.

He became more aloof. He no longer said hello to white people, even family friends, unless they greeted him first, he now says. They asked his parents, What's gotten into Elliott?

He went to La Guardia Community College—in part because Run of Run-DMC had gone there to major in mortuary science—and then to Queens College. He began writing for hip-hop publications. One day first semester, he had an interview with Kool G. Rap. School felt irrelevant. He walked out of class and never returned. He entrusted his fate to hip-hop, and hip-hop breathed possibility into his life.

"If I came out of school without hip-hop, I wouldn't have thought of owning my own business and having power," he said. "As a person of color, to be legit, you think you have to be a worker for someone. Hip-hop made me believe."

But hip-hop was full of bizarre crosscurrents. When he saw white kids simulating his behavior, he got annoyed. It was one thing if they had grown up in the culture. But those well-to-do young whites who tried to appropriate hip-hop for themselves, he says, were simply insecure "image chameleons."

40   Right here was the enigma of hip-hop: The black rappers certainly weren't preaching integration, inviting whites into their homes. They were telling their often dismal stories, the pathologies they felt had been visited on them by a racist system they yearned to escape. But so many white kids were turning that on its head. They wanted to live life large, the way the rappers did.

A REASON FOR RHYMES

The phone rang. Dog got it: "He here. We here. I'll hit you back later. You gonna be in the crib?"

It was afternoon. Like a lot of aspiring rappers, Dog and his friend Trife were living life small, passing time in Dog's rampantly messy apartment in Brooklyn's Clinton Hill section. Passing time was what they did most days. They played games, gossiped, drank Hennessy, chewed over the future. Weekends, they went bowling. They were 23, young black men seeking sanctuary from the streets by rhyming their lives.

With their friends Po and Sinbo, they had formed a rap group, Wanted and Respected. Dog's closet was stuffed with recording equipment; his specialty was creating the beats. He made some slim money doing tapes for kids with their own rap dreams ($100 a tape) and selling shirts on the street. The group had played a few clubs, always gratis. Others shuttled in and out, but life weighed on the composition: members kept getting jailed, and one had been killed.

Dog and Trife had followed a trajectory of intense poverty and outlaw life. Dog's grandmother basically raised him—a dozen relatives packed into a three-bedroom place. Trife grew up with his mother, an R & B singer, and seven others in the nearby projects; he still lived there with her.

They had belonged to a gang called the Raiders, they said, selling drugs and doing other things that landed them in prison. If a white person came into their neighborhood, they said, they robbed him. They all packed guns. "It was bad as Beirut," Dog said. Trife said he still sold drugs, and some of the others did dubious things.

A few years ago, they gravitated to rap, embracing it the way so many poor blacks have long embraced basketball. But it was better. There were more slots. And it seemed to demand less talent. "You don't even have to sing well," Dog said.

"Music is my sanity," Trife said. "If I wasn't doing this, I'd probably be doing 25 to life."

Dog laughed. "If it weren't for rap, I'd be dead."

Many older blacks felt rap denigrated their race. They hated the constant use of "nigga" in the songs. Dog and Trife shrugged this off. Rap was raw and ugly, but that was their lives, they said. Rap was a blunter truth.

Dog found it curious that whites—suburban mall rats, college backpackers—bought most rap records. "White people can listen to rap, but I know they can't relate," he said. "I hear rap and I'm saying, 'Here's another guy who's had it unfair.' They're taking, 'This guy is cool, he's a drug dealer, he's got all the girls, he's a big person, he killed people.' That is moronic."

Later, Dog said: "Hip-hop is bringing the races together, but on false pretenses to make money. Look at Trife. He's got two felonies. That means he's finished in society. But he can rap. His two felonies, in rap, man, that's a plus."

"It's messed up," Trife said. "In hip-hop, I'm valid when I'm disrespected."

Trife recited, some lyrics he had written:

You can't walk in my shoes,
If you ain't lived my life.
Hustling all day, clapping out all night.

THE COOL RICH KIDS' MOVEMENT

The road to Earlham was speckled with billboards for Tom Raper RV's, the Midwest's largest RV dealer. The trees were sheathed in glass from the freezing rain.

55   Earlham, a small Quaker college, was predominantly white, marginally into hip-hop. Upski was to give a talk, accompanied by a hip-hop group, Rubberoom.

Upski had dropped out of Oberlin College in his junior year. He had only reluctantly gone to college at all. He spent more time doing graffiti and reading magazines than going to class. He wrote an anonymous column for the black paper that scathingly denounced white people. He had a hip-hop radio show: "Yo, this is live from Chicago." Many people thought he was black.

Even so, he says, he was sporadically queasy about his hip-hop moorings. He knew his infatuation with blacks could be taken different ways. He could be accepted as credible, or taken as exploitative.

"That is the great fear of blacks," he said. " 'Oh, you'll be fascinated with us, and then go back to dominating us and you'll be better at it because you'll have inside information.'" When he had shown drafts of his writings about race to a black classmate at Oberlin, she had slipped them back under his door and stopped talking to him.

He committed himself to journalism and activism. As he put it, "I saw it as my job to get white people to talk about race."

60   In 1994, a year after his influential "wigger" article, he self-published *Bomb the Suburbs*—part memoir of a white man's life in hip-hop, part interviews with hip-hop figures, part treatise on race and social change. It sold an impressive 23,000 copies. The gangsta rapper Tupac Shakur declared it "the best book I read in prison."

Upski hitchhiked around the country, promoting the book, pushing his views on racial cohesion, further cementing his eccentric renown. "I thought white people would start listening to and liking black people," he said, but ultimately, he was discouraged.

He refocused. He would become a social-change agent, motivating whites to be activists. Last fall, he published *No More Prisons* and began the "Cool Rich Kids' Movement." He would coax cool rich kids to give money to the cause. He started the Active Element Foundation and, with an ally, a well-to-do white woman, also started a group, Reciprocity, that paid him a modest salary. This year, he began his college tour.

At Earlham, before a mostly white audience, Upski said: "The thing that drives me is getting to know people and making relationships across race and class, which doesn't happen so much in America. Some of the stuff I'm going to say is going to sound heavy, and you're going to say, 'Let me go smoke some weed and chill.'"

He bounced around the room, his manner that of the motivational speaker. He said: "My goal today is to encourage you to accept the best and worst things about yourself." He talked about how they were too comfortable in this school, and how he had been "saved" by transferring to a black school after sixth grade. And then Rubberoom performed, and a lot of people left and the remaining ones danced. Upski danced.

Upski had brought along a copy of Stress, a small hip-hop magazine published by people of color. Upski told the students to read this, not the white-owned magazines.

He used to write for *XXL*, a fledgling magazine with a white owner and publisher. In 1997, the original black editor and black staff quit after being refused an ownership stake. There were innuendos of racism, but whether it was just business or race depended on the vantage point. Upski, however, swore never to work for *XXL* again.

After all, there were always ways for a smart white guy to make money.

AGONIZING AT THE MONKEY ACADEMY

When the editor's job at *XXL* was offered to him last August, Elliott Wilson was put in a delicate spot. He was broke. In college, he accepted a flurry of credit cards and bought all the "fly" clothing. Now he owed $8,000.

He remembers thinking about how blacks needed to think more like whites. "We have a short expectancy in life," he said. "So we go for the quick buck. That's why kids sell drugs. That's why they rob. We don't feel we can be on a five-year plan to success."

The *XXL* job came with excellent pay—low six figures. But talk of racial tension stained the place. He asked himself, he said, could blacks think he was selling out? First, he had to discuss it with the Ego Trip collective. He went over to the Monkey Academy.

Two rooms in a Chelsea basement, the Monkey Academy was a shrine to hip-hop. Roosting on a shelf was a "Talking Master P" doll ("Make 'em say uhhh") and a memento from Puff Daddy's 1998 birthday gala. Rap posters adorned the wall: Snoop Doggy Dogg, RZA, Jungle Brothers.

Ego Trip was five young men of color with ambitions of hip-hop entrepreneurship: Mr. Wilson, Sacha Jenkins, Jeff Mao, Gabriel Alvarez and Brent Rollins. They saw race as a depressive undercurrent to everything, and it was the focus of their scabrous humor. "We're always talking about the blacks and the whites," Mr. Wilson said. "That's the way me and my boys are."

The very name Monkey Academy reflected their saucy attitude. As Mr. Jenkins explained it: "Call me paranoid, but when I meet with white people, I feel that with their eyes they're calling me monkey. So why not wear that proudly? Everyone in hip-hop wants to use the N-word, so why not take it to the next level? Call us monkeys." They especially liked to trace their understanding of society to the *Planet of the Apes* movies, where the light-skinned orangutans controlled the dark gorillas.

Several years ago, the group published Ego Trip, which they saw as a magazine about race disguised as a hip-hop magazine. They invented a white owner, one Theodore Aloysius Bawno, who offered a message in each issue, blurting his bigoted views and lust for Angie Dickinson. His son, Galen, was a Princeton-educated liberal who professed common cause with blacks. But in truth, he was an unaware bigot, as Mr. Wilson says he feels so many young whites are.

75 So much of the hip-hop ruling class was white. As Mr. Wilson put it, Ego Trip wanted "to strike at all the black magazines that are white-owned and act as if they're black." It was a small irony that Ego Trip's seed money of $8,000 came from a white man, but at least he was a passive partner.

Though it gained a faithful following, Ego Trip stayed financially wobbly. No new investors came forth; the collective suspected the reluctance had to do with skin color. Ego Trip gasped and expired.

Now its founders scrambled with day jobs and worked on projects like *Ego Trip's Book of Rap Lists* and a companion album. Hip-hop Web sites were proliferating, and they hoped to start one, too. They said they wanted to hear the roar of money, on their terms. "Black people create, but we don't reap the benefits," Mr. Wilson said. "We get punked and pimped. If we were white boys, we'd all be rich by now."

On that August day, he recalls, he sat on the couch, his emotions in an uproar. He had to wonder: was he now going to work for a true-life Ted Bawno? The others, he says, expressed a dim view of the *XXL* offer: "They were feeling I was pimping."

Not long before, he had been music editor of *The Source*. One duty was to rate new albums, on a scale of one to five "microphones." When he gave three microphones to "Corruption" by Corrupt, he says, the white publisher, David Mays, increased it to three and a half without telling him. When he confronted Mr. Mays, he concluded that the publisher did not respect him. Mr. Mays wouldn't give his side, but as Mr. Wilson tells it, he quit over half a microphone.

He felt strongly, he recalls, that he had to help himself. He no 80 longer saw hip-hop as a great equalizer. "Who because of hip-hop now believes, 'I've seen the light, I'm going to save the blacks'?" he would say.

Sure, there was something positive in white kids' idolizing black rappers, but "what's going to happen when these white kids lose their little hip-hop jones and go work for Merrill Lynch?" he said.

What should he do? Months later, he remembers the confusion, the vectors of his life colliding. His throat tightened and he began to cry. He went to the bathroom of the Monkey Academy and composed himself. The message left hanging in the air from the others was, Do what you got to do.

As a black man, how many opportunities would come his way? He had this unslaked desire to prove his mettle. He took the job.

TAPPING THE UNCONSCIOUS BIASES

Upski went to the laundermat. Shaking in detergent, he talked about how he was a bundle of contradictions, subject to irrational racist phantasms for which he had no cogent defense. "I have patterns like every other white guy that I'm not very aware of that play out as racist," he admitted. He laughed at racist jokes. Walking down the street at night, he felt threatened if he saw a shabbily dressed black man. "I frequently feel I have more of a level of comfort and trust with white people," he said.

He talked differently to black friends ("Yo. . . That's wack. . . 85 Peace, brother."). It infuriated his white girlfriend, Gita Drury. "I'll say to him, 'Do you know you're talking black now? Can you talk white, because that's what you are,'" she said. "I think it's patronizing." When he got on the phone, she could detect at once the caller's race. When he talked black, she would wave a sign at him: "Why are you talking like that?"

She saw this episodic behavior in other ways: "If we walk down the street and a black person walks by, he will give this nod, raise his chin a bit. He wouldn't do it with a white guy. I'll say, 'Oh, you have to prove to a black person that you're down.'"

Not long ago, Upski recalled, he spoke about race at a prominent college along with a black friend. He was paid twice as much as his friend. He spoke longer, but not twice as long. He never told his friend.

Sometimes, he said, he believed that black people were dumber than whites. Sometimes he felt the opposite. Now, as the washers ended their cycles, he hauled the wet clothes to the dryers. A stout black woman stood beside an empty cart. He asked if she was using it. She stared at him, bewildered. He asked again. Nothing.

Exasperated, he simply grabbed the cart and heaped it with his clothes.

90   Later on, he said: "When that happened, part of my gut reaction was, 'This is a black woman who has limited brain capacity, and it fits my stereotype of blacks having less cognitive intelligence.' "

Would a white woman have understood?

"It's dangerous for me to even say that," he said. "But that's what I thought."

EMBARRASSED BY RAP'S 'BABIES'

The strip club was scattered with patrons with embalmed looks, solemnly quaffing their beverages. Elliott Wilson pulled up a stool beside a dancer. A fistful of dollars flapped from a rubber band curled around her wrist, the night's rewards.

Strip clubs, in particular this one in Queens, had a powerful hold on him. Though rap was his music, he said, he liked to unwind here rather than at a hip-hop club. There, everyone wanted something. Here, no one wanted anything but his money. "I'm not caught up in me and Puffy having each other's cell phone numbers," he said.

95   He had conflicted feelings about rap and rappers. "A lot of rappers rap about sex and violence, because people are interested in it," he said. "But it's art. It's poetry. If a rapper says, 'Kill your mother' in a song, it doesn't mean kill your mother. You can't take anything at face value." The real-life violence and arrests of rappers were something else. "Rappers are babies," he said. "They don't know how to balance their success and their street life. When I hear about Jay-Z this and Puffy that, I'm embarrassed to be part of the profession."

Mr. Wilson and his friend Gabe Alvarez shared an apartment in Clinton Hill, next to Fort Greene, a gentrifying neighborhood promoted by Spike Lee before he moved to the Upper East Side.

"Part of it's good and part isn't," Mr. Alvarez said. "You go a block over and there're the drug dealers."

"It's like the classic black neighborhood," Mr. Wilson said. "The liquor store, the bodega. I want good restaurants. I don't want to live in the 'hood. Who wants to live in the 'hood?" He wanted to move to Park Slope.

It was not his thing to go out of his way to patronize black businesses. It was fruitless, he said. He had seen that so much in hip-hop. "There's always a white man somewhere making money," he said. "You can't avoid the white man. My going to a black barber or something doesn't do anything."

UPSKI MEETS DOG AND TRIFE

Upski had gone to get his hair cut at the black-owned Freakin U   100
Creations. He only went to black barbers, and part of his manifesto was to direct at least half his money to minority stores. Fort Greene afforded plenty of possibilities. All in all, though, he found the neighborhood imperfect, already too gentrified. His girlfriend lived there, so he did. He had lived in a black neighborhood in Washington. He said he felt he belonged either in a rich white neighborhood, where he could persuade residents to integrate, or in the true 'hood, where he could organize. He mused about moving to East New York.

Upski chatted with one of the owners, Justice Cephas. Two young black men waited their turn. Mr. Cephas was a hip-hop promoter on the side and was working with their group. They were Dog and Trife.

Upski said, "Don't take anything off the top."

Dog studied Upski's pate and said, "What's there to take off?"

Upski laughed. He asked how they felt about whites' moving into the neighborhood.

"Five years ago, I would have beaten you up just for sitting in   105
that barber chair," Dog told him.

"Oh," Upski said.

"But I've matured," Dog said.

Later, though, he talked about how he was still deeply bitter toward white people. No white person had ever done anything positive for him, he said. As he remarked of whites: "I've never been with you. Why would I want to be with you now?"

Trife added, "If you're not my people now, you're not my people down the line."

Dog and Trife had told Upski about their group, Wanted and   110
Respected. Trife's older brother had started a record label, Trife-Life Records, and they were working on its first album. They

hoped to sell it on the street, create some buzz. All the while, Trife said later, he was thinking, "What is this white guy doing in this barbershop?"

Upski smiled. These young men, he said, reminded him of the black friends he used to run with in Chicago. If he were younger, he mused, he might want to run with them.

THE BEATLES PARALLAX

Inside Elliott Wilson's *XXL* cubicle was a computer, a stereo and a table strewn with rap albums. The music was on—loud.

His eyes scanned the screen—copy for the next issue. He fiddled with it. "I'm adding curse words," he said. "Putting in ain'ts. Making it more hip-hop."

The publisher, Dennis Page, came in with his beneficent smile. "Hey, man, we doing O.K.?"

115   "Yeah."

Mr. Page peeked over his shoulder at the screen. He nodded: "That's dope."

They went on like that, bantering.

Mr. Wilson called his boss D.P.G.—Dennis Page Gangsta, after Snoop Doggy Dogg's crew, the Dogg Pound Gangstas. Mr. Wilson had given D.P.G. an inscribed copy of *Ego Trip's Book of Rap Lists*. He wrote, "I don't care what people say, I know your favorite color is green."

It was how he felt about the relationship. They were both there for the money, he said.

120   Dennis Page was 46. He had the black walk, the black talk. His father had run a liquor store in Trenton, and Mr. Page had hung around with black kids and absorbed their ways. Now, he says, he has no real black friends. He admits he's been called a wigger. "I feel stigmatized by black people in hip-hop who feel I'm exploiting them," he said. "I don't feel I'm exploiting. It's a business. The record companies are white-owned. But I feel I take more heat. Certain black people feel that white people shouldn't even buy hip-hop albums, no less write about it. I'm not saying a black man can't buy a Beatles record."

XXL was just going monthly, and its circulation, which it gave as 175,000, was still far below the leading magazines'—*Vibe* sold more than 700,000 copies, *The Source* 425,000. *XXL* had been heavily political, clearly aimed at blacks. To build up the white audience, Mr. Page and Mr. Wilson agreed to tone it down, focus it almost entirely on the music.

"My magazine isn't some white-boy magazine, though,"
Mr. Wilson said. "It's black, too. I'm not sacrificing what *XXL*
stands for." Even so, he added, "it can't be totally black if a white
man is signing the check."

'I PREACH TO MESS UP'

Tuesday dawned muggy. It started badly and got worse. Upski was
addressing about 250 students at Evergreen College in Olympia,
Wash. Maybe 10 weren't white.

He had gathered a panel of half a dozen students. One, Evelyn
Aako, was black. Introducing her, he said: "I don't know her very
well, but she's black. And she's going to talk about issues of being
black on campus."

Ms. Aako gave him an arch look. "That was very weird," she
recalled thinking. "Like I was a little dark object."

As Upski began talking, the white audience got defensive. One
student said: "Why do we have to talk about race? Why can't we
talk about how we're alike?"

Ms. Aako was getting disgusted. Finally she told Upski: "I've
been sitting here with an uncomfortable feeling in my stomach
about how you introduced me. I felt tokenized and on display. This
follows a tradition where black people serve as entertainment for
white people. That's not what I do."

Upski said: "I screwed up. But what can we do? The world is
screwed up."

Some white students were looking irritated. One said: "Can't
we hear Upski talk? We can talk about race later."

A black student said: "What do you mean later? We never talk
about race."

Some whites left. Virtually all the students of color followed.
Before leaving, Ms. Aako said, "It's not my job to educate you."

Later, Upski sounded no less confident of his ability to stimulate change. But perhaps, he said, he needed to refine his
approach.

"I think the main thing that keeps white people from growing
is they're afraid to look bad," he said. "So I preach to mess up. One
of my blind spots at Evergreen was that Evelyn wasn't going to
trust me, that black people and white people, we're still at war."

Increasingly, he said, he was questioning his own evolution.
Here he was intent on helping blacks, and spending most of his
time in white culture. He had had a string of black girlfriends, but
now he was with a white woman.

135   A few years ago, probably two-thirds of his friends were black and Latino. Now it had flip-flopped.

Hip-hop itself had moved away from political and racial talk and for the most part sold excess and riches, women and violence. So much of hip-hop, he said, was self-denigrating, imitative and shallow. It was candy.

"One of the things I have the least respect for about parts of black culture," he said, "is there's so much pain and insecurity that it gets medicated by aping the worst aspects of white culture."

He talked about how so many of his old black and Latino graffiti friends hadn't survived hip-hop too well. One got locked up for firebombing a car. Another fell from a fire escape while trying to rob an apartment. He is now a paraplegic, drinking away his life, Upski said.

And yet, Upski had to admit, he was cruising along. His girlfriend, Ms. Drury, had inherited money, though they lived modestly. He didn't earn a lot, but he didn't worry. Until recently, he never took cabs and rarely ate out; he called it flaunting privilege. But now he was traveling more in white circles where everyone took cabs and ate out. So he did, too. And, he acknowledged, he liked it.

140   "The part of Billy that wanted to be black for a good part of his youth, that's fading," Ms. Drury said. "One of the issues in our relationship is he's a chameleon. The thing with Billy, he wants to be liked."

He had always cared so much about how he looked through black eyes, he said. Now his success depended on how he looked through white eyes. He had always dressed poorly and now he owned three suits. Where was he going? he wondered. As you got older, holding onto your hip-hop values seemed a lot harder if you were white.

TRAPS AND TRAPPINGS OF SUCCESS

Elliott Wilson climbed the stairs to the basketball court. The old guys were already there. The doctor had told him he had high blood pressure, a real slap in the face. "I've got the black man's disease," he joked.

Who knew the factors, but he had never eaten properly. He was also feeling the pressure of his job, he said. A friend who had been editor of *The Source* said the same thing had happened to him.

His doctor put him on medication, urged exercise. So he had begun playing full-court basketball three mornings a week. There was an early crowd of young guys, but Mr. Wilson wasn't ready for them. He played with a bunch of white guys, some in their 50's and 60's, and one black guy in his 70's. He hit some baskets and missed some. He changed and headed for *XXL*.

He had now edited four issues. The first one, with DMX on the   145
cover, had outsold any previous issue. He felt he was making a mark, he said. He had his disputes with Dennis Page, but they got along. His Ego Trip comrades felt proud of him.

He was making such good money, more than three times what Upski made, but somehow, he said, that wasn't the point. What he really wanted was to "take *The Source* out in a year or two," then expand the reaches of Ego Trip. Still, there were always seeds of self-doubt.

"Do I feel secure?" he said. "No. Because I'm black and I have bad credit. Having bad credit in this country is like being a convict. You don't have a prosperity mind-set when you're a person of color. You have something, you always feel someone is going to take it. You're always on edge, wondering what next."

'I JUST WANT THE MONEY'

Dog twirled the dials and gave Trife the signal to start. In the tiny apartment, Dog and Trife and Sinbo and Po were rehearsing for their album, the one they hoped might be destiny's next chosen one.

Scrizz, Trife's brother and the C.E.O. of Trife-Life Records, was listening like a jittery father. With no product yet, Trife-Life was not a paying job for him. His background, like that of the others, was drugs and crime. At the moment, he was out on bail while fighting an assault charge.

Wanted and Respected started in on its song "All the Time."   150
Golden bars of light streaked through the windows. Scrizz tapped his foot. He, too, had a got-to-happen mentality. He didn't much care who bought the album, white or black, but he knew where the money was. "I just want them to eat it up," he said. "I just want the money."

It came down to that. A group of young black guys in Brooklyn rhyming their lives, betting on a brighter tomorrow sponsored by white kids' money.

Dog turned up the music. They cleared their throats and kept rapping.

Questions for Discussion and Topics for Writing

1. Compare the stories of Billy Wimsatt and Elliott Wilson. Are these two polar opposites? How do they complicate racial stereotypes? How do they reinforce them?
2. How do the brief stories about Dog and Trife affect Kleinfield's article? What do they reveal about the rap scene? How do they stand in contrast to the predicaments of Wimsatt and Wilson?
3. At the beginning of the 20th century, W. E. B. Du Bois proclaimed that the problem of the century would be "the color line." Considering these narratives, does that seem true? Assuming that the "color line" can be delineated, is it permeable? Is it easily crossed? What seems to happen to identity when one crosses it?
4. Write a character sketch of yourself or someone you know. Then develop an essay based on observations you have made about this person. What does the description tell you about the person? What does it tell you about the larger concept of self-representation?

Sold Out on Soul
The Corporate Annexation of Black Popular Music
MARK ANTHONY NEAL

Mark Anthony Neal is Associate Professor of Black Popular Culture in the Program in African-American Studies at Duke University. Neal's scholarly work includes the following books: What the Music Said: Black Popular Music and Black Public Culture, Soul Babies: Black Popular Culture and the Post-Soul Aesthetic, *and* Songs in the Key of Black Life: A Rhythm and Blues Nation. *Neal is also co-editor with Murray Forman of* That's the Joint! The Hip-Hop Studies Reader. *The following work is taken from the Fall 1997 issue of* Popular Music and Society.

———————————— ✦ ————————————

It has been less than 40 years since Berry Gordy institutionalized black popular music as a viable and profitable fixture across America's popular landscape in the form of the Motown Corporation. Gordy's subsequent success in marketing black popular music to largely white audiences served as the future blueprint for Corporate America's later annexation of the black popular music industry, a process that placed significant constraints on black expressive culture, even as the historic parameters associated with black expression in a segregated society began to erode. Subsequently, black popular music was no longer solely mediated by the communal masses within segregated black locales, but by Corporate America's own mecurical desires for the marketplace.

Ambitiously naming his music the "Sound of Young America," Gordy's efforts were also motivated by broader national issues rooted in the Civil Rights movement. The ascent of the Motown Corporation paralleled the significance of integration for many African Americans during the early Civil Rights era. Gordy's project surmised that the mass consumption of "Soul," via an efficient mass production process, was a natural corollary to broader efforts for blacks to integrate American society in general and corporate boardrooms in particular. Gordy's strategy was prudent as the large white consumption of Motown recordings established Motown as a hegemonic force within the popular music industry. Motown became a very visible icon of the economic and social opportunities afforded African Americans during the early 1960s.

By the time a young band from working class Gary, Indiana, emerged with tunes like "I Want You Back," "The Love You Save," "ABC," and "I'll Be There,"—all four tunes reached number one pop status between January of 1970 and March of 1971—Gordy had successfully conquered young America's popular musical taste. The Jackson Five was the last major act produced by Motown prior to its relocation to Los Angeles, lifting up from its roots in the industrialized urban Midwest, and severing its connection with black working-class concerns. What is significant here is that the corporate annexation of black popular music begins precisely at the moment that Motown is witnessing its greatest success marketing and selling black popular music in the form of Michael Jackson and the Jackson Five.

SOUL FOR SALE: THE MARKETING OF BLACK MUSICAL EXPRESSION

The cornerstones of Corporate America's annexation of the black popular music tradition were the implementation of strategies developed by Berry Gordy himself; namely to market Soul music, if not Blackness itself, to a mainstream and youthful consumer base and as a purveyor of youthful sensibilities for older audiences, but also as a measurement of racial and social difference that could be construed as enticing, appealing, or wholly repugnant, as market taste demanded, particularly when mediated through the various prisms of race, class, age, geographical location, and sexual preference. Furthermore, many corporate marketing strategies aimed to exploit post-Civil Rights movement narratives that often implied the inclusion of African Americans and African American culture into mainstream American life by, ironically, embracing modes of black nationalist discourse, though many corporations in reality rarely offered African Americans significant autonomy and agency in their commercial products.

5   In an influential essay initially published in *Esquire* magazine, author Claude Brown writes, "The language of Soul—or, as it might be called, "Spoken Soul" or "colored English"—is simply an honest portrayal of black America. The roots of it are more than one hundred years old" (135). Brown's comments bespeak the larger social and cultural connotations of the word Soul. Generally associated with the genre of music which bore its name, throughout the 1960s Soul became primarily linked to evocations of black communal pride. Soul music, the popular and secular offspring of Thomas Dorsey's innovations in Gospel music, relied upon what Geneva Smitherman has called "tonal semantics." As she relates, "To both understand and 'feel' tonal semantics requires the listener to be of a cultural tradition that finds value and meaning in word sound" (135). Influenced by West African tone languages, the practice of tonal semantics allows for different meanings to be derived from the tonal quality of a particular word or phrase. Denied access to the predominant instruments of rhythmic expression, the vocal quality of first- and second-generation African Slaves began to mimic the very diversity of tones and colors that were inherent to the African polyrhythms of the past. The practice of "polytonal" expression or "polytonality," in which complex and varying meanings were conveyed via vocal tones, represents a unique process emblematic of the African American experience.

Because the practice of slavery obliterated distinctions between public and private life for those enslaved, much of black liberatory expression was initially inspired by the desire to create covert spaces that, on the one hand, would provide the physical parameters in which to recover humanity, but also the space to develop more meaningful forms of resistance. I suggest that the practice of polytonal expression, particularly when premised by the type of public/social formations and surveillance that accompanied slave labor, created the context for the creation of covert social space(s) in which the parameters were not physical, but aural. Furthermore notions of social space infer a framework in which community could be constituted. The desire to create community and the pursuit of covert social space remained two of the dominant existential tensions within the African American Diaspora well into the 20th century. I would further suggest that the practice of polytonal expression, particularly within the context of field labor or other social formations in which blacks were communally constructed, represented the reconstitution of community within the parameters of aurally defined social space.

In its essence Soul music represented the conflation of "polytonal" vocal expression over a layered musical landscape of Rhythm and Blues and Gospel. The process of "polytonality" represented the creolization of various discourses and energies to create a mode of expression that is uniquely African (pretext), uniquely American (context), and capable of liberatory (subtext) interpretations. Thus Soul music represented a powerful "bricolage" or collage of black public formations, whose presence can be dated to the antebellum South. As polytonal expression constructed aural notions of community and social space, Rhythm and Blues and Gospel music represented music that was distinctly created for transmission within two of the dominant social spaces within the Black Public Sphere of the 20th century. Soul music thus represented the construction of "hypercommunity" in that both physical and metaphysical notions of space and community, and all the political and social meanings that underlie such formations, converge within its aesthetic sensibilities. Soul music became the ideal artistic medium to foreground the largest mass social movement to emerge from within the African American experience.

With the subsequent annexation of black popular music, in which the Soul genre was then the dominant popular form, at least in terms of popularity, the larger meanings of Soul were also deconstructed for use within mass market culture. Divorced from its politicized and organic connotations, "Soul" became a malleable market resource merchandised to black and white consumers alike in the form of music, television shows, and haircare products. This process underscores a major facet of contemporary mass consumer culture, which has often sought to separate the iconography of political struggle from the organic sources and purposes of such struggles. The commodification of "Soul" had a particularly compelling impact on African American popular expression, in that political resistance was often parlayed as an element of style. This is not to suggest that the Afro hairdo or the Dashiki was as politically meaningful as sit-ins or mass rallies, but that many of the icons of black social movement were invested with some vestige of oppositional expression. Nevertheless the mass commodification of Soul reduced Blackness to a commodity that could be bought and sold—and this is important—without the cultural and social markers that have defined Blackness.

As the decade of the 1970s progressed and the Black Public Sphere began to exhibit early signs of deterioration, predicated on black middle-class flight, the demise of central cities, and the postindustrial transformation of urban economies, black identity—in other words Blackness—became largely mediated and thus determined by the mechanisms of mass consumer culture. But corporate efforts to annex the black popular music tradition also challenged African American efforts to build and maintain community, in that black popular music was historically integral to black communal formations and the production and distribution of communally derived narratives. In this regard, the mass commodification of black expression undermined many of the processes associated with the development of narratives of resistance from within the black community. Furthermore this occurred as structural changes in the economy and in black urban spaces were literally challenging efforts to maintain community. . . .

POSTINDUSTRIAL SOUL: BLACK POPULAR
MUSIC SINCE THE 1980s

10   Demographic shifts within the black urban landscape were reflected in black consumer taste in the post-Civil Rights era, particularly as represented in the popularity of recordings like Smokey Robinson's *A Quiet Storm*. Released in 1975, the seven-minute title track to *A Quiet Storm* would become the aesthetic cornerstone of a more upscale and sophisticated Soul sound that would captivate an older, mature, and largely black middle-class audience as a Howard University communications student appropriated Robinson's title and introduced the "Quiet Storm" format to black radio programmers. The generally late-night format basically consisted of Soul ballads, interspersed with some Jazz and possibly a little blues. By the early 1980s, the format would be a fixture in virtually every major radio market that programmed black music or, as it came to be known by the late 1980s, Urban Contemporary music. As important as this recording was to Robinson's then-fading career, it would prove more important to black radio programmers searching to maintain programming that appealed to a growing black middle class with disposable income. While the "Quiet

Storm" format was in part shaped by middle-class sensibilities, particularly given its Howard University roots, it was a music that cut across class lines because it appealed to adult sensibilities. "Quiet Storm" recordings were in most cases devoid of any significant political commentary and maintained a strict aesthetic and narrative distance from issues relating to black urban life, though the increased length of recordings did allow for complex explorations of male-female relations (see George 131–35, 172–73).

Luther Vandross and Anita Baker are perhaps the two artists who most visibly benefitted from the development of "Quiet Storm" radio. The success of Vandross and Baker in the mid-1980s was the first corporate acknowledgment of the considerable buying power of the black middle class (with both artists achieving Gold and Platinum status with a largely black listening audience) which was cultivated by black radio as opposed to corporate promotion. Unfortunately for many of these artists, their successes occured as a second baby-boom generation began to become the very young consumers that Gordy et al. courted almost two decades earlier—an audience that represented growth potential that urban and adult contemporary could never deliver. Instead, many corporate labels watched closely as three young black men from Hollis, Queens, recording on the independent Priority label, and their white protégés The Beastie Boys, recording for independent Def Jam Records, sold more than six million records in 1986 of a "new" genre of music known as Hip-Hop or Rap (see George 186–88).

The rudimentary elements of Hip-Hop music precede the commercial success of Run-DMC by more that a decade. Like Be-Bop before it, Hip-Hop's politics were initially a politics of style, which created an aural and stylistic community to buffer the erosion of community within the postindustrial city and the mass commodification of organic expression. Perhaps more than any previous popular form, Hip-Hop thrived on its own creative and aesthetic volatility by ironically embracing such volatility as part of its stylistic traditions. This has allowed the form to maintain an aesthetic and narrative distance from mass-market limitations, though I must acknowledge that it is often a transient distance. The relative commercial uninterest in the form during its developing years allowed for its relatively autonomous development. Relying largely on word of mouth and live performance as means of promotion, like black popular forms prior to the Civil Rights era, Hip-Hop perhaps represents the last black popular form to be wholly derived from the experiences and texts of the black urban landscape.

Like Be-Bop, Hip-Hop appropriated popular texts, often refiguring them to serve Hip-Hop sensibilities. This phenomenon contextually questions and ultimately undermines the notion of corporate ownership of popular music and would have legal ramifications well into the decade of the 1990s. Released on the black-owned indie label Sugar Hill, "Rapper's Delight," with a bass line strikingly similar to Chic's "Good Times," sold more than two million copies in 1979–1980. Initially viewed as simply a fad music—Surf music for a ghetto underclass—the release of "Rapper's Delight" began a fairly productive relationship between independent labels and Hip-Hop artists. The rise of independent labels like Profile, Def Jam, Tommy Boy, and 4th and Broadway was largely subsidized by the marketing and selling of Hip-Hop and urban dance music. Despite the commercial success of Kurtis Blow's 1980 release, "The Breaks," and the critical acclaim afforded Grand Master Flash's "The Message" and Afrika Baambataa's "Looking for the Perfect Beat," corporate labels virtually ignored Hip-Hop music until the mid-1980s.

In retrospect, Corporate America's subsequent though limited investment in Hip-Hop represented savvy business acumen. Hip-Hop was a relatively inexpensive art form to produce in that the music did not rely on live musicians, particularly during the period when sampling practices were loosely monitored, and, unfortunately, young urban Hip-Hop artists could be paid a fraction of the rate of more established adult acts because of ineffective representation, unsophisticated negotiating strategies, ignorance of the recording industry, and racism. Two years after the release of Run-DMC's landmark *Raisin' Hell* (1986) recording, many independent recording labels that featured Hip-Hop entered into distribution deals with corporate conglomerates. The Def Jam label's sale to conglomerate CBS/Columbia was strikingly reminiscent of the conglomerate's relationship with Gamble and Huff more than a decade earlier. The acquisition of Def Jam and its roster of popular artists like LL Cool J and Public Enemy, who both had multiplatinum releases for the "new" corporate label, gave CBS/Columbia access to cutting edge artists and producers. MCA Records would enter the same relationship with former Def Jam staffer, and protégé of Def Jam President Russell Simmons, Andre Harrell. By the end of the 1980s, Def Jam and Uptown would represent the second generation of corporate-supported, urban-defined "boutique" labels, serving as the foundations for the multi-billion-dollar black music industry of the 1990s.

Hardly radio-friendly, Hip-Hop garnered a necessary promo-   15
tional boost with the debut of *Yo! MTV Raps* on MTV in the fall of
1988. Regional offerings like Ralph MacDaniel's *Video Music Box*
in New York City initially created a forum for video treatments of
Hip-Hop recordings during MTV's apartheid-like programming
during the early 1980s. Given the paucity of likely video outlets
and the lack of promotion for Hip-Hop prior to 1988, many of the
videos represented poorly conceived and crudely executed ideas.
The mainstreaming (a relative term here, really) of Hip-Hop music video would open the form to an audience of mid-American
youths, who relished the subversive "otherness" that the music
and its purveyors represented. By the time "Gangsta Rap" (an often cartoonish portrayal of black masculinity, ghetto realism, and
gangster sensibilities) became one of the most popular genres of
Hip-Hop, a significant portion of the music was largely supported
by young white Americans.

Hip-Hop was the music of a generation of young black urbanites affected by urban deterioration, economic decay, and the proliferation of recreational drugs. This is not to say the music was
solely defined by this focus (artists Run-DMC and LL Cool J, for
instance, were products of black middle-class Queens, NY) but
that a significant number of the artists were in fact working-class
and working poor urbanites. Hip-Hop offered these elements, rendered invisible by communal dislocation and isolation, a forum to
critique the conditions that defined their existence. If Gamble and
Huff created music that spoke to an African American Diaspora,
Hip-Hop was the music of the most neglected and despised members of that Diaspora. But like Soul music a generation earlier,
Hip-Hop was essentialized and sold as the "authentic" distillation
of contemporary "Blackness," though in fact the form rendered
"Blackness" as postmodern as Hip-Hop was itself and thus as difficult to essentialize, though its value as a mass commodity was
predicated on consumer acceptance that Hip-Hop represented an
essential "Blackness" that was urban, youthful, and threatening.

Because such essentialization projects were premised on
notions of Blackness that were socially interpreted by mainstream
culture as intensely deviant, the mass commodification of
Hip-Hop for white consumers was much more effective than that
of Soul a generation earlier, because Hip-Hop itself contained the
very narratives of difference that drove corporate efforts to market
contemporary "Blackness." As the children of the Silent Generation
embraced Motown and black culture as a critique and rejection of

their parents, the children of Yuppie America embraced Hip-Hop as a measurement of their own disgust with contemporary American life. This was particularly compelling when poor white youth were allowed to build class alliances with "ghetto" black youth in the form of Gangsta Rap critiques of police brutality. Considering police brutality as an equal-opportunity offense, narratives like the NWA anthem "Fuck tha Police" would resonate amongst trailer-park youth in the Midwest.

Ironically, the mass commodification of Hip-Hop countered historical sensibilties that often rejected mass-mediated forms of black expression on the basis of inauthenticity. Hip-Hop's intense desire to "keep it real" by distributing narratives close to emerging styles and crises within the postindustrial landscape countered the more profound desire for the economic stability that a successful recording career could afford. The literal demise of viable commercial venues for Hip-Hop performance in the late 1980s and 1990s has rendered questions of authenticity, as related to mass commodification, obsolete as the marketplace has emerged as the dominant province for Hip-Hop expression. Contemporary notions of authenticity within Hip-Hop have little to do with aesthetic quality, and more to do with narrative commitments to the realities of black urban life—the more vivid, the more real. This is the logical manifestation of a community dislocated and isolated from the larger black community and mainstream American culture.

The often visible and demonstrative critiques of Hip-Hop by black religious and political leaders reflected the growing distance between older black middle-class elements and their younger working-class/working poor counterparts. The mainstream attacks on Hip-Hop and its purveyors bespeak the silence that engulfs informed readings of black life in the postindustrial city and Hip-Hop's commitment to give voice to those experiences via the marketplace. Not simply a generation gap, this distance represents a very different worldview regarding the success of the Civil Rights movement and the realities of contemporary life within the African-American Diaspora. Black radio's early rejection of Hip-Hop, excepting the few late-night programming slots given to well-known Hip-Hop DJs in the major markets, reflected the sentiments of the black middle class regarding Hip-Hop, particularly with regard to the notion of Hip-Hop as essentialized Blackness, which in effect rendered the black middle class invisible as consumers or otherwise, and in part reflected a historical trend among the black middle class regarding popular art forms that emit from the black working-class experience.

Like the Soul tradition two decades earlier, Corporate America   20
intensified its annexation of the black popular music tradition in the
early 1990s. Reflecting the furious consolidation that has taken
place in the entertainment industry, more than 80 percent of all music recorded in the United States was controlled by six major corporate entities. Black popular forms accounted for approximately
25 percent of the total sales of recorded music. The commodification of Hip-Hop was intensified, in part, because of the lack of
formal sites of production, critique, and distribution within the
postindustrial city. Hip-Hop emerged as the first form of black
popular expression that was not initially afforded the process of
communal critique prior to its subsequent mass production and distribution. In other words, unlike previous forms of black popular expression that were critiqued prior to their distribution beyond
segregated black enclaves in democratic communal spaces like
New York's Apollo Theater or the Central Avenue strip in Los Angeles, Hip-Hop emerged as the first popular form of black expression
not subject to such communal processes. This reflects a unique situation of intense corporate commodification in an era when the
physical sites of communal exchange were in decline, as represented by postindustrial transformations of black public spaces. . . .

Works Cited

Brown, Claude. "The Language of Soul." *Rappin' and Stylin' Out*. Ed. Thomas
Kochman. Urbana: U of Illinois P, 1972.
George, Nelson. *The Death of Rhythm and Blues*. New York: Pantheon, 1988.
Goldberg, David Theo. "Polluting the Body Politic: Racist Discourse and Urban
Location." *Racism, the City and the State*. Ed. Malcolm Cross and Michael
Keith. New York: Routledge, 1993.
Haymes, Stephen. *Race, Culture and the City: A Pedagogy for Black Urban
Struggle*. Albany: State U of New York P, 1995.
Smitherman, Geneva. *Talkin' and Testifyin': The Language of Black America*.
Detroit: Wayne State UP, 1977.

Questions for Discussion and Topics for Writing

1. Early in his essay, Neal discusses the importance of West African languages to
the formation of African-American music. In particular, he mentions
"polytonal" expression. Neal's language is technical, but his argument is extremely interesting and crucial to an understanding of African-American
music. Carefully reread the passages where he discusses polytonality. How
does Neal connect this term to the conditions of slavery? What role does
polytonality have in the formation of community?

2. A key purpose of Neal's essay is to teach us about the role of corporate culture in the production of music. At one point he describes how the forces of "mass consumer culture" attempt to "separate the iconography of political struggle from the organic sources and purposes of such struggle." Write a summary of the two paragraphs leading up to the one from which this quotation is extracted. As you do so, attempt to answer this question: Why is corporate United States interested in the "iconography of political struggle"? If a large part of the market for black music is the white consumer, why are signs of political struggle considered good for sales?

3. Neal's discussion moves from soul to hip hop. As with soul, the marketing of hip hop involves selling "blackness" to white consumers. In what specific ways does Neal's analysis of hip hop parallel his discussion of soul?

4. Write a two-page summary of Neal's reading. Neal's argument is intricate and challenging. Be sure to look up terms that you do not understand. Early in your summary, be sure to identify key elements of Neal's thesis. Once you have done this, the rest of your summary should follow clearly and logically.

5. Write an essay that combines the insights of Cheryl Keyes ("The Roots and Stylistic Foundations of the Rap Music Tradition") and Neal. In particular, focus on how African-American popular music makes use of West African oral forms. How does Neal help us understand ideas about the relationship between African and American culture that are only hinted at in the Keyes reading?

Elvis, Wiggers, and Crossing Over to Nonwhiteness
DAVID R. ROEDIGER

David Roediger is Kendrick C. Babcock Professor of History at the University of Illinois Urbana–Champaign. Roediger's research interests include race and class in the United States, and the history of U.S. radicalism. His books include Our Own Time: A History of American Labor and the Working Day, The Wages of Whiteness: Race and the Making of the American Working Class, *and* Towards the Abolition of Whiteness. *The following article is taken from his 2002 book,* Colored White: Transcending the Racial Past.

———————— ◆ ————————

. . . *Wigger* first came to my attention as a slur used at Cabrini High School in a Detroit suburb in about 1989. When white Detroiters enrolled at the school, bringing with them "black-influenced" styles and friendships with African Americans, some of the suburban white students caused a stir by calling the newcomers wiggers, meaning "white niggers" or whites acting "too black." Similar recent uses of wigger as a slur against whites by whites have been reported in Madison, Wisconsin, and in Warren, Ohio. What brought the term briefly to the nation's attention were dramatic 1993 events in very rural Morocco, Indiana, where the hiphop fashions and musical tastes of two young white sisters resulted in their being called wiggers, suspended from their virtually all-white school, and spat upon and threatened with death by white male students who demanded that they "dress white" (or paint themselves another color and move to "the slums of Chicago"). The resulting discussions of the controversy on *Montel Williams*, and other major talk/outrage shows, as well as in the pages of *Esquire* and *VIBE*, catapulted the Moroccans into notoriety. By December 1993, after an *Oprah* show centered on *wiggers*, *The Source*, a leading hip-hop magazine, declared the term and the controversy "officially played and over." It wasn't.[1]

The sense of *wigger* described above is consistent with uses of *white nigger* as a white-on-white epithet (*like smoked Irishman, guinea, black Dutch, nigger lover,* and *Black Republican*) dating back at least to the nineteenth century, although *white nigger* was then more likely to be applied to a white either accepting "nigger work" or politically breaking with what was seen as proper behavior for whites than to a suspected cultural dissenter from whiteness. In 1868, for example, a Confederate veteran who voted with the Republican opponents of white supremacy was seized by a Tennessee mob, placed on a mock auction block, and sold as a "white nigger." Closer to modern uses was the branding of Johnny Cash as a "white nigger" during his rockabilly days. Wigger as a culturally based white-on-white slur existed in Buffalo in the early 1970s. The white rapper MC Serch, heard it in the early 1980s when white classmates reacted to his adoption of hiphop clothing by calling him a wigger or a "black wanna-be"—shortly before many of them adopted the style themselves.[2]

However, at the same time that Serch was called a *wigger* derisively by whites, another young East Coast hiphopper, Gary Miles, was being called one affectionately by African Americans. Miles, self-described as only "phenotypically white," was when I contacted him a University of California–Los Angeles graduate student who forcefully argued that *wigger* originated among African Americans to denote whites who seriously embraced African

American cultural forms and values, in contrast to "wannabe" dabblers in the external trappings of rap. The meaning was still "white nigger," but *nigger* in the rehabilitated sense proliferating in rap. Often pronounced *wigga*, the term signals the same sort of inclusion as a greeting "That's my nigga" might. In this sense, wigger would echo earlier African American uses of words such as *hillbilly cat* in early rock and roll and some Latina uses of "Whatina" for white women who share their struggles. Miles allowed that the approbation implied by *wigga* could sometimes change on short notice, however.[3]

In Milwaukee, another usage of *wigger* appeared. Although one young white informant there saw it as used in his inner-city high school as a flat (neither friendly nor mocking) description of those whites who "want to identify with black culture," another account found black Milwaukee high schoolers using it to discuss with contempt white suburban school kids who "wear the jackets . . . and try to talk black [but] who wouldn't last a minute" in the city. This comports with long-standing African American uses of *white nigger* as a derogatory term for "a white person with Negro affectations."[4]

5   The case for *wigger* as a coinage of African Americans—this does not rule out whites independently creating the term at another place and time—is buttressed by two further considerations. As both Miles and Sundiata Cha-Jua have pointed out, substituting *w* or *wh* at the beginning of existing words to create new words to describe whites or white institutions is not infrequent in African American speech—hence *witch* for "*white bitch*" and *whitianity* for "white Christianity." Second, and here the tremendous hybridity of American slang complicates easy racial distinctions, *wigger* clearly gestures toward earlier uses of *wig* and *wigged out* by both Black and white jazz musicians and beat poets. *Wigged*, variously connoting overstimulated, intellectualized, laudably crazy, and stressed, could hardly have failed to strike Black-influenced musical subcultures as an apt cousin for *wigger*.[5]

Further variations exist. Youth culture journalist Charles Aaron reports *wigger's* use by "whites who embrace black culture to call out whites who defame black culture." In a letter to *VIBE*, one reader adopted this "calling-out" usage in criticizing the "ignorant, redneck pieces of racist white trash" in Morocco, Indiana, as the "real '*wiggers*'" and as a "disgrace to the white heritage they fight so desperately to protect." Where my older son went to junior high school, *wigger* was at the same time acceptingly applied by Blacks to whites, disparagingly applied by racist whites to other whites, dismissively applied by whites adopting Black styles to whites who were seen as doing so inauthentically, and used approvingly by white would-be-hiphoppers to describe each other. One high schooler in the north suburbs of Chicago, who had recently moved there from the city, proudly saw herself as a wigger—as one of the white students who "wished they were black"—but had never thought of the term as derived from *nigger*.[6]

This is not the place to evaluate fully the political importance of wiggers, let alone their wisdom. The broader white hiphop audience is rather easily ridiculed. Hiphop magazines, marketed in large part to white audiences, who now are estimated to buy from 50% to 70% of rap recordings sold, often themselves ridicule wiggers and wannabes as middle-class, superficial, voyeuristic, apolitical, consumerist, dumb, and even racist. There is little reason to doubt these charges or to suppose that white fans are underrepresented among those whom Greg Tate derides as "all the B-boy wannabes who like to say *ho!*"[7]

When Italian American youth in New York City in the 1980s chose to identify themselves with elements of African American style, they at times proudly called themselves guineas. In doing so, they rehabilitated a term used earlier in the century to slur Italian immigrants and to connect Italians with Blacks. But those guineas, as Donald Tricarico writes, "resist[ed] identification" with African Americans on other levels and bit "the hand that feeds them style." For whites to easily appropriate a form of *nigger* is likewise fraught with difficulties. Venise Wagner's excellent San Francisco *Examiner* article on "wiggas" concluded with the words of a chastened white convert to Islam, formerly a wigger: "They [wiggers] would like to imagine themselves as not part of the problem. But we are all part of the problem." Moreover, being a wigger is often an adolescent phase, calling to mind Leslie Fiedler's remark that white American males spend their early years as imaginary Indians and their teens as imaginary Blacks before settling into a white adulthood (not to mention Janis Joplin's curious hope that "being black for a while will make me a better white").[8]

As the courageous high schoolers of Morocco, Indiana, show, wiggers are by no means all male, but they often are aggressively so and identify with violence, scatology, homophobia, and sexism in rap rather than with Black music and culture more broadly. Indeed, Robin D.G. Kelley's fine work on hiphop reminds us that one impetus toward sexual violence in the lyrics is precisely that it sells well to white adolescent males. Bay area hiphop DJ Davey D's recent warning that some of the music and marketing leaves the impression that "calling a woman a . . . 'ho' is black culture," reveals the stakes involved in such a marketing approach. Recent controversies over the misogyny and homophobia of the white megastar Eminem raise the larger threat that such hatred will be the lowest common denominator uniting young male audiences across color lines. In her inspired rant "Owed to Eminem," the great poet June Jordan writes that she is "tired of wiggas that whine as they squeal/about bitches and faggots and little girls too." Brent Staples's *New York Times* opinion piece "Dying to Be Black," roots the wigger's embrace of gangsta rap in the feeling that blackness has the "power to generate fear," a power "particularly seductive to adolescent boys in the suburbs." One expert recently explained to *American Demographics* that marketers hope to reach white suburban consumers, and middle-class Black youth, precisely by developing the "hardest-core element" in hiphop. Consumerism, sexuality, and male supremacy can hardly be separated in either the music or the fan magazines, not when Benetton uses the center spread of the inaugural issue of *VIBE* to gesture toward both *Playboy* and *National Geographic* with a large photo of topless African women, including one who is albino to make the advertisement somehow subversive of racial boundaries.[9]

10   But the very matters that warn us against romantically mistaking wiggers for the vanguard of antiracism ought also to allow us to see that the proliferation of wiggers cannot simply be dismissed. The dynamics of cultural hybridity have long featured much that is deeply problematic on the white side. From minstrelsy to the blackfaced antebellum mobs who victimized African Americans, to the insidious recent film *Soul Man*, the superficial notion that blackness could be put on and taken off at will has hounded hybridity. Aggressive male posturing, sexual and otherwise, accompanied fascination with Black culture long before rap. Surely no wigger has gone further over the top in this regard than Norman Mailer's 1950s essay "The White Negro," which squarely premised an admiration for Black culture on that culture's capacity to produce orgasms in white males. Nor is the commodification of Black cultural forms by white promoters, artists, and audiences new. A century and a half ago, minstrels likened themselves to dealers in slaves on the African coast, joking that both made money by "taking off the niggers." Not only individual Black artists, but also whole genres have been impoverished in the process the minstrels began. When Elvis "discovered" Big Mama Thornton, Amiri Baraka reminds us, she was "dis'd" and her music "covered."[10]

Crossover, in a manifestly unequal society, has as often been the product of tragic, tawdry, and exploitive forces as of romantic ones. Whether we judge the beauty and solidarity created by the crossing of cultural color lines in the interstices of racial capitalism to outweigh the associated slights and tragedies is on one level immaterial. The process goes on, superficially and at times deeply. If to abdicate studying it were to abdicate only understanding that mythical thing called "white culture," the consequences would be bearable. But such an abdication also entails giving up on understanding the astonishing variety within U.S. culture and within African American culture, the latter having as one of its essential elements the ability to borrow creatively from others and to engender mixed and new forms.[11]

The specific perils, and openings, created by whites trying on and taking off African American culture change profoundly, even amidst continuities. In the case of wiggers, for example, the tendency to essentialize Blackness as male, hard, and violent is considerably more pronounced than was the case in earlier white attachments to rhythm and blues and to soul. Not only does violence loom larger in the marketing and mythmaking of hiphop than in the case of the older forms, but romance has, until recently, tended not to be for sale, even as sex surely has been. (The overlap of categories complicates matters here. Contemporary "rhythm and blues," which includes the inheritors of soul as well as some "pop-sounding" rappers and does market romance, at times outsells both hiphop and rock.) The physical separation of the races in the ultrasegregated United States combines with the seeming intimacy of MTV and videos to give a large field for adolescent fantasies of sex and violence. One 1997 student paper at Bowling Green State University aptly suspected that "because they listen to violence in the music," wiggers come to think "that they are a part of it." The student added, "In a way they are right."[12]

Indeed any serious account of wiggers must come to grips with place of fantasy and of electronically disseminated culture in their emergence. Most studies to date emphasize their presence in what the anthropologist Matthew Durington calls "suburban space." The most revealing film on wiggers, *Whiteboyz*, sets its tragicomedy in whitest Iowa. There Danny Hoch's rural wannabe character can develop, in total isolation from lived experiences with urban African Americans, the notion that his mole defines his real skin color and all else is just a huge white birthmark. In her superb reporting on Indiana wiggers, Farai Chideya casts MTV as the "cultural common denominator" fueling their imaginations and actions.[13] On the other hand, from Charles Murray's phantasms of the wigger to the uses of the word at Cabrini High, wiggers are also at times portrayed as emerging, and in fact do emerge, from racially mixed neighborhoods and from poverty shared with people of color. As former wigger Brendan Rogers described his own background, "If you don't have a lot of money, and you live in place that isn't predominantly white, you have trouble identifying with other white people."[14]

The challenges of disentangling the imaginary and the lived are great, and thinking in terms of either/or (and still less in terms of authentic/inauthentic) does not help us. For example, in the case of two white teenagers branded wiggers (or "wannabe gangsters") and victimized as such in the tiny, 98 percent white town of North Branch, Minnesota, in 1996, the temptation is to see young, video-driven imaginations run wild in a replay of events in Morocco, Indiana. However, the boys had recently moved from the Twin Cities and were ultimately exiled by authorities to St. Paul rather than sent to jail. Moreover, as Rose Farley's reporting on the case shows, the Black population of North Branch, though tiny, was a focus of surveillance and fear in the town. Even in the Indiana case, the area was not all-white, and proximity to the city of Gary clearly shaped intolerance in the town.[15] Nor, of course, does lived urban experience inoculate against vivid imaginations regarding the ease of racial crossings. William Upski Wimsatt, a bright, middle-class Chicagoan, is deservedly among the most often cited writers on wiggers. In 1993 he described his own transformation. "My school was predominantly black," Wimsatt wrote, "so I became black too."[16]

15   Likewise intricate and important are the changed ways in which white interpretations of music developed mainly by African American artists have found a market. Except perhaps for the very young, white hiphop consumers do not seek out music made by white entertainers who claim to be authentically Black or who endeavor to sanitize rap. The preference is for African American artists. There is little room for the sorts of pale, safe imitations provided in Elvis's time by Pat Boone. Nor is claiming to be a wigger viable in the long run. When white rappers attack each other, the charge of "wannabe" is routinely leveled. Here is Everlast, who sometimes answers to the name "Whitey Ford," on MC Serch: ". . . he might as well have been wearing a T-shirt that said I WISH I WAS BLACK . . . nobody's gonna really respect that." And Everlast on House of Pain (featuring Everlast): "We came out, 'Yo, we're peckerwoods, we're white trash . . . and we love hip-hop.'" Eminem's

breakthrough Rolling Stone cover sported the huge headline "LOW DOWN AND DIRTY WHITE BOY RAP."[17]

Notes

1. Telephone interview with Terry Moore in Detroit (October 25, 1992); Denise Sanders, "Black Is In," (Madison) *Isthmus* (October 29, 1993), 1, 20; letter to author from Tom Sabatini in Warren, Ohio (November 7, 1993); Richard Rocper, "Fashion Statement Gets an Ugly Reply," (Chicago) *Sun Times* (November 29, 1993), 11; "Wiggers Attacked," MTV News (November 24, 1993); Kathy Dobie, "Heartland of Darkness," *VIBE* 2 (August 1994), 63–67, 124, 126; E. Jean Carroll, "The Return of the White Negro," *Esquire* (June 1994), 100–107; Pistol Pete, "Media Watch," *Source* (December 1993), 17.

2. On these usages, see Roediger, *Wages of Whiteness*, 68, 145; and "Guineas, Wiggers and the Dramas of Racialized Culture," *American Literary History* 7 (Winter 1995), 654–58; Steve Pond, "The Hard Reign of a Country Music King," *Rolling Stone* (December 10, 1992), 122; Serch quoted in David Samuels, "The Rap on Rap," *The New Republic* (November 11, 1991), 24–29. On the 1868 incident, see Michael Newton and Judy Ann Newton. *Racial and Religious Violence in America: A Chronology* (New York: Garland, 1991), 200.

3. Telephone interview with Gary Miles in Los Angeles (November 15, 1992); Alice Echols, " 'We Gotta Get Out of This Place': Notes Toward a Remapping of the Sixties," *Socialist Review* 22 (1992), 9–34. For "Whatinas," see Becky Thompson and White Women Challenging Racism, "Home/Work: Antiracism Activism and the Meaning of Whiteness," in Fine, Weis, Powell, and Wong, eds., *Off White*, 358.

4. Telephone interview with Steve Meyer in Milwaukee (November 29, 1992); Abra Quinn, "Field Notes from Milwaukee on *Wigger*" (December, 1992); Clarence Major, *From Juba to Jive: A Dictionary of African-American Slang* (New York: Penguin, 1994), 122.

5. Miles interview and interview with Sundiata Cha-Jua in Columbia, Missouri (January 25, 1993); Clarence Major, *Dictionary of Afro-American Slang* (New York: International Publishers, 1970), 122; "Notes on *Wigged*," Peter J. Tamony Collection, Western Historical Manuscripts Collection, Ellis Library, University of Missouri at Columbia. The link to jazz usages meaning "crazy" is proposed in Robert Chapman, ed., *American Slang* (New York: HarperPerennial, 1998), 546–47.

6. Aaron, "Black Like Them": Interview with Brendan Roediger in Columbia, Missouri (March 16, 1993); Interview with name withheld in Cambridge, MA (February 20, 1993); Nadia Shihata, to *VIBE* 2 (November 1994), 26; Conversation with Noel Ignatiev in Lowell, MA (June 4, 1993).

7. Ledbetter, "Imitation of Life," 112–14; William Upski Wimsatt, "We Use Words Like 'Mackadocious,' " *Source* (May 1993), 64–66: Tate, "Sound and Fury," 15. See Also Wimsatt, "*Wigger:* Confessions of a White Wannabe," (Chicago) *Reader* (July 8, 1994), 1; Aaron, "Black Like Them," on the demographics of rap purchasers.

8. Donald Tricarico, "Guido: Fashioning an Italian-American Youth Style." *Journal of Ethnic Studies* 19 (1991), 56–57; Venise Wagner, "Crossover: The Rest of America Is Still Deeply Divided by Race. So How Come So Many White Suburban Youths Want to Be Black?" (San Francisco) *Examiner* (November 10, 1996); Leslie Fiedler, *Waiting for the End* (New York: Stein and Day, 1964), 134; Joplin, in Ledbetter, "Imitation of Life," 114.

9. Robin D. G. Kelley, "Straight from Underground," *Nation* (June 8, 1992), 793–96; Brent Staples, "Dying to Be Black," *New York Times* (December 9, 1996). Barbara Ransby and Tracye Matthews, "Black Popular Culture and the Transcendence of Patriarchal Illusions." *Race and Class* 35 (1993), 57–68; Leerom Medovoi, "Mapping the Rebel Image," *Cultural Critique* 20 (1991–1992), 153–88; *VIBE* Special Preview Issue (September 1992), center spread. On nudity in *National Geographic*, see Catherine A. Lutz and Jane L. Collins, *Reading National Geographic* (Chicago: University of Chicago Press, 1993), esp. 172–78; June Jordan, "Owed to Eminem," *VIBE* (January 2003); Davey D as quoted in Wagner, "Crossover." For "hardest-core element," see Norman Kelley, "Rhythm Nation: The Political Economy of Black Music," *Black Renaissance Noire* 2 (Summer 1999), 16, 8–22. Compare, in the same issue, Davarian Baldwin, "Black Empires, White Desires: The Spatial Politics of Identity in the Age of Hip-Hop," esp. 146–50.

10. Norman Mailer, "The White Negro," in *Advertisements for Myself* (New York: Putnam, 1959), 341, 349; on *Soul Man*, see Margaret M. Russell, "Race and the Dominant Gaze: Narrative of Law and Inequality in Popular Film," in Richard Delgado, ed., *Critical Race Theory: The Cutting Edge* (Philadelphia: Temple University Press, 1995), 59–63; Roediger, *Wages of Whiteness*, 119; Amiri Baraka in William J. Harris, ed., *The Le Roi Jones/Amiri Baraka Reader* (New York: Thunder's Mouth Press, 1995), xiii.

11. On "white culture," see Roediger, *Towards the Abolition of Whiteness* (London and New York: Verso, 1994), 1–17; on hybridity in Black culture, see Lester Bowie's remarks in Dave Marsh, "Grave Dancers Union," *Rock and Rap Confidential* (September 1993), 7; Stuart Hall, "What Is This 'Black' in Black Popular Culture?" *Social Justice* 20 (1993), 104–14.

12. Wagner, "Crossover," unpaginated. I thank Professor Rachel Buff (history) for sending me the unsigned Bowling Green State University paper. See also Mumia Abu-Jamal's acute "A Rap Thing" in his *All Things Censored*. Noelle Hanrahan, ed. (New York: Seven Stories Press, 2000), 124–25.

13. Matthew Durington, "Racial (Co)option: Visualizing Whiteness in Suburban Space" (unpublished paper, American Anthropological Association, Temple University, 1998) and available at http://astro.temple.edu/ruby/aaa/matt.html. See also Rhonda B. Sewall, "Black Like Me," (St. Louis) *Post-Dispatch* (November 23, 1999); Farai Chideya, *The Color of Our Future* (New York: Morrow, 1999), 86–112. On Hoch, see Charles Aaron. "What the White Boy Means When He Says Yo," *Spin* 14 (November, 1998), 124–26 and passim.

14. Rogers, as quoted in Wagner, "Crossover," unpaginated.

15. Rose Farley, "Wiggers," *Twin Cities Reader* (March 6–12, 1996), 8–14.

16. For Wimsatt's quote, which first appeared in *In Context* in 1993, see http://www.context.org./CLTB/permiss.htm.

17. Charles Baron, "Even Homeboys Get the Blues," *Spin* 15 (June 1999), 86, in an insert titled "Signifying Whiteys." Emphasis original. On Eminem's positioning, see Anthony Bozza, "Eminem Blows Up," *Rolling Stone* 811 (April 29, 1999), 43–47, 72. See also the issue's front cover.

Questions for Discussion and Topics for Writing

1. Highlighting complexity, Roediger shows the myriad and contradictory ways the word *wigger* is used by both black and white youth. Delineate the ways in which the word is used. What conclusions can you draw from these multifarious and often contradictory meanings? Do you think the word can still be meaningful despite its many uses?

2. Near the end of the essay, Roediger makes an impassioned argument for understanding *wigger* as a means of "disentangling the imaginary and the lived." What do you think is at stake in the phenomenon of "wiggers"? Do you agree with Roediger that "the proliferation of wiggers cannot simply be dismissed"? Why or why not?

3. The controversy around the word *wigger* shows the power and importance of diction or word choice. Consider writing a diction paper of your own. Choose a highly charged or evocative word and explore its meaning. Describe its etymology (its historical roots) and then construct an argument about the word's use and significance. You may choose to use hip hop or another cultural form to give context and specificity to the word (see also Michel Marriott, "Rap's Embrace of 'Nigger' Fires Bitter Debate").

4. It is clear that part of Roediger's argument is that it is ineffective to see things in terms of "either/or" or "authentic/inauthentic." Can you think of another term or cultural phenomenon that is oversimplified when considered in terms of either/or? Write an essay discussing the multiple meanings of this term or phenomenon, highlighting the contradictions rather than resolving them. Instead of taking sides, use the argument to show multiple perspectives and the ways in which they can coexist even if they contradict each other.

Rap's Embrace of 'Nigger' Fires Bitter Debate

MICHEL MARRIOTT

A technology reporter, Michel Marriott has written articles appearing in the "Circuits" section of The New York Times. *He is the author of* The Matrix Cultural Revolution: How Deep Does the Rabbit Hole

Go? *The following article is from the January 24, 1993, issue of* The New York Times.

─────────── ✦ ───────────

One of America's oldest and most searing epithets—"nigger"—is flooding into the nation's popular culture, giving rise to a bitter debate among blacks about its historically ugly power and its increasingly open use in an integrated society.

Whether thoughtlessly or by design, large numbers of a post-civil rights generation of blacks have turned to a conspicuous use of "nigger" just as they have gained considerable cultural influence through rap music and related genres.

Some blacks, mostly young people, argue that their open use of the word will eventually demystify it, strip it of its racist meaning. They liken it to the way some homosexuals have started referring to themselves as "queers" in a defiant slap at an old slur.

But other blacks—most of them older—say that "nigger," no matter who uses it, is such a hideous pejorative that it should be stricken from the national vocabulary. At a time when they perceive a deepening racial estrangement, they say its popular use can only make bigotry more socially acceptable.

5   "Nigger," of course, has long been an element of black vernacular, almost an honorific of the streets but strictly, and still, off limits to whites. But as the word has found voice in black music, dance and film, the role of black culture in popular culture has driven it into the mainstream.

'THAT MUCH I FLAUNT'

For the last several years, rap artists have increasingly used "nigger" in their lyrics, repackaging it and selling it not just to their own inner-city neighborhoods but to the largely white suburbs. In his song "Straight Up Nigga," Ice-T raps, "I'm a nigga in America, and that much I flaunt," and indeed, a large portion of his record sales are in white America.

In movies and on television, too, "nigger" is heard with unprecedented regularity these days. In *Trespass*, a newly released major-studio film about an inner-city treasure hunt, black rappers portraying gang members call one another "nigger" almost as often as they call one another by their names.

And every Friday at midnight, Home Box Office televises "Russell Simmons' Def Comedy Jam," a half-hour featuring many black, cutting-edge comedians who frequently use "nigger" in their acts.

Sometimes, the use of the word is simply a flat-out repetition of the street vernacular. In rap and hip-hop music, a genre in which millions of listeners adopt the artists' style and language, "nigger" is virtually interchangeable with words like "guy," "man" or "brother."

But often the songs themselves become discussions of the 10 word's various uses and meanings in society, black or white. Not only is black popular culture the focus of the debate, it is often the medium for it.

'MAKES MY TEETH WHITE'

Paul Mooney, a veteran black stand-up comic and writer, recently released a comedy tape titled "Race." On the tape, which includes routines called "Nigger Vampire," "1-900-Blame-a-Nigger," "Niggerstein," "Nigger Raisins" and "Nigger History," Mr. Mooney explains why he uses the word so often.

"I say nigger all the time," he said. "I say nigger 100 times every morning. It makes my teeth white. Nigger-nigger-nigger-nigger-nigger-nigger-nigger-nigger-nigger. I say it. You think, 'What a small white world.'"

Blacks who say they should use the word more openly maintain that its casual use, especially in the company of whites, will shift the word's context and strip "nigger" of its ability to hurt. That is precisely what blacks have been doing for years, say linguists who study black vernacular. By using the word strictly among themselves, the linguists say, they change its context and in doing so dull its edge whenever whites use it.

Kris Parker, a leading rap artist known as KRS-One, predicts that through black culture's ability to affect popular American culture through the electronic media, "nigger" will be de-racialized by its broader use and become just another word.

MEANING IN AMERICA

"In another 5 to 10 years, you're going to see youth in elementary 15 school spelling it out in their vocabulary tests," he said. "It's going to be that accepted by the society."

But other blacks, especially members of the generation for whom Malcolm X and the Rev. Dr. Martin Luther King, Jr. were living heroes, say no one should ever be permitted to forget what "nigger" has meant, and still means, in America.

"That term encapsulates so much of the indignities forced on our people," said the Rev. Benjamin F. Chavis, Jr., a longtime civil-rights leader who is executive director of the United Church of Christ Commission for Racial Justice. "That term made us less than human, and that is why we must reject the usage of that term.

"We cannot let that term be trivialized," he said. "We cannot let that term be taken out of its historical context."

Some blacks say they are so traumatized by the oppressive legacy of "nigger," that they cannot even bring themselves to say the word. Instead, they choose linguistic dodges like "the N-word" or simply spelling the word out. Other blacks say they are "ambivalent" about the growing public use of "nigger."

EARLIER HATEFUL TERMS

20   "Does it signal a new progressive step forward toward a new level of understanding or a regressive step back into self-hate?" asked Christopher Cathcart, a black 29-year-old public relations special-ist in New York. "I fear it is the latter."

Throughout history, nearly minority groups have found them-selves branded by hateful terms. Early in the century, such seem-ingly innocent words as "Irish" and "Jew" were considered pejoratives, said Edward Bendix, a professor of linguistic anthro-pology at the Graduate Center of the City University of New York.

In time the groups have used some of the same terms as pass-words to their particular groups, which is what happened with "nigger" in the black vernacular. Indeed, Bob Guccione, Jr., editor and publisher of the popular music magazine *Spin*—which reports extensively on the rap music scene—said that while whites are very reluctant to use "nigger" because it has "such an incredible weight of ugliness to it," blacks often use it in the presence of whites as a verbal demarcation point.

'THAT'S HARDER'

"In a sense, it empowers the black community in the white main-stream," said Mr. Guccione, who is white. "They can use a very pow-erful word like a passkey, and whites dare not, or should not, use it."

But seldom has a word like "nigger" been pushed into the mainstream while its negative connotations exist, said Dr. Robin Lakoff, a social linguist and author of the book, *Talking Power*, (Basic Books, 1990). "That's harder with 'nigger,' especially with so many people around who still use it in its racist meaning," said Dr. Lakoff, a professor of linguistics at the University of California at Berkeley.

Many of the blacks who defend their open use of the word ac-   25 knowledge that whites still cannot publicly say "nigger" without stirring up old black-white antagonisms.

"Race in America is like herpes because you can never get rid of it," said James Bernard, who is black and senior editor of *The Source*, a magazine that covers the rap and hip-hop scene. "There is still a line."

'A HORRENDOUS WORD'

The magazine's multiracial staff recently published a story about Spike Lee and the basketball star Charles Barkley under a headline "NINETIES NIGGERS." Kris Parker, the rapper, said such uses represent progress. But to the white Chicago writer Studs Terkel, whose latest book, *Race* (The New Press, 1992), is a series of interviews with blacks and whites about race in America, the increased use of "nigger" represents anything but progress.

"It is a horrendous word," he said, adding that the new permissiveness may have more to do with the "wink and nod" of the Reagan-Bush years of dismantling civil rights gains than with rap artists naming themselves N.W.A., for Niggas With Attitude.

Examples abound that "nigger" has not lost its wounding power when used by whites. Whether scratched into a restroom stall or scrawled on the house of a black family in a white neighborhood, "nigger" remains a graffito of hate—the most commonly heard epithet used during anti-black crimes, the authorities say.

When a black man from New Jersey was abducted and set   30 ablaze by three white men in Florida on New Year's Day, one of the first things they said to him, according to the victim's mother, was "nigger."

On Friday, an all-white fraternity at Rider College in New Jersey was disciplined after college officials learned the fraternity had sponsored a "nigger night" on which potential pledges were told to dress like blacks and emulate Stepin Fetchit as they cleaned the fraternity house.

BLURRING A LINE

The changing uses of the word have made for some curious situations on the white side of an increasingly blurred line.

Alex T. Noble, a white public relations intern in New York, said he has white friends who use "nigger" with one another as a term of endearment. Mr. Noble, who works with rappers, said when a black friend calls him a "nigger," "I feel flattered, like I'm part of something."

But, he adds, he is extremely reluctant to return the salutation.

35   "As a white person I would never go up to a black person and say, 'Yo, nigger,'" Mr. Noble said. "I think it's hard to outrun the legacy of oppression that word signifies. Anytime a white person says that word it is troublesome."

The attempts to demystify "nigger" are by no means new. One of the more publicized cases came in the early 1970's, when Richard Pryor used "nigger" in his stand-up comedy act with the express purpose of defanging its racist bite. He titled his seminal comedy album in 1974 *That Nigger's Crazy*. Some years later, however, after a trip to Africa, Mr. Pryor told audiences he would never use the word again as a performer. While abroad, he said, he saw black people running governments and businesses. And in a moment of epiphany, he said he realized that he did not see any "niggers."

Jocelyn Jerome was born of the civil-rights generation, and when she hears the term it cuts her like a knife.

'FEEL LIKE CRYING'

"When I hear it, it makes me angry and very sad," said Ms. Jerome, a 53-year-old mother of three grown children and the director of a program that tries to encourage more minority students to become physicians. "There are times when I honestly feel like crying."

She says she has made it her mission to discourage young black people from using the racial epithet.

40   In a recent incident, a group of young blacks got on Ms. Jerome's bus and spoke in a conversation that consisted of little more than nigger this and nigger that, Ms. Jerome said. She decided to speak up.

"I put my newspaper down and said, 'Look, I know my talking is not going to make you change today or tomorrow, but I have a question: why are you constantly using that word? Do you know what that word means?'"

She said the youngsters listened to her respectfully, occasionally telling her that "nigger" was a term of endearment among young blacks.

Little changed, but that has not weakened her resolve.

"As far as I'm concerned," Ms. Jerome said, "no one has the license to use it."

Questions for Discussion and Topics for Writing

1. Marriott offers many opinions about the meaning and the use of the word *nigger*. Make a list of pros and cons, citing on the "pro" list reasons for using the word and on the "con" list reasons against. Then assert your own argument either for or against using the word. In your conclusion, consider the consequences of becoming desensitized to the word or, alternatively, censoring the word. Are either of these alternatives desirable? If not, can you think of a better way to understand and/or use the word?

2. Marriott discusses both the attitude of Kris Parker (KRS-ONE) and the opinion of Rev. Benjamin F. Chavis, Jr. toward the word *nigger*. Summarize each opinion. Is there a way in which you can reconcile these diametrically opposed views or are they hopelessly polarized?

3. The controversy surrounding the word *nigger* shows the power and importance of diction or word choice. Consider writing a diction paper of your own. Choose a highly charged or evocative word and explore its meaning. Describe its etymology (its historical use) and then construct an argument about the word's use and significance. You may choose to use hip hop or another cultural form to give context and specificity to the word (see also Roediger's "Elvis, Wiggers, and Crossing Over to Non-Whiteness").

4. Using this essay as an example, consider the relationship between words and ideas. Do you think that changing the definition of a word will necessarily change ideas or attitudes the word engenders? Offer examples from your experience to support your point of view.

The Hip-Hop Nation
Whose Is It? In the End, Black Men Must Lead
TOURÉ

A fiction writer and journalist, Touré is also a correspondent for Black Entertainment Television (BET). He is the author of the novel Soul City, The Portable Promised Land *(a collection of short stories), and* Never Drank the Kool-Aid, *a collection of his work for magazines. His writing has appeared in* Rolling Stone, The New Yorker, The New York Times, The Best American Essays of 1999, *and the* Da Capo Best Music Writing of 2004. *The following article appeared in* The New York Times *on August 22, 1999.*

———————— ✦ ————————

ILIVE in a country no map maker will ever respect. A place with its own language, culture and history. It is as much a nation as Italy or Zambia. A place my countrymen call the Hip-Hop Nation, purposefully invoking all of the jingoistic pride that nationalists throughout history have leaned on. Our path to nationhood has been paved by a handful of fathers: Muhammad Ali with his ceaseless bravado, Bob Marley with his truth-telling rebel music, Huey Newton with his bodacious political style, James Brown with his obsession with funk.

We are a nation with no precise date of origin, no physical land, no single chief. But if you live in the Hip-Hop Nation, if you are not merely a fan of the music but a daily imbiber of the culture, if you sprinkle your conversation with phrases like off the meter (for something that's great) or got me open (for something that gives an explosive positive emotional release), if you know why Dutch Masters make better blunts than Phillies (they're thinner), if you know at a glance why Allen Iverson is hip-hop and Grant Hill is not, if you feel the murders of Tupac Shakur and the Notorious B.I.G. in the 1997–98 civil war were assassinations (no other word fits), if you can say yes to all of these questions (and a yes to some doesn't count), then you know the Hip-Hop Nation is a place as real as America on a pre-Columbus atlas. It's there even though the rest of you ain't been there yet.

The Nation exists in any place where hip-hop music is being played or hip-hop attitude is being exuded. Once I went shopping for a Macintosh. The salesman, a wiry 20-something white guy, rattled on about Macs, then, looking at the rapper, or what we call an MC, on my T-shirt, said: "You like Nas? Did you hear him rhyme last night on the 'Stretch and Bobbito' show?" I felt as if my jaw had dropped. He had invoked a legendary hip-hop radio show broadcast once a week on college radio at 2 in the morning. It was as if we were secret agents, and he had uttered the code phrase that revealed him to be my contact. We stood for an hour talking MC's and DJ's, beats and flows, turning that staid computer store into an outpost of the Hip-Hop Nation.

The Nation's pioneers were a multiracial bunch—whites were among the early elite graffiti artists and Latinos were integral to the shaping of DJing and MCing, b-boying (break dancing) and general hip-hop style. Today's Nation makes brothers of men black, brown, yellow and white. But this world was built to worship urban black maleness: the way we speak, walk, dance, dress, think. We are revered by others, but our leadership is and will remain black. As it should.

We are a nation with our own gods and devils, traditions and   5
laws (one of them is to not share them with outsiders), but there has never been and never will be a president of the Hip-Hop Nation. Like black America, we're close-knit yet still too fractious for one leader. Instead, a powerful senate charts our future. That senate is made up of our leading MC's, their every album and single a bill or referendum proposing linguistic, musical and topical directions for the culture. Is Compton a cool spot? Can Edie Brickell, an embodiment of American female whiteness, be the source for a sample? Is a thick countrified Southern accent something we want to hear? Is police brutality still a rallying point? Like a politician with polls and focus groups, an MC must carefully calibrate his musical message because once his music is released, the people vote with their dollars in the store and their butts in the club, ignoring certain MC's and returning them to private life while anointing others, granting them time on our giant national microphone.

Unlike rhythm-and-blues, hip-hop has a strong memoiristic impulse, meaning our senator-MC's speak about themselves, their neighborhoods, the people around them, playing autobiographer, reporter and oral historian. Telling the stories as they actually happened is what is meant by the catch phrase keeping it real. Outsiders laugh when that hallowed phrase is seemingly made hollow by obvious self-mythologizing—materialistic boasts that would be beyond even the Donald or tales of crimes that would be envied by a Gotti. But this bragging is merely people speaking of the people they dream of being, which, of course, is a reflection of the people they are.

How do you get into this senate? The answer is complex, involving both rhyming technique and force of personality. To be a great MC you must have a hypnotizing flow—a cadence and delivery that get inside the drum and bass patterns and create their own rhythm line. You must have a magnetic voice—it can be deliciously nasal like Q-Tip's, or delicate and sing-songy like Snoop Doggy Dogg's, or deep-toned like that of Rakim, who sounds as commanding as Moses—but it must be a compelling sound. And you must say rhymes with writerly details, up-to-the-minute slang, bold punch lines, witty metaphors and original political or sociological insights.

But, again like a politician, to be a great MC you must seem like an extension of the masses and, simultaneously, an extraordinary individual. There must be a certain down-homeness about you, a way of carrying yourself that replicates the way people in your home base feel about life. You must be the embodiment of your audience.

At the same time, you must seem greater than your audience. You must come across as supercool—an attitude based on toughness or sex appeal or intellect or bravado that inspires your listeners to say, I'd like to be you.

10   In the first decade and a half after the first hip-hop record was released in 1979, hip-hop was a national conversation—about urban poverty and police brutality, the proliferation of guns and the importance of safe sex, as well as the joy of a good party—in which the only speakers were black men.

In recent years that conversation has opened up. Hip-hop has become more democratic, cracking the monopoly that black men from New York and L.A. have long held over the Hip-Hop Nation senate.

Traditionally, hip-hop has been hypermodern, disdaining the surreal for gritty images of urban life. But Missy Elliott and her producer, Timbaland, have constructed a post-modern esthetic that manifests itself, on her latest album, *Da Real World*, in references to the sci-fi film *The Matrix* and videos in which Missy dresses as if she were in a scene from the 1982 movie *Blade Runner*. Her music also has a futuristic feel, from Timbaland's spare, propulsive beats filled with quirky sounds that evoke science-fiction to Missy's experiments with singing and rhyming, as well as using onomatopoeia in her rhymes. The duo have become part of the Nation's sonic vanguard, as well as door-openers for a new genre: hip-hop sci-fi.

Groups from the South Coast like GooDie Mob, Eightball and MJG and Outkast have also brought new perspectives. (The Hip-Hop Nation reconfigures American geography with a Saul Steinberg-like eye, maximizing cities where the most important hip-hop has come from, microscoping other places. When we speak of the East Coast, we mean the five boroughs of New York, Long Island, Westchester County, New Jersey and Philadelphia; by West Coast we mean Los Angeles, Compton, Long Beach, Vallejo and Oakland; and the region made up of Atlanta, New Orleans, Virginia, Miami and Memphis is called the South Coast.)

Outkast is a pair of Atlanta MC's, Dre (Andre Benjamin) and Big Boi (Antwan Patton), who are not new to many in the Hip-Hop

Nation. But with the success of *Aquemini*, their third album, and months of touring as the opening act for Lauryn Hill, they are new to power within hip-hop. Their hip-hop mixes the cerebralness of New York rappers and the George Clinton-drenched funk favored out West with a particularly Southern musicality, soulfulness, twang-drenched rhymes and Baptist churchlike euphoric joy.

But the most polarizing and revolutionary new entry to the 15 hip-hop senate is Eminem (born Marshall Mathers). There have been white MC's before him, but none have been as complex. Either they were clearly talentless (like Vanilla Ice) or they worshiped blackness (like MC Serch of 3rd Bass). Eminem is different. The fervency of fans, black and white, marveling at his skill and laughing at his jokes, has kept him in office, despite those offended by his whiny white-boy shock-jock shtick.

He is an original voice in the national conversation that is hip-hop because he speaks of the dysfunctionality of his white-trash world—his absentee father, his drugged-out mom, his daughter's hateful mother, his own morally bankrupt conscience. With Eminem the discussion turns to problems in the white community, or at least—because he is from a black neighborhood in Detroit—to the problems of whites in the black community. On a recent song (called "Busa Rhyme" from Missy's new album *Da Real World*) Eminem rhymes darkly: "I'm homicidal/ and suicidal/ with no friends/ holdin' a gun with no handle/ just a barrel at both ends." Finally someone has arrived to represent the Dylan Klebolds and Eric Harrises of America.

A rash of overprotectiveness within our nation keeps many fans from enjoying the hip-hop of a sneering white MC, but why shouldn't we welcome a frank discussion of white maladies into our homes when millions of white people allow our MC's into their homes to talk about our disorders every day?

The Hip-Hop Nation senate is swelling to include whites, women and Southerners, but don't expect that senate to become a true melting pot anytime soon. As long as upper-class white men stay in charge of the United States Senate, urban black men will remain our leading speakers. Hip-hop's history is long enough to grant us the maturity to open our world, but America is still white enough that we know we need our own oasis.

It all began with a few parties. Jams in New York city parks thrown by DJ's like Kool Here, Grandmaster Flash and Afrika Bambaataa. To your eyes it would've appeared to be a rapper in a public park, a DJ behind him, his cables plugged into the street lamp, the police not far away, waiting for just the right moment to shut it all down. But to us those parks were the center of a universe. The cops—or rather, five-oh (from the television series *Hawaii Five-O*)—were Satan. The music—James Brown, Sly Stone, Funkadelic and anything with a stone cold bass and drum rhythm you could rhyme over—breathed meaning and substance and soul into our bodies. It gave life. It was God.

20   From behind the turntables in his roped-off pulpit in the park, the DJ gave a rousing sermon sonically praising God's glory. Then up stepped the High Priest, the conduit between God and you—the MC. How crucial was he? In 1979, in its seminal song, "Rapper's Delight," the Sugar Hill Gang explained that even Superman was useless if he couldn't flow: "He may be able to fly all through the night/ But can he rock a party til the early light?"

A few years later, in the early 80's, a trickle of cassettes began appearing in urban mom-and-pop record stores like Skippy White's on Blue Hill Avenue in Mattapan Square in Boston. As a 12-year-old I would walk there from my father's office. Every other month or so a new hip-hop tape would arrive, direct from New York City: Run-DMC . . . MC Shan . . . the Fat Boys. A kid on an allowance could own all the hip-hop albums ever made. For all the force of the music, the culture was so small and precious you held it in your hands as delicately as a wounded bird.

In the mid-80's hip-hop won the nation's attention and was branded a fad that would soon die like disco. Hip-hoppers closed ranks, constructed a wall and instituted a siege mentality. We became like Jews, a tribe that knew how close extinction was and responded to every attack and affront, no matter how small, as if it were a potential death blow. Where Jews battle anti-Semitic attitudes and actions, we fought fans who are not orthodox and music not purely concerned with art. Where Jews hold holidays that celebrate specific legends, ancestors and miracles, hip-hoppers spoke of the old school with a holy reverence and urged new jacks to know their history. Our Zionism was the Hip-Hop Nation.

By the late 80's and early 90's mainstreaming had arrived bringing powerful gifts, as the devil always does. Now our music was broadcast on prime-time MTV, and our political views, via Chuck D and KRS-One, were heard on CNN and *Nightline*. Hip-hop, like jazz and rock-and-roll before it, had become the defining force of a generation. It was not going to die. The siege mentality subsided.

The guards at the gate were retired. The fan base grew, and the music diversified, which caused the fan base to grow larger still and the music to diversify further. But we continue to live in

America, to suffer the daily assaults of racism. And our sanity continues to rely on having a place where the heroes look like us and play by our rules. As long as being a black man is a cross to bear and not a benediction, you can find me and my comrades locked inside one of those mass therapy sessions called a party, inside that tri-coastal support group called the Hip-Hop Nation.

Questions for Discussion and Topics for Writing

1. How does Touré define the Hip-Hop Nation? To answer this question, go through his essay (originally an article in *The New York Times*), and look for particular terms or images that he uses to develop his theme of Nation. About what kind of nation is he writing?

2. The subtitle of Touré's piece is "In the End Black Men Must Lead." How inclusive is the author's Hip-Hop Nation? Who is included? Does Touré have a pluralistic vision of this imagined community? If so, why does he portray his nation as having a black leadership?

3. At the end of his essay Touré tells us why the Hip-Hop Nation is important. How does he define the Nation's role? More generally, what claim does he seem to be making about the role of culture, especially musical culture, in people's lives?

4. Write an essay putting Touré's essay in dialogue with Kleinfield's "Guarding the Borders of the Hip-Hop Nation." Give your paper the following focus: Does anyone own culture? Is it right to say that any one ethnic or racial group should be in charge of something like the Hip-Hop Nation? Ultimately, what you will do in this paper is decide whether you agree with or object to Touré's conclusion in "The Hip-Hop Nation."

5. Research the concept of the *imagined community*, a term generally attributed to writer Benedict Anderson. Does the term apply to the Hip-Hop Nation? Write an essay that uses Anderson's term in framing a discussion of Touré's key ideas.

Making Connections

1. Watch Spike Lee's movie, *Do the Right Thing*. Then listen to Public Enemy's song "Fight the Power." How might the song help us understand the racial dynamics expressed in Lee's movie?
2. Listen to the Goodie Mob song, "Cell Therapy." How is the theme of surveillance racialized in the song? Do you think the song's allusions to Hitler and the holocaust are justified in this context? Why or why not?
3. Look up the "N" word in the Oxford English Dictionary. What is the word's etymology? How has the word been used historically, from its early uses to its present day manifestations? How is the "N" word used in hip hop culture? How is hip hop's use of the word unique or new? Write an essay debating the use of the "N" word in hip hop or in ordinary conversation.
4. Watch the movie *Whiteboyz* starring Danny Hoch. How does Danny Hoch's depiction of a midwestern white youth who embraces gangsta rap expose racial contradictions within hip hop culture?

CHAPTER 3

Your Momma's a Mack Daddy: Gender Construction in Hip Hop

The fights between the anti-rap crusader C. Delores Tucker and the rapper Tupac Shakur in the early- to mid-90s are part of hip hop legend and lore. Forever memorialized in lyrics and on Tupac's album *All Eyez on Me*, their beef both highlighted the public perceptions of the violence and misogyny in rap music and, at the same time, brought hip hop immediately into the political arena. While Tupac eloquently if derisively addressed Tucker in his albums, redressing the critiques she made concerning the music, Tucker appeared as a guest speaker on many news specials devoted to debating the deleterious effects of hip hop. Because both personalities emerged from the black Civil Rights Movement—Tucker by her association with figures such as Martin Luther King and Shakur as the son of prominent Black Panthers—the dispute was not only charged with political but also historical meaning. The legacy of the Civil Rights Movement was a fundamental concern girding this debate. Importantly, such a monumental struggle was not posed in complex philosophical or sociological terms; rather, with Tucker calling Tupac's lyrics "smut" and Shakur calling Tucker a "bitch," this fight to define the prevailing perceptions of the black community—while highly political and carrying deep social consequences—played itself out in terms of gender. More specifically, the argument revolved around the way hip hop uses gender dynamics, or the social constructs that identify us as men and women, to assert social, ideological, and even aesthetic claims.

Rappers use gender to hew out various kinds of identities as well as to forge significant critiques of those tendencies within a culture that denigrates women. The beef between Tucker and Tupac, for example, is often understood as a fight between the prudishness of censorship and libertinism of virulent sexuality, but this stigmatization overlooks the ways in which Tupac undercuts what might even be his own misogynist impulses. On the same album where Tupac ridicules Tucker, he writes tributes to his mother. When Tupac uses denigrating monikers such as "bitch," he often uses the debased connotations as a metaphor to address the destructiveness of promiscuous behavior or as a rhetorical tool to criticize Tucker's political position. While certainly there are many rappers who repeat popular culture's gross glamorization of violent domination, there are many like Tupac who exploit the trope to make a larger social statement. The notion that hip hop is misogynist rant oversimplifies its wealth of attitudes and positions about what men and woman are and the roles they play. Repressing the statements of hip hop as Tucker set out to do not only smacks of censorship but also ignores and even silences some of rap music's most trenchant and bold critiques of the systematic oppression of women and the concomitant male identities that reinforce such destructive dynamics.

Many women rappers have used the word as a means of ironic identification and as a focal point of a larger social critique. The Boss, a Detroit-born gangsta rapper, makes it into a term of empowerment. In the song "Recipe of a Ho," she drives a denotative wedge between pejorative names and proclaims that not all "bitches" are "ho's." Turning these usually analogous terms into opposites, Boss infuses "bitch" with a sense of fierce resistance to misogynist attitudes. She dresses down the men who puff themselves up by denigrating women, insisting that she is a "bitch" who doesn't "stutter." By implying that she possesses lyrical, rapping, and rhyming skills that rival or exceed those of most men, Boss forges a link between rhetoric and social power, an important connection for a female rapper when the implied authorial position of the MC is male.

Some women rappers have taken up this "male" position as a means of neutralizing implied male dominance. For example, the Lady of Rage in her song "Lyrical Gangbang" speaks, acts, and sounds like her male counterparts and is ultimately indistinguishable from them. More subtly, Brooklyn rapper Jean Grae uses the male authorial position to flip the script. In a feat of poetic justice, Grae tropes masculinity in her song "Knock" in order to critique the male-dominated recording industry. Her lyrics, she argues, penetrate the ears of her male listeners, an act that if performed by hip hop's sex queens would give the listener "gonorrhea." In strong sexual terms, this virile rhyme metaphorically puts Grae in the dominant male position and the male-dominated music industry in the subordinate female position. The line simultaneously critiques those "chicks" flashing "T and A" who conform willingly to the music industry's subordination and objectification of women.

In her song "U.N.I.T.Y.," Queen Latifah goes further and traces the effect of these seemingly inert gender roles. She begins by retaliating against men's catcalls and denigrating attitudes. Using the word "bitch" as a refrain, she asks defiantly who it is that is calling her a bitch. She then tells the story of a time she was called "bitch" by a "little dude" who was trying to "break fly" because he was with "his boys." In response, she "punched him dead in his eye." Here, Latifah reverses stereotypical gender roles and beats the guy up. In this funny episode, she appropriates a masculine identity as a means of retaliation. However, this gender flip, while seemingly innocuous, leads to a much grimmer scene.

In the next stanza, Latifah describes her own abusive relationship in which she is beaten while her threats to leave her abuser remain idle. Despite feeling like a "personal whore," Latifah cannot bring herself to end the relationship. Afraid to leave her abuser, she seems to have internalized his attitude that she is nothing without him. It is only through real struggle that Latifah comes to see that the exact opposite is true: she is nothing *with* him. The story is a savvy critique of the first, more humorous event. In this narrative of domestic violence, the real danger in current gender roles becomes apparent. Even if the roles are reversed, the violence remains and women are more often the victims than the assailants. Latifah also painfully acknowledges her complicity in the situation: it is not only the violent ideas of masculinity but also the submissive ideas of femininity that conspire to create these intolerably destructive relationships.

This recognition is implicit in the third stanza, where Latifah roundly criticizes a woman for taking up a masculine "gangsta" role in an effort to be "hard." For Latifah, being a "gangsta bitch" is both oxymoronic and moronic, perpetuating stereotypes that are not only misogynist but inherently destructive for both men and women. In the end, she appeals to women to unify and reject these identifications (both masculine and feminine), demanding that they let men know they are neither bitches nor "ho's."

Men have also criticized the position of male domination, recognizing misogyny's deleterious effects on men and women alike. One of the most perceptive critiques of this conventional masculine authoritative position is by The Coup in the song "Me and Jesus the Pimp." The song tells the story of a prostitute killed by her pimp, Jesus, as witnessed by her young son who, in need of a father figure, ironically starts to look up to the pimp after the murder until, eventually, he comes to his senses. In the end, the boy stands up to Jesus, killing him in retribution for his mother's murder. While at first this may seem to be an act of revenge, the boy's reason for killing Jesus disturbingly repeats the pimp's definition of masculinity. The pimp, recognizing the ghetto's gendered distinction between hard and soft personalities, admonishes the boy not to be a Micro*soft*, but rather a Macintosh with a *"hard* drive." The boy tragically takes up a masculine identification that generates misogyny in order to destroy it. He kills Jesus the pimp and avenges his mother's death, but in doing so he reveals how these male attitudes of violence and misogyny are not only connected but also how, even when rejected, they get recycled. In the terms of the song, the problem is larger than personal identification. By calling the pimp "Jesus," The Coup alludes to Christianity's religious patriarchy, thereby implicating the dominant culture's socioreligious mores in its gender critique and suggesting the breadth and depth of the problem.

Despite many deft gender critiques, the question remains whether these have any relationship to the "real" world of hip hop. Even if they "flip the script" or redefine the terms of gender, can women really have a place in an industry and a music that remains so male-dominated? The existence of artists like Missy Elliot belies any simplistic view that hip hop is principally for men and against women. Not only is Missy Elliot one of hip hop's great talents, she is also one of its most savvy business*men:* when many of even the most successful male rappers signed on to record labels, giving away both control and money in order to acquire recognition and distribution, Missy held out until she was given her own record label and now boasts her own reality TV show. Missy has achieved what most male rappers can't even imagine and has taken the *miss* right out of *dismissive* and *submissive.*

Hip-Hop Women Shredding the Veil
Race and Class in Popular Feminist Identity
MARCYLIENA MORGAN

Associate Professor in the Department of Communication at Stanford, Marcyliena Morgan teaches courses on hip hop; discourse; language and identity; race, class, and gender; the ethnography of

communications; and representation in the media. She has authored
Language, Discourse and Power in African-American Culture *and*
edited Language and the Social Construction of Identity in Creole
Situations. *Morgan is also executive director of Stanford's Hip Hop*
Archive. The piece that follows is excerpted from the Summer 2005
issue of South Atlantic Quarterly.

——————————— ✦ ———————————

DO RIGHT WOMAN

. . . In the midst of hip-hop's rise into America's consciousness, concern over both the representation and involvement of women often
has been in the form of scandal, moral panic, and cultural and political hysteria. Since the mid-1990s, politicians and public figures
such as C. Delores Tucker, as well as respected musicians like Dionne
Warwick, have publicly derided hip-hop artists for what they deem
to be widespread misogyny and violence in lyrics, videos, and staged
performances.[1] In contrast, scholars and many feminists, while
highly critical of sexism and violence in hip-hop, argue that it is a
product and representation of male-dominated culture and should
be criticized within American culture and media representation.[2]
While well intentioned, this public debate does not improve the day-
to-day life of the young women hip-hop fans and artists. Their reality is fraught with numerous physical threats and stereotypical
media images of young urban women who are frequently cast in
sexist, racist, paternalistic, contested, and convoluted notions of
the strong, angry, promiscuous, childbearing, wild black woman.
Moreover, the representations of these notions of young urban
women occur within a panoply of discursive practices and symbols
of womanhood, motherhood, sexuality, class, authority, race, influence, and desire. It should come as no surprise that hip-hop women
are not only aware of representations of their generation but are also
invested in understanding the musical, social, political, and cultural
history of black women that led to these representations. Female
MCs use hip-hop to develop and display their lyrical skills as well as
present and challenge what it means to be a young black woman in
America and the world. They do not use their musical and verbal
genre to destroy the veil of race, gender, and class discrimination.
They prefer to render it diaphanous, so that it can be seen and
manipulated as symbol, warning, and memory of what it meant to
live under its tyranny and the dangers of underestimating dominant
society's desire to erect it once again.

African American musical traditions often connect younger generations to mothers, women, workers, singers, activists, and organizers who have struggled to place the lives and values of black working-class women within general American and African American culture. Musical forms have a central role in African American culture as a major source of socialization, social change, political thought, and expression of desire, religious belief, and love.[3] The music, history, and memories of past generations are the seeds of the hip-hop generation, and the women prepare to both run with them and use them to incinerate race and gender stereotypes—if necessary. The history that these musicians deliver to the hip-hop generation includes details of how black women were treated as property under slavery and denied rights to their bodies and any argument of femininity, family, and motherhood. Evidence of a sense of connectedness to their female predecessors often appears as responsibility and entitlement in the practiced lyrics of artists. One strategy is the performance of racially marked and "strong woman/sister" authenticity that challenges pernicious stereotypes and uses figures such as Angela Davis (e.g., the artist Medusa) to represent uncompromising revolutionary commitment and spirit. Others look to Mother Africa (embodied in, say, Queen Latifah), explicitly promote self-respect, and engage in educational dialogue with men and women who lack knowledge of their history and culture. Still others offer a variety of street-smart perspectives (e.g., Eve, Rah Digga, Missy Elliott) and that of the down-to-earth, thoughtful, and conscious woman (e.g., Lauryn Hill, Mystic).

Irrespective of style, hip-hop women share the same value of performance: hard, skillful, provocative, and intelligent rhyming. They are skilled MCs, and they represent the lives of women in hip-hop and the world. Medusa, a prominent underground MC, describes herself as "One Bad Sista" who speaks with her ancestors by her side and contemplates their sacrifices and triumphs through the power ("gangsta") and wisdom of her womb and vagina as she croons, "This pussy gangsta."[4] This explicit reference is simultaneously sexual and nonsexual, defiant and compliant. It is the unambiguous telling of the black woman's story as she carries, produces, and attempts to protect that which she holds dear.

AIN'T NO WAY

Female MCs devour and set to rhyme black women's history, social life, and dreams of being treated with respect as women in America. Virtually every female rapper has "shouted out" the names of strong, talented women who were symbols of excellence

and leadership. These names include Angela Davis, Harriet Tubman, Sojourner Truth, Rosa Parks, Nina Simone, Bessie Smith,
Billie Holiday, Aretha Franklin, and more.[5] Though not all female
MCs are versed on the details of the treatment of black women in
the United States, they are well aware that black women had to
struggle to be valued as both women and black people in American history. For many black women, a claim to womanhood has
been a matter not only of social practice but also of the courts.

The tragic 1855 case *State of Missouri v. Celia* set the stage for   5
how black women would be treated and viewed by society for
decades to come. After attempting to resist repeated rapes by her
master that left her pregnant and sick, Celia struck and killed him
and then tried to destroy the evidence. During her trial for murder,
the defense's argument was that in the state of Missouri, women
are protected from rape and therefore Celia should be subject to a
lesser sentence. The court ruled that the assault did not constitute
rape, since she was a slave rather than a woman, and thus could
not be adjudicated under laws that protect women.[6] The precedent
had been set. Because she was a slave, Celia was not a woman.
Later, because black women worked to support their families,
unlike many white women, their claims to womanhood were
treated as dubious. As Evelyn Higginbotham argues, "Gender, so
colored by race, remained from birth until death inextricably
linked to one's personal identity and social status. For black and
white women, gendered identity was reconstructed and represented in very different, indeed antagonistic, racialized contexts."[7]

This racialized context was also one that regulated the public
attitude and behavior of blacks. During U.S. slavery and until the
1960s in the South, blacks could not exhibit linguistic agency, nor
could they initiate verbal interactions with whites under the threat
of death.[8] Submission to white supremacy demanded nonverbal
communication as well. Thus, while the place of black women in
the legal history concerning women's rights is truly disturbing,
control and surveillance were relentless and occurred within all
aspects of black life, especially in terms of day-to-day interactions.
Since discursive practices of all black people were regulated by
white supremacists, all black communication with whites in general was performed as powerless, agentless, childlike, and thus
feminine. Interaction styles included nearly every conservative,
overly polite verbal and nonverbal expectat7ion of women's
speech, such as: use formal address when speaking to a white person, do not speak unless spoken to, do not speak assuredly (use
hedges), do not make statements (overuse tag questions), and so
on. The discursive requirements also included nonverbal rules

such as stepping aside when a white person approaches, keeping one's head lowered, and not looking someone directly in the eye. Thus linguistic and conversational cues of subservience and dependence were necessary as performatives to corroborate the defense for slavery, and later Jim Crow segregation.

While the speech of all blacks was monitored to address the needs and demands of white patriarchy, this was true for white women's speech as well. White women's speech has historically been relegated to subservient status in the role of servant or sex object.[9] The "normal" woman's speech was thus described as less informal and more standard and conservative than men's. This designation did not result in equality in conversation. Instead, white women were treated to more interruptions from males and the frequent use of back channels (urging others to continue). Rather than initiating conversations on their own, they focused on helping others keep their turn at talk. In contrast to stereotypes of the dominant, subversive, emasculating, uncaring black woman, feminist psychology and linguistic theory portrayed middle-class white women as indiscriminate "people pleasers," concerned with harmony and with being accepted in life and in conversation. Signifying, loud-talking black women simply didn't stand a chance.[10] Rejecting the cult of the good woman who speaks without agency, hip-hop women have chosen a discourse style that is not only independent of patriarchal censorship and control but also freely critiques the loss of power and responsibility of the good woman.

I SAY A LITTLE PRAYER

The power of women to discursively claim a space and challenge both patriarchy and feminism was born during the discursive struggles of the black power movement. While many identify the black power movement as the beginning of collective black pride, it was also the end of discursive compliance with white supremacy. The civil rights movement employed the polite and nonconfrontational discursive style of the middle class in order to construct the image of the equal, worthy, intelligent citizen. Once the black power movement reframed the struggle for civil rights as one that demanded the same entitlements as whites, a discourse style was ushered in that did not simply address, confront, and resist compliant African American discourse. The new discourse annihilated the old and considered it a symbol of a slave and self-hate mentality. Suddenly, to speak in a deferential manner marked one as a lackey of white supremacists (an Uncle Tom). The new discourse style confronted white supremacy and neither complied nor demanded rights within it. Instead, the discourse style asserted a black presence on its terms, one that reflected a different consciousness and a sense of entitlement. As a result, African American speech in white-dominated contexts went from childlike, feminine, overly polite, and self-effacing to aggressive, impolite, direct, and in-your-face threatening.

Black women found themselves caught in the crevices of the movement from powerless and feminine discourse to a powerful one symbolizing not simply masculinity but a powerful black masculinity that challenges, threatens, and competes with white masculinity. To assert equal entitlements meant negotiating both feminine and masculine discourses, with racist and sexist baggage embedded in both. Thus, while this discursive space is potentially a powerful one, it is also one of unending contestation and mediation. This space was occupied not only by black women after slavery but also by the women of the blues, who in singing about women's realities introduced their strategies and methods for change and representation. Their only alternatives were to portray or defend cultural values about accurately describing people and treating them fairly and equally. It is not surprising that at the core of black communities are women who were prepared and compelled to confront racial, class, and gender injustice. There are rewards for women who are adept at handling discourse concerning these subjects, and there is punishment for those who are naive and fail to recognize the power they and those in power have over their words. As a result, there are two intertwined themes throughout African American women's discourse. One is associated with representing individual and group identity and the other with representing racial, gender, and class injustice. Consequently, any critique of gender hegemony is also a critique of race. . . .

Notes

1. C. Delores Tucker was chair of the National Political Congress of Black Women and Chair of the Democratic National Committee Black Caucus. In the 1990s, she participated in a national campaign against violent lyrics in rap music. In 1997, she and her husband sued the estate of Tupac Shakur for $10 million over lyrics in which Shakur rhymed her name with an obscenity. Her lawsuit alleged, among other things, that her husband, William Tucker, had suffered loss of "consortium."

2. See, for instance, bell hooks, *Outlaw Culture: Resisting Representations* (New York: Routledge, 1994).

3. Angela Davis, *Blues Legacies and Black Feminism: Gertrude "Ma" Rainey, Bessie Smith and Billie Holiday* (New York: Pantheon, 1998): Michael C. Dawson,

Black Visions: The Roots of Contemporary African-American Political Ideologies (Chicago: University of Chicago Press, 2001); Tricia Rose, *Black Noise: Rap Music and Black Culture in Contemporary America* (Hanover, NH: Wesleyan University Press, 1994); Dionne Bennett, "The Love Difference Makes: Inter-subjectivity and the Emotional Politics of African American Romantic Ritual" (PhD diss., University of California, Los Angeles, 2003).

4. Medusa, "My Pussy's Gangsta."

5. The performers invoking these names include Medusa, Lauryn Hill, Lil' Kim, MC Lyte, Rah Digga, and more.

6. See Evelyn Brooks Higginbotham, "African-American Women's History and the Metalanguage of Race," *Signs* 17 (1992): 251–74.

7. Ibid., 8. Thus while Butler (1990) interrogates the meaning of women within historical and political contexts regarding sexuality, Harris (1996) is concerned with when the legal status of black women moved from "property" to "woman." Judith Butler, *Gender Trouble: Feminism and the Subversion of Identity* (London and New York: Routledge, 1990); Cheryl L. Harris, "Finding Sojourner's Truth: Race, Gender, and the Institution of Property," *Cardozo Law Review* 18 (1996): 306–409.

8. Marcyliena Morgan, *Language, Discourse, and Power in African American Culture* (Cambridge: Cambridge University Press, 2002).

9. Robin Lakoff, *Language and Woman's Place* (New York: Harper & Row, 1975).

10. These, of course, are references to African American verbal genres. See Morgan, *Language, Discourse, and Power in African American Culture*; Claudia Mitchell-Kernan, *Language Behavior in a Black Urban Community* (Berkeley, CA: Language Behavior Research Laboratory, 1971); Geneva Smitherman, *Talkin That Talk: Language, Culture and Education in African America* (London: Routledge, 2000).

Questions for Discussion and Topics for Writing

1. Marcyliena Morgan argues that female MCs prefer to "render [the veil of race, gender, and class discrimination] diaphanous, so that it can be seen and ma-nipulated as symbol, warning, and memory of what it means to live under its tyranny and the dangers of underestimating dominant society's desire to erect it once again." Explain Morgan's claim, and then use her quotation in a paragraph explaining how female rappers use their music to articulate their position in society.

2. Morgan cites the 1855 case *State of Missouri v. Celia*. How does Morgan's citation of the Celia case help her lay a foundation for her discussion of female MCs? What were the specific linguistic outcomes of the case? In other words, how did the case help create a racialized context affecting the ways black women could express themselves in public?

3. Regarding the expressive practices of women, Morgan also discusses white women's speech in a context of patriarchal control. How were white women affected by the "cult of the good woman"? How do hip hop women construct a discourse style that differentiates them from the "good woman"?

4. Research the *State of Missouri v. Celia* case and write an essay that builds on Morgan's own analyses. Go into more detail than Morgan does, and, based on your research, construct an argument that either confirms or complicates Morgan's claims.

5. Research either of the other two cases that Morgan cites, the K-BOO case or the controversy involving the rapper Nelly and the uproar he created because of a planned concert at Spelman College. Use your research to help explain some of Morgan's more difficult claims, such as the following: "[There] are two intertwined themes throughout African American women's discourse. One is associated with representing individual and group identity and the other with representing racial, gender, and class injustice." How does such a claim manifest itself in the two cases cited above?

Beyond Racism and Misogyny
Black Feminism and 2 Live Crew
KIMBERLE CRENSHAW

Kimberle Crenshaw is a professor of law at UCLA and Columbia. Crenshaw has been published in the Harvard Law Review, *the* National Black Law Journal, *the* Stanford Law Review, *and the* Southern California Law Review. *She has lectured around the world on race matters, addressing audiences in Europe, Africa, and South America. Her publications include* Critical Race Theory *and* Words That Wound: Critical Race Theory, Assaultive Speech, and the First Amendment. *The following article first appeared in* Boston Review *in 1991.*

————————— ✦ —————————

In June 1990, the members of the rap group 2 Live Crew were arrested and charged under a Florida obscenity statute for their performance in an adults-only club in Hollywood, Florida. The arrests came just two days after a federal court judge had ruled that the sexually explicit lyrics in 2 Live Crew's album, *As Nasty As They Wanna Be*, were obscene. Although the members of 2 Live Crew were eventually acquitted of charges stemming from the live performance, the Federal court determination that *As Nasty As They Wanna Be* is obscene still stands. This obscenity judgment, along with the arrests and the subsequent trial, prompted an intense public controversy about rap music, a controversy that merged with a broader debate about the representation of sex and violence in popular music, about cultural diversity, and about the meaning of freedom of expression.

I

Two positions dominated the debate about 2 Live Crew. Writing in *Newsweek*, political columnist George Will staked out a case against the Crew, arguing that *Nasty* was misogynistic filth and characterizing their lyrics as a profoundly repugnant "combination of extreme infantilism and menace" that objectified Black women and represented them as legitimate targets for sexual violence.

The most prominent defense of 2 Live Crew was advanced by Professor Henry Louis Gates, Jr., an expert on African-American literature. In a *New York Times* Op-Ed piece, and in testimony at the criminal trial, Gates portrayed 2 Live Crew as brilliant artists who were inventively elaborating distinctively African-American forms of cultural expression. Furthermore, Gates argued, the characteristic exaggeration featured in their lyrics served a political end: to explode popular racist stereotypes about Black sexuality precisely by presenting those stereotypes in a comically extreme form. Where Will saw a misogynistic assault on Black women by social degenerates, Gates found a form of 'sexual carnivalesque' freighted with the promise to free us from the pathologies of racism.

II

As a Black feminist, I felt the pull of each of these poles, but not the compelling attractions either. My immediate response to the criminal charges against 2 Live Crew was ambivalence: I wanted to stand together with the brothers against a racist attack, but I wanted to stand *against* a frightening explosion of violent imagery directed at women like me. My sharp internal division—my dissatisfaction with the idea that the "real issue" is race or that the "real issue" is gender—is characteristic of my experience as a Black woman living at the intersection of racial and sexual subordination. To that experience Black feminism offers an intellectual and political response: aiming to bring together the different aspects of an otherwise divided sensibility, it argues that Black women are commonly marginalized by a politics of race alone or gender alone, and that a political response to either form of subordination must be a political response to both. When the controversy over 2 Live Crew is approached in light of such Black feminist sensibilities, an alternative to the dominant poles of the public debate emerges.

5   At the legal "bottom line" I agree with the supporters of 2 Live Crew that the obscenity prosecution was wrongheaded. But the reasons for my conclusion are not the same as the reasons generally offered in support of 2 Live Crew. I will come to those reasons shortly, but first I should emphasize that after listening to 2 Live

Crew's lyrics, along with those of other rap artists, my defense of 2 Live Crew, (qualified though it is) did not come easy.

The first time I listened to 2 Live Crew, I was stunned. The issue had been distorted by descriptions of "As Nasty As They Wanna Be" as simply "sexually explicit." "Nasty" is much more: it is virulently misogynist, sometimes violently so. Black women are cunts, "'ho's," and all-purpose bitches: raggedy bitches, sorry-ass bitches, lowdown slimy-ass bitches. Good sex is often portrayed as painful and humiliating for women. . . .

. . . Those of us who are concerned about the high rates of gender violence in our communities must be troubled by the possible connections between these images and tolerance for violence against women. Children and teenagers are listening to this music, and I am concerned that the range of acceptable behavior is being broadened by the constant propagation of anti-women imagery. I'm concerned, too, about young Black women who, like young men, are learning that their value lies between their legs. Unlike men, however, their sexual value is a depletable commodity; by expending it, girls become whores and boys become men.

Nasty is misogynist, and a Black feminist response to the case against 2 Live Crew must start from a full acknowledgment of that misogyny. But such a response must also consider whether an exclusive focus on issues of gender risks overlooking aspects of the prosecution of 2 Live Crew that raise serious questions of racism. And here is where the roots of my opposition to the obscenity prosecution lie.

III

An initial problem concerning the prosecution was its apparent selectivity. A comparison between 2 Live Crew and other mass-marketed sexual representations suggests that race played some role in distinguishing 2 Live Crew as the first group ever to be prosecuted for obscenity in connection with a musical recording, and one of only a handful of recording artists to be prosecuted for a live performance. Recent controversies about sexism, racism, and violence in popular culture point to a vast range of expression that might well provide targets for censorship, but that have not been targeted. Madonna has acted out masturbation, portrayed the seduction of a priest, and depicted group sex on stage, yet she has never been prosecuted for obscenity. While 2 Live Crew was performing in an adults-only club in Hollywood, Florida, Andrew Dice Clay was performing nationwide on HBO. Well-known for his racist "humor," Clay is also comparable to 2 Live Crew in sexual explicitness and misogyny. In his show, for example, Clay offers:

"Eenie, meenie, minee, mo, suck my [expletive] and swallow slow,"
or "Lose the bra bitch." Moreover, graphic sexual images—many
of them violent—were widely available in Broward County where
the performance and trial took place. According to the trial testimony of Vice Detective McCloud, "nude dance shows and adult
bookstores are scattered throughout the county where 2 Live Crew
performed." But again, no obscenity charges were leveled against
the performers or producers of these representations.

10   In response to this charge of selectivity, it might be argued that
the prosecution of 2 Live Crew demonstrates that its lyrics were
uniquely obscene. In a sense, this argument runs, the proof is in
the condemnation—if their music was not uniquely obscene, it
would not have been deemed so by the Court. However, the elements of 2 Live Crew's representation that contributed to their
selective arrest continued to play out as the court applied the
obscenity standard to the recording.

To clarify this argument, we need to consider the technical use
of "obscenity" as a legal term of art. For the purposes of legal argument, the Supreme Court in the 1973 case of Miller v. California
held that a work is obscene if and only if it meets each of three conditions: (1) "the average person, applying community standards,
would find that the work, taken as a whole, appeals to the prurient
interest"; (2) "the work depicts or describes, in a patently offensive
way, sexual conduct specifically defined by the applicable state
law"; and (3) "the work, taken as a whole, lacks serious literary,
artistic, political, or scientific value." The Court held that it is consistent with First Amendment guarantees of freedom of expression
for states to subject work that meets all three parts of the Miller
test to very restrictive regulations.

Focusing first on the "prurient interest" prong of the Miller
test, we might wonder how 2 Live Crew could have been seen as
uniquely obscene by the lights of the "community standards" of
Brossard County. After all, as Detective McCloud put it, "patrons
[of clubs in Broward] can see women dancing with at least their
breasts exposed" and bookstore patrons can "view and purchase
films and magazines that depict vaginal, oral and anal sex, homo-
sexual sex and group sex." In arriving at its finding of obscenity,
the court placed little weight on the available range of films, magazines, and live shows as evidence of the community's sensibilities.
Instead, the court apparently accepted the Sheriff's testimony that
the decision to single out *Nasty* was based on the number of complaints against 2 Live Crew, "communicated by telephone calls,
anonymous messages, or letters to the police."

Evidence of this popular outcry was never substantiated. But even if it were, the case for selectivity would remain. The history of social repression of Black male sexuality is long, often-violent, and all-too-familiar. Negative reactions against the sexual conduct of Black males have traditionally had racist overtones, especially where that conduct threatens to "cross over" into the mainstream community. So even if the decision to prosecute did reflect a widespread community perception of the purely prurient character of 2 Live Crew's music, that perception itself might reflect an established pattern of vigilante attitudes directed toward the sexual expression of Black males. In short, the appeal to community standards does not undercut a concern about racism; rather, it underscores that concern.

A second troubling dimension of the case against 2 Live Crew was the court's apparent disregard for the culturally rooted aspects of 2 Live Crew's music. Such disregard was essential to a finding of obscenity, given the third prong of the Miller test requiring that obscene material lack any literary, artistic, or political value. 2 Live Crew argued that this test was not met since the recording exemplified such African-American cultural modes as "playing the dozens," "call and response," and "signifying." As a storehouse of such cultural modes, it could not be said that *Nasty* was completely devoid of literary or artistic value. Yet the court denied the group's clause of cultural specificity by re-characterizing those modes claimed to be African-American in more generic terms. For example, the court reasoned that "playing the dozens" is "commonly seen in adolescents, especially boys, of all ages." "Boasting," the court observed, appears to be "part of the universal human condition." And the court noted that the cultural origins of one song featuring "call and response"—a song about oral sex in which competing groups chanted "less filling" and "tastes great"—were to be found in a Miller beer commercial, and thus not derived from any African-American cultural tradition. The possibility that the Miller beer commercial may have itself evolved from an African-American cultural tradition was lost on the court.

In disregarding testimony about cultural specificity, the court denied the artistic value in the form and style of *Nasty* and, by implication, rap music more generally. This disturbing dismissal of the cultural attributes of rap, and this effort to universalize African-American modes of expression, flattens cultural differences. The court's analysis here manifests in legal terms a frequently encountered strategy of cultural appropriation. African-American contributions that have been accepted by the mainstream culture are eventually absorbed as simply "American" or found to be

15

"universal." Other modes associated with African-American culture that resist absorption remain distinctive and are either ignored, or dismissed as "deviant."

An additional concern has as much to do with the obscenity doctrine itself as with the court's application of it to 2 Live Crew. The case illustrates the ways that obscenity doctrine invites racially selective enforcement while at the same time pressing into focus the wrong questions about sexual expression.

As I mentioned earlier, obscenity requires a determination that the material, taken as a whole, appeals to the prurient interest. Although the prurient interest requirement eludes precise definition it seems clear that prurient material must appeal in some immediate way to sexual desire. While it is difficult to say definitively what constitutes such an appeal, one might surmise that the twenty-five cent peep shows that are standard fare in Broward County rank considerably higher on this scale than the sexual tall tales of 2 Live Crew. But the obscenity doctrine is, as justice Stevens said, "intolerably vague," and the result is that "grossly disparate treatment of similar offenders is a characteristic of the criminal enforcement of obscenity law." More precisely, as the case of 2 Live Crew suggests, the vagueness of the doctrine operating in a world of racial subordination represents an invitation to racially selective enforcement.

While 2 Live Crew should be one of the lesser candidates in the prurient interests sweepstakes mandated by the obscenity doctrine, it is also a lesser contender by another measure that lies entirely outside of obscenity: violence. Compared to such groups as N.W.A., Too Short, Ice Cube, and the Geto Boys, 2 Live Crew's misogynistic hyperbole sounds minor league. Sometimes called "gangsta' rap," the lyrics offered by these other groups celebrate violent assault, rape, rape-murder, and mutilation. Nevertheless, had these other groups been targeted rather than the comparatively less offensive 2 Live Crew, they may have been more successful in defeating the prosecution. The graphic violence in their representations militates against a finding of obscenity by suggesting an appeal not to prurient interests but instead to the fantasy of the social outlaw. Against an historical backdrop that prominently features the image of the Black male as social outlaw, gangsta' rap might be read as a subversive form of opposition that aims to challenge social convention precisely by becoming the very social outlaw that society has proscribed. For this reason, their lyrics might even be read as political, and if they are political they are not obscene. So long, then, as prurience remains an obsession of First Amendment argument, and violent imagery is seen as distinct from sexuality, rap artists may actually be able to strengthen their legal shield by heightening the level of violence in their lyrics.

I do not mean to suggest here that the distinction between sex and violence ought to be maintained in obscenity, nor, more specifically, that the violent rappers ought to be protected. To the contrary, these groups trouble me much more than 2 Live Crew does. My point instead is to emphasize that the obscenity doctrine itself does nothing to protect the interests of those who are most directly implicated in such rap—Black women. Because the doctrine is vague, it opens the door to selecting offenders on the basis of race. Because it separates out sexuality and violence, it shields the most violently misogynistic rappers from prosecution. For Black women who are hurt by both racism and misogyny, it does no good at all.

Although Black women's interests were quite obviously irrele- 20 vant in this obscenity judgment, their bodies figured prominently in the public case supporting the targeting of 2 Live Crew. This brings me to my final concern: George Will's *Newsweek* essay provides a striking example of how Black women were appropriated and deployed in the broader attack against 2 Live Grew. Commenting on "America's Slide into the Sewers," Will tells us that "America today is capable of terrific intolerance about smoking, or toxic waste that threatens trout. But only a deeply confused society is more concerned about protecting lungs than minds, trout than black women. We legislate against smoking in restaurants; singing "Me So Horny" is a constitutional right. Secondary smoke is carcinogenic; celebration of torn vaginas is "mere words."

Notwithstanding these expressions of concern about Black women, Will's real worry is suggested by his repeated references to the Central Park jogger. He writes that "Her face was so disfigured a friend took fifteen minutes to identify her. 'I recognized her ring'." *Do you recognize the relevance of 2 Live Crew?'* (Emphasis added.) While the connection between the threat of 2 Live Crew and the specter of the Black male rapist was suggested subtly in the public debate, it is manifest throughout Will's discussion and in fact bids fair to be its central theme. "Fact: Some members of a particular age and societal cohort—the one making 2 Live Crew rich—stomped and raped the jogger to the razor edge of death, for the fun of it." Will directly indicts 2 Live Crew in the Central Park jogger rape through a fictional dialogue between himself and the defendants. Responding to one defendant's alleged comment that the rape was fun, Will asks: "Where can you get the idea that sexual violence against women is fun? From a music store, through Walkman earphones, from boom boxes blaring forth the rap lyrics of 2 Live

Crew." Since the rapists were young Black males and *Nasty* presents Black men celebrating sexual violence, surely 2 Live Crew was responsible. Apparently, the vast American industry that markets every conceivable form of misogynistic representation is irrelevant to understanding this particular incident of sexual violence.

Will invokes Black women twice—as victims of this music. But if he were really concerned with the threat to Black women, why does the Central Park jogger figure so prominently in his argument? Why not the Black woman in Brooklyn who was gang-raped and then thrown down an airshaft? For that matter, what about the twenty-five other women—mostly women of color—who were raped in New York City during the same week the Central Park jogger was raped? In Will's display of concern, Black women appear to function as a stand-in for white women. The focus on sexual violence played out on Black women's bodies seems to reflect concerns about the threat of Black male violence against the security of the white community. In this, Will's use of the Black female body to press the case against 2 Live Crew recalls the strategy of the prosecutor in Richard Wright's novel *Native Son*. Bigger Thomas, the Black male protagonist, is on trial for killing Mary Dalton, a white woman. Because Bigger burned her body, however, it cannot be established whether Mary was raped. So the prosecutor brings in the body of Bessie, a Black woman raped by Bigger and left to die, in order to establish that Bigger had raped Mary.

These considerations about selectivity, about the denial of cultural specificity, and about the manipulation of Black women's bodies convince me that race played a significant if not determinative role in the shaping of the case against 2 Live Crew. While using anti-sexist rhetoric to suggest a concern for women, the attack simultaneously endorsed traditional readings of Black male sexuality. The fact that most perpetrators and victims are of the same race is overshadowed by the mythical image of the Black male as the agent of sexual violence and the white community as his victim. The subtext of the 2 Live Crew prosecution thus becomes a rereading of the sexualized racial politics of the past.

IV

While concerns about racism fuel my opposition to the obscenity prosecution, I am also troubled by the uncritical support for, and indeed celebration of, 2 Live Crew by other opponents of that prosecution. If the rhetoric of anti-sexism provided an occasion for racism, so, too, the rhetoric of anti-racism provided an occasion for defending the misogyny of Black male rappers.

The defense of 2 Live Crew took two forms, one political and 25 one cultural, both of which were advanced most prominently by Henry Louis Gates. The political argument was that 2 Live Crew represents an attack on Black sexual stereotypes. The strategy of the attack is, in Gates's words, to "exaggerate [the] stereotypes" and thereby "to show how ridiculous the portrayals are." Thus, Gates concludes, 2 Live Crew and other rap groups are simply pushing white society's buttons to ridicule its dominant sexual images.

I agree with Gates that the reactions by Will and others to 2 Live Crew confirm that the stereotypes still exist and still evoke basic fears. But even if I were to agree that 2 Live Crew intended to explode these mythic fears, I still would argue that their strategy was wholly misguided. These fears are too active, and African-Americans are too closely associated with them, not to be burned when the myths are exploded. More fundamentally, however, I am deeply skeptical about the claim that the Crew was engaged— either in intent or effect—in pursuing a postmodern guerilla war against racist stereotypes.

Gates argues that when one listens to 2 Live Crew the ridiculous stories and the hyperbole make the listener "bust out laughing." Apparently the fact that Gates and many other people react with laughter confirms and satisfies the Crew's objective of ridiculing the stereotypes. But the fact that the Crew are often successful in prompting laughter neither substantiates Gates's reading nor forecloses serious critique of its subordinating dimensions.

In disagreeing with Gates, I do not mean to suggest that 2 Live Crew's lyrics are to be taken literally. But rather than exploding stereotypes as Gates suggests, I believe that they were simply using readily available sexual images in trying to be funny. Trading in racial stereotypes and sexual hyperbole are well-rehearsed strategies for getting some laughs. 2 Live Crew departs from this tradition only in its attempt to up the ante through more outrageous boasts and more explicit manifestations of misogyny. Neither the intent to be funny, nor Gates's loftier explanations, negate the subordinating qualities of such humor. Examining parallel arguments in the context of racist humor suggests why neither claim functions as a persuasive defense for 2 Live Crew.

Gates's use of laughter as a defensive maneuver in the attack on 2 Live Crew recalls similar strategies in defense of racist humor. Racist humor has sometimes been defended as an effort to poke fun at, or to ridicule racism. More simply, racist humor has often been excused as just joking; even racially motivated assaults are often defended as simple pranks. Thus, the racism and sexism of

Andrew Dice Clay could be defended in either mode as an attempt to explode the stereotypes of white racists, or simply as humor not meant to be taken seriously. Implicit in these defenses is the assumption that racist representations are injurious only if they are devoid of any other objective or are meant to be taken literally.

30   Although these arguments are familiar within the Black community, I think it is unlikely that they would be viewed as a persuasive defense of Andrew Dice Clay. African-Americans have frequently protested such humor, suggesting a general recognition within the Black community that "mere humor" is not inconsistent with subordination. The question of what people find humorous is of course a complicated one, sometimes involving aggression, in-group boundary policing, projection, and other issues. The claim that a representation is meant "simply as a joke" may be true, but it functions as humor within a specific social context and frequently reinforces patterns of social power. Moreover, even though racial humor may sometimes be intended to ridicule racism, the close relationship between the stereotypes and the prevailing images of marginalized people complicates this strategy. Clearly, racial humor does not always distance the audience from the racist subject, nor does it indict the wider society in which the jokes have meaning. The endearment of Archie Bunker suggests at least this much. Thus, in the context of racist humor, neither the fact that people actually laughed at racist humor nor the usual disclaimer of intent has functioned to preclude incisive and often quite angry criticism of such humor within the African-American community.

Although a similar set of arguments could be offered in the context of sexist humor, images marketed by 2 Live Crew were not condemned but, as Gates illustrates, defended, often with great commitment and skill. Clearly, the fact that the Crew and the women it objectifies are Black shaped this response. Had 2 Live Crew been white in blackface, for example, all of the readings would have been different. Although the question of whether one can defend the broader license given to Black comedians to market stereotypical images is an interesting one, it is not the issue here. 2 Live Crew cannot claim an in-group privilege to perpetuate misogynistic humor against Black women. They are not Black women, and more importantly, they enjoy a power relationship over them. Sexual humor in which women are objectified as packages of body parts to serve whatever male-bonding/male competition needs men have subordinates women in much the same way that racist humor subordinates African-Americans. That these are "just jokes" and not meant to be taken literally does little to blunt their demeaning quality—nor for that matter, does the fact that the jokes are told within a tradition of intra-group humor.

Gates advances a second, cultural defense of 2 Live Crew: the idea that *Nasty* is in line with distinctively African-American traditions of culture and entertainment. It is true that the "dozens" and other forms of verbal boasting have been practiced within the Black community for some time. It is true as well that raunchy jokes, insinuations, and boasting of sexual prowess were not meant to be taken literally. Nor were they meant to disrupt conventional myths about Black sexuality. They were meant simply to be laughed at, and perhaps to gain respect for the speaker's word wizardry.

Ultimately, however, little turns on whether the "word play" performed by 2 Live Crew is a postmodern challenge to racist sexual mythology or simply an internal group practice that has crossed over into mainstream America. Both versions of the defense are problematic because they each call on Black women to accept misogyny and its attendant disrespect in service of some broader group objective. While one version argues that accepting misogyny is necessary to anti-racist politics, the other argues that it is necessary to maintaining the cultural integrity of the community. But neither presents a sufficient reason for Black women to tolerate such misogyny. The message that these arguments embrace—that patriarchy can be made to serve anti-racist ends is a familiar one with proponents ranging from Eldridge Cleaver in the sixties to Sharazad Ali in the nineties. In Gates's variant, the position of Black women is determined by the need to wield gargantuan penises in a struggle to ridicule racist images of Black male sexuality. Even though Black women may not be the intended targets, they are necessarily attached to these gargantuan penises and are thus made to absorb the impact. The common message of all such strategies is that Black women are expected to be vehicles for notions of "liberation" that function to preserve their own subordination.

To be sure, Gates's claims about the cultural aspects of 2 Live Crew's lyrics do address the legal issue about the applicability of the obscenity standard. As I indicated earlier, their music does have artistic value: I believe the Court decided this issue incorrectly and Will was all-too-glib in his dismissal of it. But these criticisms do not settle the issue within the community. "Dozens" and other word plays have long been a Black oral tradition, but acknowledging this fact does not eliminate the need to interrogate either the sexism within that tradition or the objectives to which that tradition has been pressed. To say that playing the dozens, for example, is rooted in a Black cultural tradition or that themes represented by mythic

folk heroes such as Stackalee are "Black" does not settle the question of whether such practices are oppressive to women and others
within the community. The same point can be made about the relentless homophobia expressed in the work of Eddie Murphy and
many other comedians and rappers. Whether or not the Black community has a pronounced tradition of homophobia is beside the
point; the question instead is how these subordinating aspects of
tradition play out in the lives of people in the community, people
who otherwise share a common history, culture, and political
agenda. While it may be true that the Black community is more familiar with the cultural forms that have evolved into rap, that familiarity should not end the discussion of whether the misogyny
within rap is acceptable. Moreover, we need to consider the possible relationships between sexism within our cultural practices and
the problem of violence against women.

35   Violence against women of color is not presented as a critical
issue in either the anti-racist or anti-violence discourses. The "different culture" defense may contribute to the disregard for women
of color victimized by rape and violence, reinforcing the tendency
within the broader community not to take intra-racial violence seriously. Numerous studies have suggested that Black victims of
crime can count on less protection from the criminal justice system
than whites. This is true for rape victims as well—their rapists are
less likely to be convicted and on average serve less time when they
are convicted. Could it be that perpetuating the belief that "Blacks
are different" with respect to sexuality and violence contributes to
the familiar disregard of Black female rape victims like Bessie in
Native Son or the woman thrown down an airshaft in Brooklyn?

    Although there are times when Black feminists should fight for
the integrity of the culture, this does not mean that criticism must
end when a practice or form of expression is traced to a particular
aspect of culture. We must determine whether the practices and
forms of expression are consistent with our fundamental interests.
The question of obscenity may be settled by finding roots in the culture, but obscenity is not our central issue. Performances and representations that do riot appeal principally to "prurient interests,"
or that may reflect expressive patterns that are culturally specific,
may still encourage self-hatred, disrespect, subordination, and
other manifestations of intra-group pathology. These problems require group dialogue. While African-Americans have no plenary
authority to grapple with these issues, we do need to find ways of
using group formation mechanisms and other social spaces to reflect upon and reformulate our cultural and political practices.

I said earlier that the political goals of Black feminism are to construct and empower a political sensibility that opposes misogyny and racism simultaneously. Converging this double vision into an analysis of the 2 Live Crew controversy, it becomes clear that despite the superficial defense of the prosecution as being concerned with the interests of women, nothing about the anti-2 Live Crew movement is about Black women's lives. The political process involved in condemning the representations that subordinate Black women does not seek to empower Black women; indeed, the racism of that movement is injurious to us.

But the implication of this conclusion is not that Black feminists should stand in solidarity with the supporters of 2 Live Crew. The spirited defense of 2 Live Crew was no more about defending the Black community than the prosecution was about defending women. After all, Black women—whose very assault is the object of the representation—are part of that community. Black women can hardly regard the right to be represented as bitches and whores as essential to their interests. Instead the defense of 2 Live Crew primarily functions to protect the cultural and political prerogative of male rappers to be as misogynistic and offensive as they want to be.

The debate over 2 Live Crew illustrates how race and gender politics continue to marginalize Black women, rendering us virtually voiceless. Black feminism endeavors to respond to this silencing by constructing a political identity for Black women that will facilitate a simultaneous struggle against racism and patriarchy. Fitted with a Black feminist sensibility, one uncovers other issues in which the unique situation of Black women renders a different formulation of the problem than the version that dominates in current debate. Ready examples include rape, domestic violence, and welfare dependency. A Black feminist sensibility might also provide a more direct link between the women's movement and traditional civil rights movements, helping them both to shed conceptual blinders that limit the efficacy of each.

The development of a Black feminist sensibility is no guarantee   40
that Black women's interests will be taken seriously. In order for that sensibility to develop into empowerment, Black women will have to make it clear that patriarchy is a critical issue that negatively impacts the lives not only of African-American women, but men as well. Within the African-American political community, this recognition might reshape traditional practices so that evidence of racism would not constitute justification for uncritical rallying around misogynistic politics and patriarchal values. Although collective opposition to racist practice has been and continues to be crucially important in

protecting Black interests, an empowered Black feminist sensibility would require that the terms of unity no longer reflect priorities premised upon the continued subordination of Black women.

Questions for Discussion and Topics for Writing

1. Crenshaw discusses both racism and misogyny. How are these related? How do these two discourses conspire to silence black women and obscure their interests and needs?
2. How can humor be used to subordinate? How does humor work to protect racist remarks from censure? Does this make racist comments said in jest more insidious than those that are said in earnest? Does the context in which a joke is told matter?
3. What is a "black feminist sensibility" and how does it change the terms of the debate about race and gender? Use the trial of 2 Live Crew to support your view.
4. At the end of her essay, Crenshaw asserts that patriarchy negatively impacts black men as well as black women. How is this so? Use the essay to show how patriarchy can negatively affect men.
5. Research the 2 Live Crew case. Try in particular to locate testimony by Henry Louis Gates, a black scholar hired for the defense. What was the nature of Gates's testimony? Write an essay that looks at the competing issues of (a) supporting the one's racial community as a whole vs. (b) supporting one's gender. How were such competing loyalties reflected in this case?

When Black Feminism Faces the Music, and the Music Is Rap

MICHELE WALLACE

Michele Wallace is a professor in the Department of English at City College in New York. Her research specialties include African-American literature and poetics, feminist literature and poetics, gender and sexuality, queer theory, literary theory, American cinema and film theory, and American popular culture. Her publications include Invisibility Blues *and* Black Macho and the Myth of the Superwoman. *The following article first appeared in* The New York Times, *July 29, 1990.*

◆

Like many black feminists, I look on sexism in rap as a necessary evil. In a society plagued by poverty and illiteracy, where young black men are as likely to be in prison as in college, rap is a welcome articulation of the economic and social frustrations of black youth.

In response to disappointments faced by poor urban blacks negotiating their future, rap offers the release of creative expression and historical continuity: it draws on precedents as diverse as jazz, reggae, calypso, Afro-Cuban, African and heavy-metal, and its lyrics include rudimentary forms of political, economic and social analysis.

But with the failure of our urban public schools, rappers have taken education into their own hands; these are oral lessons (reading and writing being low priorities). And it should come as no surprise that the end result emphasizes innovations in style and rhythm over ethics and morality. Although there are exceptions, like raps advocating world peace (the W.I.S.E. Guyz's "Time for Peace") and opposing drug use (Ice-T's "I'm Your Pusher"), rap lyrics can be brutal, raw and, where women are the subject, glaringly sexist.

Given the genre's current crossover popularity and success in the marketplace, including television commercials, rap's impact on young people is growing. A large part of the appeal of pop culture is that it can offer symbolic resolutions to life's contradictions. But when it comes to gender, rap has not resolved a thing.

Though styles vary—from that of the X-rated Ice-T to the 5 sybaritic Kwanee to the hyperpolitics of Public Enemy—what seems universal is how little male rappers respect sexual intimacy and how little regard they have for the humanity of the black woman. Witness the striking contrast within rap videos: for men, standard attire is baggy outsize pants; for women, spike heels and short skirts. Videos often feature the ostentatious and fetishistic display of women's bodies. In Kool Moe Dee's "How Ya Like Me Now," women gyrate in tight leather with large revealing holes. In Digital Underground's video "Doowutchyalike," set poolside at what looks like a fraternity house party, a rapper in a clown costume pretends to bite the backside of a woman in a bikini.

As Trisha Rose, a black feminist studying rap, puts it, "Rap is basically a locker room with a beat."

The recent banning of the sale of 2 Live Crew's album *As Nasty as They Wanna Be* by local governments in Florida and elsewhere has publicized rap's treatment of women as sex objects, but it also made a hit of a record that contains some of the bawdiest lyrics in rap. Though such sexual explicitness in lyrics is rare, the assumptions about women—that they manipulate men with their bodies— are typical.

In an era when the idea that women want to be raped should be obsolete, rap lyrics and videos presuppose that women always desire sex, whether they know it or not. In Bell Biv DeVoe's rap-influenced pop hit single "Poison," for instance, a beautiful girl is considered poison because she does not respond affirmatively and automatically to a sexual proposition.

bell hooks, author of *Yearning: Race, Gender, Cultural Politics* (Southend, 1990), sees the roots of rap as a youth rebellion against all attempts to control black masculinity, both in the streets and in the home. "That rap would be anti-domesticity and in the process anti-female should come as no surprise," Ms. hooks says.

10   At present there is only a small platform for black women to address the problems of sexism in rap and in their community. Feminist criticism, like many other forms of social analysis, is widely considered part of a hostile white culture. For a black feminist to chastise misogyny in rap publicly would be viewed as divisive and counterproductive. There is a widespread perception in the black community that public criticism of black men constitutes collaborating with a racist society.

The charge is hardly new. Such a reaction greeted Ntozake Shange's play *For Colored Girls Who Have Considered Suicide When the Rainbow Is Enuf,* my own essays, "Black Macho and the Myth of the Superwoman," and Alice Walker's novel *The Color Purple,* all of which were perceived as critical of black men. After the release of the film version of *The Color Purple,* feminists were lambasted in the press for their supposed lack of support for black men; such critical analysis by black women has all but disappeared. In its place is *A Black Man's Guide to the Black Woman,* a vanity-press book by Shahrazad Ali, which has sold more than 80,000 copies by insisting that black women are neurotic, insecure and competitive with black men.

Though misogynist lyrics seem to represent the opposite of Ms. Ali's world view, these are, in fact, just two extremes on the same theme: Ms. Ali's prescription for what ails the black community is that women should not question men about their sexual philandering, and should be firmly slapped across the mouth when they do. Rap lyrics suggest just about the same: women should be silent and prone.

There are those who have wrongly advocated censorship of rap's more sexually explicit lyrics, and those who have excused the misogyny because of its basis in black oral traditions.

Rap is rooted not only in the blaxploitation films of the 60's but also in an equally sexist tradition of black comedy. In the use of four-letter words and explicit sexual references, both Richard Pryor and Eddie Murphy, who themselves drew upon the earlier examples of Redd Foxx, Pigmeat Markham and Moms Mabley, are conscious reference points for the 2 Live Crew. Black comedy, in turn, draws on an oral tradition in which black men trade "toasts," stories in which dangerous bagmen and trickster figures like Stackolee and Dolomite sexually exploit women and promote violence among men. The popular rapper Ice Cube, in the album *Amerikkka's Most Wanted*, is Stackolee come to life. In "The Nigga Ya Love to Hate," he projects an image of himself as a criminal as dangerous to women as to the straight white world.

Rap remains almost completely dominated by black males 15 and this mind-set. Although women have been involved in rap since at least the mid-80's, record companies have only recently begun to promote them. And as women rappers like Salt-n-Pepa, Monie Love, M.C. Lyte, L.A. Star and Queen Latifah slowly gain more visibility, rap's sexism may emerge as a subject for scrutiny. Indeed, the answer may lie with women, expressing in lyrics and videos the tensions between the sexes in the black community.

Today's women rappers range from a high ground that doesn't challenge male rap on its own level (Queen Latifah) to those who subscribe to the same sexual high jinks as male rappers (Oaktown's 3.5.7). M.C. Hammer launched Oaktown's 3.5.7., made up of his former backup dancers. These female rappers manifest the worst-case scenario: their skimpy, skintight leopard costumes in the video of "Wild and Loose (We Like It)" suggest an exotic animalistic sexuality. Their clothes fall to their ankles. They take bubble baths. Clearly, their bodies are more important than rapping. And in a field in which writing one's own rap is crucial, their lyrics are written by their former boss, M.C. Hammer.

Most women rappers constitute the middle ground: they talk of romance, narcissism and parties. On the other hand, Salt-n-Pepa on "Shake Your Thang" uses the structure of the 1969 Isley Brothers song "It's Your Thing" to insert a protofeminist rap response: "Don't try to tell me how to party. It's my dance and it's my body." M.C. Lyte, in a dialogue with Positive K on "I'm Not Havin' It," comes down hard on the notion that women can't say no and criticizes the shallowness of the male rap.

Queen Latifah introduces her video, "Ladies First," performed with the English rapper Monie Love, with photographs of black political heroines like Winnie Mandela, Sojourner Truth, Harriet Tubman and Angela Davis. With a sound that resembles scat as much as rap, Queen Latifah chants "Stereotypes they got to go" against a backdrop of newsreel footage of the apartheid struggle in South Africa. The politically sophisticated Queen Latifah seems worlds apart from the adolescent, buffoonish sex orientation of most rap. In general, women rappers seem so much more grown up. Can they inspire a more beneficent attitude toward sex in rap? What won't subvert rap's sexism is the actions of men; what will is women speaking in their own voice, not just in artificial female ghettos, but with and to men. . . .

Questions for Discussion and Topics for Writing

1. According to Wallace, why do women meet with resistance when they speak out against sexism and misogyny in rap music? What do you think the root of such opposition might be?

2. Wallace notes that rap's misogyny is often excused because of its "basis in black oral traditions." However, she doesn't explain why this view seems justified to its proponents. Write a paragraph in which you try to fill in this gap in Wallace's piece. Note: Kimberle Crenshaw makes a very similar point in her essay, also found in this chapter.

3. Wallace mentions a character from black oral traditions called Stackolee. Research this character. One good source would be an article titled "Godfather of Gangsta," which is easily located on the Web. Write a paper in which you examine the controversy involving the African-American oral tradition vs. sexism and misogyny in rap music.

4. Write an essay that looks at female rappers and their response to mainstream hip hop's depictions of women. Since Wallace wrote her article have any women MCs emerged who are "speaking in their own voice," as she puts it? One artist you might consider looking at is the Brooklyn-based MC, Jean Grae.

The Venus Hip Hop and the Pink Ghetto
Negotiating Spaces for Women
IMANI PERRY

Imani Perry, a law professor at Rutgers Law School, received a Ph.D. in the History of American Civilization from Harvard University and a J.D. from Harvard Law School. Perry's work is transdisciplinary, combining African-American legal and cultural studies. Her research uses the methods and materials of law, literature, history, and popular culture. In addition to numerous scholarly articles, Perry wrote Prophets of the Hood: Politics and Poetics in Hip Hop *(2004), from which the following piece is excerpted.*

—————————— ✦ ——————————

It seemed to happen suddenly. Every time one turned on BET (Black Entertainment Television) or MTV, one encountered a disturbing music video: Black men rapped surrounded by dozens of black and Latina women dressed in bathing suits, or scantily clad in some other fashion. Video after video proved the same, each one more objectifying than the former. Some took place in strip clubs, some at the pool, at the beach, or in hotel rooms, but the recurrent theme was dozens of half-naked women. The confluence of cultural trends leading to this moment merits more extended scholarly attention than it will receive here, but, in short, it occurred as pornography became increasingly mainstreamed and alluded to in objectifying shows such as *Baywatch*, as the tech boom gave rise to a celebration of consumption and widespread wealth, and as hip hop continued its pattern of shifting dominant foci—from political consciousness to social realism to gangsterism to humor to in this moment, a hedonist conspicuous consumption previously largely associated with Miami Bass music.

The sexist message embraced here proves complex. Its attack on black female identity is multifaceted. First, and most obviously, the women are commodified. They appear in the videos quite explicitly as property, not unlike the luxury cars, Rolex watches, and platinum and diamond medallions also featured. The male stars of the videos do not have access to these legions of women because of charisma or sexual prowess, but rather because they are able to "buy" them due to their wealth. The message is not, "I am a Don Juan," but instead, "I am rich and these are my spoils." Not only are the women commodified, but sex as a whole is.

Moreover the women are often presented as vacuous, doing nothing in the videos but swaying around seductively. Often, they avert their eyes from the camera, allowing the viewer to have a voyeuristic relationship to them. Or they look at the camera, eyes fixed in seductive invitation, mouth slightly open. Any signs of thought, humor, irony, intelligence, anger, or any other emotion, prove extremely rare. Even the manner in which the women dance signals cultural destruction. Black American dance is discursive in that sexuality is usually combined with humor, and that the body is used to converse with other moving bodies. Yet the women who appear in these videos usually dance in a two-dimensional fashion, in a derivative but nonintellectual version of black dance more reminiscent of symbols of pornographic male sexual fantasy than the ritual, conversational, and sexual traditions of black dance. Despite all the gyrations of the video models, their uninterested, wet-lipped languor stands in sharp contrast to (for example) the highly sexualized booty dancing of the Deep South, which features polyrhythmic rear end movement, innuendo, and sexual bravado.

This use of black women in the music videos of male hip hop artists often makes very clear reference to the culture of strip clubs and pornography. Women dance around poles, and porn actresses and exotic dancers are often the stars of the videos, bringing the movement-based symbols of their trades with them. The introduction of porn symbols into music videos is consistent with a larger movement that began in the late 1990s, in which pornographic imagery, discourses, and themes began to enter American popular culture. Powerful examples may be found in the *Howard Stern Show*, E! Entertainment Television, and daytime talk shows. Porn film stars attain mainstream celebrity, exotic dancers are routine talk show guests, and the public face of lesbianism becomes not a matter of the sexual preference of women, but of the sexual consumption and fantasy life of men. The videos discussed here make for an appropriate companion piece to this wider trend. While the music videos are male-centered in that they assume a heterosexual male viewer who will appreciate the images of sexually available young women, it is clear that young women watch them as well. The messages such videos send to young women are instructions on how to be sexy and how to look in order to capture the attention of men with wealth and charisma. Magazines geared toward young women have given instructions on how women should participate in their own objectification for decades, but never before has a genre completely centralized black women in this process.[1]

5   The beauty ideal for black women presented in these videos is as impossible to achieve as the waif-thin models in *Vogue* magazine are for white women. There is a preference for lighter-complexioned women of color, with long and straight or loosely curled hair. Hair that hangs slick against the head when wet as the model emerges out of a swimming pool (a common video image) is at a premium too. Neither natural tightly curled hair nor most coarse relaxed hair becomes slick, shining, and smooth when wet. It is a beauty ideal that contrasts sharply to the real hair of most black women. When brown-skinned or dark-skinned women

appear in the videos, they always have hair that falls well below shoulder length, despite the fact that the average length of black women's natural hair in the United States today is four to six inches, according to Barry Fletcher.[2]

Camera shots linger on very specific types of bodies. The videos have assimilated the African American ideal of a large rotund behind, but the video ideal also features a very small waist, large breasts, and slim shapely legs and arms. Often, while the camera features the faces of lighter-complexioned women, it will linger on the behinds of darker women, implying the same thing as the early 1990s refrain from Sir Mix-A-Lot's "Baby Got Back," "L.A. face with an Oakland booty."[3] That is, the ideal features a "high-status" face combined with a highly sexualized body read by the viewer as the body of a poor or working-class woman.[4] Color is aligned with class, and women are created or valued by how many fantasy elements have been pieced together in their bodies.

While one might argue that the celebration of the rotund behind signals an appreciation of black women's bodies, the image taken as a whole indicates how difficult a beauty ideal this proves to attain for anyone. A small percentage of women, even black women, have such Jessica Rabbit proportions. As journalist Tomika Anderson wrote for *Essence* magazine, "In movies, rap songs and on television, we're told that the attractive, desirable and sexy ladies are the ones with 'junk in their trunks.' And even though this might seem ridiculous, some of us actually listen to (and care about) these obviously misogynistic subliminal messages—just as we are affected by racialized issues like hair texture and skin tone."[5]

Americans have reacted with surprise to abundant social scientific data showing that black girls comprise the social group that scores highest on self-esteem assessments and that they tend to have much better body images than white girls. While these differences in esteem and body image are to a large extent attributable to cultural differences, with black girls having been socialized to see beauty in strong personality characteristics and grooming rather than in particular body types, I believe the media plays a role as well. White girls find themselves inundated with images of beauty impossible for most to attain: sheets of blond hair, waif-thin bodies, large breasts, no cellulite, small but round features, and high cheekbones. Over the years, black women have remained relatively absent from public images of beauty, an exclusion which may have saved black girls from aspiring to impossible ideals. But with the recent explosion of objectified and highly idealized images of black women in music videos, it is quite possible that the body images and even self-esteem of black girls will begin to drop, particularly as they move into adolescence and their bodies come under scrutiny. Many of the music videos feature neighborhood scenes including children. In them, little black girls are beautiful. They laugh, smile, play double Dutch, and more. They are full of personality, and they emerge as cultural celebrations with their hair plaited, twisted, or curled and adorned with colorful ribbons to match their outfits in characteristic black girl grooming style. And yet the adult women generally remain two-dimensional and robbed of personality. Is this what puberty is supposed to hold for these girls?

A FEMINIST RESPONSE?

In such troubling moments, we should all look for a gender-critical voice—in the world, in ourselves. Where do we find a response to this phenomenon that will compellingly argue against such characterizations of black women, where do we find a hip hop feminism? Hip hop has seen a feminist presence since the 1980s in such figures as Salt-N-Pepa, Queen Latifah, and MC Lyte, and hip hop feminism continues to exist despite the widespread objectification of black female bodies. We can find numerous examples of feminist and antisexist songs in hip hop and hip hop soul. Mary J. Blige, Lauryn Hill, Destiny's Child, Missy Elliot, Erykah Badu, and others each have their individual manner of representing black female identity and self-definition.

10   Alicia Keys, one of the crop of singer-songwriters who fit into the hip hop nation, presents an image that contrasts sharply with the video models. The classically trained pianist who has claimed Biggie Smalls and Jay-Z among her music influences appeared in her first music video for the song "Fallin'" in a manner both stylish and sexy but decidedly not self-exploiting. Her hair in cornrows, wearing a leather jacket and fedora, she sings with visible bluesy emotion. She describes repeatedly falling in love with a man who is not good for her. In the music video, Keys travels by bus to visit the man in prison. This element figures as an important signifier of hip hop sensibilities, as rap music is the one art form that consistently engages with the crisis of black imprisonment and considers imprisoned people as part of its community. As Keys rides in the bus, she gazes at women prisoners working in a field outside the window. They sing the refrain to the song, "I keep on fallin', in and out, of love with you/I never loved someone

the way I love you."[6] The women on the bus riding to visit men in prison mirror the women outside of the bus, who are prison laborers. This visual duality comments on the often overlooked problem of black female imprisonment in conversations about the rise of American imprisonment and black imprisonment in particular. It makes reference to two issues facing black women. One is that many black women are the mates of imprisoned men. The second is that many black women wind up in prison because they unwittingly or naively became involved with men participating in illegal activities.[7] The video poignantly alludes to these social ills with a close-up of a stone-faced woman in prison clothing with a single tear rolling down her cheek. Although, like Badu, Keys frequently appeared on her first albums to be narratively enmeshed in a "stand by your man" ethos that propped up male-centered heteronormativity, both of their voices and images offer dramatic feminist moments notable for their departure from objectifying and exploitative depictions.

Singer-songwriter India Arie offers another critical example of a black feminist space in the hip hop world. A young brown-skinned and dread-locked woman, she burst on the music scene with her song and companion music video "Video" which criticize the image of women in videos. In the refrain she sings, "I'm not your average girl from a video/My body's not built like a super-model but/I've learned to love myself unconditionally/because I am a queen."[8]

Similar lyrics assert that value is found in intelligence and integrity rather than expensive clothes, liquor, and firearms. The video celebrates Arie who smiles and dances and pokes fun at the process of selecting girls for music videos. She rides her bicycle into the sunshine with her guitar strapped across her shoulder. Arie refuses to condemn artists who present a sexy image but has stated that she will not wear a skirt above calf length on stage and that she will do nothing that will embarrass her family. Musically, while her sound is folksy soul, she does understand her work as being related to hip hop. "I'm trying to blend acoustic and hip-hop elements," she explains. "I used the most acoustic-sounding drum samples, to have something loud enough to compete with other records, but to keep the realistic, softer feel."[9] Arie understands her work as inflected with hip hop sensibilities, more than with the music's compositional elements. She says: "I don't define hip-hop the way a record company would. The thread that runs though both my music and hip-hop is that it's a very precise expression of my way of life. It's like blues; it's very real and honest output of emotion into a song. Because of that legacy, my generation now has an opportunity to candidly state our opinions. That's what my album is about. I just wanna be me."[10]

Arie's definition of hip hop as honest self-expression is true to the ideology at the heart of the genre at its beginnings, a concept that multitudes of hip hop artists continue to profess to. Yet that element of hip hop stands in tension with the process of celebrity creation. The "honest" words in hip hop exist in a swamp of image making. It does not suffice to examine the clear and simple feminist presences in hip hop; we must consider the murkier ones as well. When it comes to feminist messages, often the words and language of a hip hop song may have feminist content, but the visual image may be implicated in the subjugation of black women. Unlike the individualistic and expressive visuals we have of Arie, Keys, Jill Scott, or Missy Elliot, other artists are often marketed in a manner quite similar to the way in which objectified video models are presented.

TENSIONS BETWEEN TEXTS

Wholesome young stars like Arie and Keys present both strong and respectable images of black womanhood, yet those women who are "sexy" in particular have a much more difficult time carving out a feminist space for themselves. In an earlier piece, "It's My Thang and I'll Swing It the Way that I Feel: Sexual Subjectivity and Black Women Rappers," I argued for the existence of a feminist space in hip hop in which women articulated sexual subjectivity and desire.[11] While I still do believe this is possible, I find it more difficult to achieve now. When the women articulating subjectivity are increasingly presented in visual media as objects rather than subjects, as they are now, their statement to the world is ambiguous at best, and, at worst, the feminist message of their work will become undermined. Joan Morgan reflects on the tension that this presents in her work, which details the conflicts facing a woman with a feminist identity and the erotics of a hip hop market culture: "Am I no longer down for the cause if I admit that while total gender equality is an interesting intellectual concept, it doesn't do a damn thing for me erotically. That, truth be told, men with too many feminist sensibilities have never made my panties wet, at least not like that reformed thug nigga who can make even the most chauvinistic 'wassup baby' feel like a sweet wet tongue darting in and out of your ear."[12] The question is whether the appeal to the erotics of male desire proves too strong to still make the sexy female MC a voice "for the cause."

A musical artist occupies a multitextual space in popular culture. Lyrics, interviews, music, and videos together create a collage, often finely planned, from which an audience is supposed to form impressions. But the texts may conflict with one another. Lil' Kim, the much discussed, critiqued, and condemned nasty-talking bad girl of hip hop, is a master of shock appeal. Her outfits often expose her breasts, her nipples covered by sequined pasties color-coordinated with the rest of her attire. Despite Kim's visual and lyrical vulgarity, many of her critics admit to finding her endearing. Her interviewers know her as sweet-natured and generous. But Lil' Kim stands as a contradiction because while she interviews as a vulnerable and sweet woman, she raps with the hardness adored by her fans. She has an impressive aggressive sexual presence, and she has often articulated a sexual subjectivity through words, along with an in-your-face camera presence. However, as Kim has developed as an entertainer, it has become clear that her image is complicit in the oppressive language of American cinematography in regard to women's sexuality. She has adopted a Pamela-Anderson-in-brown-skin aesthetic, calling on pornographic tropes but losing the subversiveness sometimes apparent in her early career. Andre Leon Talley of *Vogue* magazine noted her transformation from an "around the way girl" with a flat chest, big behind, and jet black (or green, or blue) weave to the celebrity Kim who shows off breast implants and shakes her long blond hair.[13] In her videos, the camera angles exploit her sexuality. In the video for the song "How Many Licks," she appears as a Barbie-type doll, her body parts welded together in a factory. The video stands as an apt metaphor for her self-commodification and use of white female beauty ideals. The video closes off its own possibilities. The doll factory image might have operated as a tongue-in-cheek criticism of image making or white female beauty ideals, but, instead the video functions as a serious vehicle for Kim to be constructed as beautiful and seductive with blond hair and blue eyes. To be a doll in American popular culture is to be perfect, and she will satisfy many male fantasies as many times as she is replicated. Over several years, Kim has become defined more by her participation in codes of pornographic descriptions of women than by her challenging of concepts of respectability or her explicit sexuality.

It is a delicate balance, but it is important to distinguish between sexual explicitness and internalized sexism. While many who have debated the image of female sexuality have put "explicit" and "self-objectifying" on one side and "respectable" and "covered-up" on the other, I find this a flawed means of categorization. The nature of sexual explicitness proves important to consider, and will become more so as more nuanced images will emerge. There is a creative possibility for liberatory explicitness because it may expand the confines of what women are allowed to say and do. We just need to refer to the history of blues music—one full of raunchy, irreverent, and transgressive women artists—for examples. Yet the overwhelming prevalence of the Madonna/whore dichotomy in American culture means that any woman who uses explicit language or images in her creative expression is in danger of being symbolically cast into the role of whore regardless of what liberatory intentions she may have, particularly if she does not have complete control over her image.

Let us turn to other examples to further explore the tensions between text and visual image in women's hip hop. Eve has emerged as one of the strongest feminist voices in hip hop today. She rhymes against domestic violence and for women's self-definition and self-reliance. She encourages women to hold men in their lives accountable for disrespectful or less-than-loving behavior. Yet the politics of Eve's image are conflicted. She has appeared in music videos for songs on which she has collaborated with male hip hop artists, videos filled with the stock legions of objectified video models. On the one hand, Eve's provocative dress validates the idea of attractiveness exemplified by the models. But the rapper is also distinguished from these women because she is the star. She appears dignified and expressive, while they do not. Her distinction from the other women supports their objectification. She is the exception that makes the rule, and it is her exceptionalism that allows her to have a voice. Similar dynamics have appeared in videos featuring hip hop singer Lil' Mo. In fact, a number of women hip hop artists who claim to be the only woman in their crews, to be the only one who can hang with the fellas, through their exceptionalism make arguments that justify the subjugation of other women, even the majority of women.

Moreover, both Eve and Lil' Kim often speak of the sexual power they have as deriving from their physical attractiveness to men. It is therefore a power granted by male desire, rather than a statement of the power of female sexual desire. While neither artist has completely abandoned the language of empowering female subjectivity in her music, any emphasis on power granted through conventional attractiveness in this media language limits the feminist potential of the music. In one of the songs in which

Eve most explicitly expresses desire, "Gotta Man," the desire is rooted in the man's ability to dominate. She describes him as "the only thug in the hood who is wild enough to tame me,"[14] and therefore she is "the shrew," willingly stripped of her defiant power by a sexual union. Instead of using her aggressive tongue to challenge prevailing sexist sexual paradigms, she affirms them by saying that she simply needs a man stronger than most, stronger than she, to bring everything back to normal.

The tensions present in hip hop through the interplay of the visual and the linguistic, and the intertextuality of each medium, are various. Even Lauryn Hill, often seen as the redeemer of hip hop due to her dignified, intellectually challenging, and spiritual lyricism has a complicated image. As a member of the Fugees, she often dressed casually in baggy yet interesting clothes thoroughly rooted in hip hop style. It seems no accident that she became a celebrity, gracing the covers of British *GQ*, *Harper's Bazaar*, and numerous other magazines, when her sartorial presentation changed. Her skirts got shorter and tighter, her cleavage more pronounced, and her dreadlocks longer. When she began to sport an alternative style that nevertheless garnered mainstream acceptability, she was courted by high-end designers like Armani. As Lauryn's image became more easily absorbable into the language of American beauty culture, her celebrity grew. She even appeared on the cover of *Sophisticates Black Hair Magazine*, a black beauty guide that usually relegates natural hair to a couple of small pictures of women with curly afros or afro weaves, while the vast majority of its photos show women with long straight weaves and relaxers. The hip hop artist was certainly one of the few *Sophisticates* cover models ever to have natural hair, and the only with locks. (Interestingly, the silhouette of the locks was molded into the shape of shoulder-length relaxed hair.) In the issue of British *GQ* that featured Lauryn as a cover model, journalist Sanjiv writes, "She could be every woman in a way Chaka Khan could only sing about—the decade's biggest new soul arrival with the looks of a supermodel and Hollywood knocking at her door."[15]

In September of 1999, Lauryn appeared on the cover of *Harper's Bazaar*. The article inside discussed her community service projects, and the cover celebrated her model-like beauty. Of course, the cover had something subversive to it. Dark-skinned and kinky-haired Lauryn Hill was beautiful, and the image was ironic. Her locks were styled into the shape of a Farah Fawcett flip, a tongue-in-cheek hybridization at once referencing the seventies heyday of unprocessed afro hair and that era's symbol of white

20

female beauty, Farah Fawcett. The hybrid cover proves analogous to the diverse elements used in the creation of the new in hip hop. Nevertheless, it is important to note that Lauryn became widely attractive when her silhouette—thin body and big hair—matched that of mainstream beauty. So even as the artist has been treated as the symbol of black women's dignity and intelligence in hip hop (and rightfully so given her brilliant lyricism), she too found herself pulled into the sexist world of image making. Although she has made some public appearances since cutting off her long hair, getting rid of the makeup, and returning to baggy clothes, publicity about her has noticeably dropped.[16]

In contrast to Lauryn Hill, Erykah Badu has remained unapologetically committed to the drama of her neo-Afrocentric stylings in her image making, and she therefore has only achieved limited mainstream beauty acceptance. After she shaved her head, doffed her enormous head wrap, and wore a dress shaped like a ball gown (although in reality it was a deconstructed, rough textured "warrior princess," as she called it, work of art), Joan Rivers named her the best-dressed attendee at the 2000 Grammy Awards. Yet she also, rather than simply complimenting her dress or style, said that this was the best Badu had ever looked and that she was an extremely beautiful woman. Rivers appeared to insinuate that the singer was receiving recognition for coming closer to looking "as beautiful as she really is," not for truly being the best dressed. A 2001 *Vogue* article discussed Badu in the context of how ugliness could prove beautiful and how fine the line between the beauty and ugliness was, making reference to her unusual attire, again a sign of how disturbing the beauty industry finds her unwillingness to fit into standard paradigms of female presentation, even as her large hazel eyes and high cheekbones undeniably appeal to individuals in that industry.

I used the examples of Lil' Kim, Eve, Lauryn Hill, and Erykah Badu—all very distinct artists—to draw attention to the kinds of tensions that might exist between a feminist content in hip hop lyrics and the visual image of the artist. I hope these examples encourage readers, as viewers and listeners of popular culture, to become attuned to the multitextual character of the music world and to read as many layers of the media as possible.

THE COLONIZER AND COLONIZED

In her essay "Language and the Writer," novelist and cultural critic Toni Cade Bambara reminds us that "the creative imagination has been colonized. The global screen has been colonized. And the audience—readers and viewers—is in bondage to an industry. It has the money, the will, the muscle, and the propaganda machine oiled up to keep us all locked up in a delusional system—as to even what America is."[17] Musical artists are cultural actors, but those backed by record labels are hardly independent actors. In music videos and photo layouts, they exist within what Cade Bambara has described as a colonized space, particularly in regard to race and gender. In a context in which a short, tight dress and a camera rolling up the body, lingering on behinds and breasts, holds particular power with regard to gender and personal value, we must ask how powerful words can be that intend to contradict such objectification. How subversive are revolutionary words in a colonized visual world full of traditional gender messages?

Notes

1. The most prominent black women's magazines, *Essence* and *Honey*, as well as *Girl*, geared toward a multicultural audience of adolescent girls, all have an explicitly feminist agenda. Readers of these magazines are not offered articles about how to seduce men or how to appear sexy, the typical fare of such publications as *Cosmopolitan*, *YM*, and *Glamour*.

2. Barry Fletcher, *Why Black Women are Losing their Hair* (New York: Unity Publishing, 2000), ii.

3. Sir Mix-A-Lot, "Baby Got Back," (Mix a Lot Records 1993).

4. There are many hip hop lyrics that identify the voluptuous body with women who live in housing projects or who come from the hood. Additionally, the assumption that lighter-complexioned black women are of a higher socioeconomic status, or have greater sexual desirability, constitutes a long-standing aspect of black American culture. Although this cultural phenomenon was challenged in the late civil rights era, it flourishes in the images that appear in many television shows, movies, books, and in the tendency of black male celebrities and athletes to choose very light-complexioned spouses if they marry black women.

5. Tomika Anderson, "Nothing Butt the Truth," *Essence*, November 2001, 116.

6. Alicia Keys, "Fallin'" *Songs in A Minor* (BMG/J, 2001).

7. President Clinton pardoned Kendra Smith, the most famous representative of this population, who spent years in prison as the result of her boyfriend's crimes.

8. India Arie, "Video," *Acoustic Soul* (Motown, 2001).

9. India Arie, interview, available at http://www.mtv.com.

10. Ibid.

11. Imani Perry, "It's My Thang and I'll Swing It the Way that I Feel: Sexual Subjectivity and Black Women Rappers," in *Race, Class, and Gender in the Media*, ed. Gaul Dines and Jean M. Humez (Thousand Oaks, CA: Sage Press, 1994).

12. Joan Morgan, *When Chickenheads Come Home to Roost: My Life as a Hip-Hop Feminist* (New York: Simon and Schuster, 1999).

13. Andre Leon Talley, "Style Fax," *Vogue* November 1999, 18.

14. Eve, "Gotta Man," *RuffRyders* (Interscope, 2000).

15. Sanjiv, "Queen of the Hill: Lauryn Fugee Finds Her Voice," *GQ* (UK), October 1998, 188.

16. At the time of the publication of this book, I have found no interviews or articles addressing the reason for Lauryn Hill's second transformation, but it will be interesting to see if she understands it as a rejection of the way in which she was styled in order to be palatable to a widespread audience.

17. Toni Cade Bambara, "Language and the Writer," in *Deep Sightings and Rescue Missions: Fiction, Essays, and Conversations*, ed. Toni Morrison (New York: Pantheon, 1996), 140.

Questions for Discussion and Topics for Writing

1. Analyzing the images of Black and Hispanic women in rap music videos, Perry insists that the portrayals of such women are "commodified." She argues, implicitly, that such images are not merely "sexualized." What does *commodification* mean and how does this phenomenon affect the specific content of music videos?

2. Perry tells us that African-American women—in most surveys and research—present higher levels of self-esteem than their white counterparts. What is her explanation for this difference? Does she see this difference changing? Why or why not?

3. What positive or alternative visual images of Black women does pop culture offer? Examine the specific examples Perry discusses. What is different about these artists and the videos they use to market their talents and images?

4. Imani Perry is generally recognized as one of the best young scholars of hip hop culture working today, continuing a tradition of female hip hop scholarship begun a decade ago with the brilliant work of Tricia Rose. Her work is intricately argued and difficult, but she rewards your patience if you take the time to read her slowly and carefully. As an exercise in close reading, write an essay that re-traces Perry's multilayered argument about the image of African-American women in hip hop. In the midst of the shifts and subtleties of Perry's analysis, do you see any clear position emerging in her work?

5. Choose two of the artists about whom Perry writes. Locate their images through Internet research. Extend Perry's argument about these artists by performing your own close reading of specific images. How does Perry's essay help you understand the images you see?

The Coolness of Being Real

BELL HOOKS

bell hooks is Distinguished Professor of English at City College in New York. One of the leading scholars and public intellectuals of her generation, hooks has written dozens of articles and books on the intersecting issues of race, feminism, and politics. Her published works include Ain't I a Woman? Black Women and Feminism, Feminist Theory from Margin to Center, Talking Back: Thinking Feminist, Thinking Black, *and* Teaching to Transgress: Education as the Practice of Freedom. *The piece that follows appeared in hooks's 2004 work,* We Real Cool: Black Men and Masculinity.

◆

Once upon a time black male "cool" was defined by the ways in which black men confronted the hardships of life without allowing their spirits to be ravaged. They took the pain of it and used it alchemically to turn the pain into gold. That burning process required high heat. Black male cool was defined by the ability to withstand the heat and remain centered. It was defined by black male willingness to confront reality, to face the truth, and bear it not by adopting a false pose of cool while feeding on fantasy; not by black male denial or by assuming a "poor me" victim identity. It was defined by individual black males daring to self-define rather than be defined by others.

Using their imaginations to transcend all the forms of oppression that would keep them from celebrating life, individual black males have created a context where they can be self-defining and transform a world beyond themselves. Critic Stanley Crouch attests to this power in the *All-American Skin Game, Or, the Decoy of Race* when he writes about Louis Armstrong: "Lifting his trumpet to a scarred embouchure, he rose from the gumbo pot of the Western Hemisphere like a brown Poseidon of melody. Armstrong was then calling up the heroic, Afro-American lyricism of hope swelling out beyond deep recognition of tragedy, and was also enriching our ambivalent sense of adult romance through the beat of that matchless dance in which all of the complexities of courtship and romantic failure seem to have located themselves in the Argentinian steps of endless ballroom couples so expressive of passion nuance they seem forever mythic. The transcending power of such combinations is symbolic of the affirmative, miscegenated heat necessary to melt down the iron suits of history." If every young black male in America simply studied the history, the life, and work of black musicians, they would have blueprints for healing and survival. They would see clearly the roads they can take that will lead to a life of suffering and pain and the roads they can take that will lead to paradise, to healing, to a life lived in community.

In the opening statement of his autobiography *Blues All Around Me* B.B. King declares: "When it comes to my own life, others may know the cold facts better than me. . . . Truth is, cold facts don't tell the whole story. . . . I'm not writing a cold-blooded history. I'm writing a memory of my heart. That's the truth I'm after—following my feelings no matter where they lead. I want to try to understand myself, hoping that you . . . will understand me as well." In previous chapters I have talked about the blues as a musical form black males once chose because it allowed them to express a range of complex emotions, from the most intense joy to profound heartbreak and sorrow.

Sharing what the blues meant to him as a boy King states: "Blues meant hope, excitement, pure emotion. Blues were about feelings." Just as today's gangsta rap invites black males to adopt a cool pose, to front and fake it, to mask true feelings, the blues was an invitation to black men to be vulnerable, to express true feelings, to break open their hearts and expose them. Black males have helped create the blues, more than any other music, as a music of resistance to the patriarchal notion that a real man should never express genuine feelings. Emotional awareness of real-life pain in black men's lives was and is the heart and soul of the blues. When the guitar player sings, "I found a leak in my building, and my soul has got to move. I say my soul has got to move," he is singing about the pain of betrayal, about the soul's need not to be abandoned, to find shelter in a secure emotional place. He is giving lyric voice to all that Thomas Moore writes about in his bestselling book *Care of the Soul.*

5   Writing about the transformative power of the blues, Stanley Crouch offers this powerful insight: "The blues is the sound of spiritual investigation in a secular frame, and through its very lyricism, the blues achieves its spiritual penetration." Were masses of young blacks listening to the blues they would make the connection between, on the one hand, a serious politics of cool that is about recognizing the meaning of spiritual quest in a secular life

where self-actualization requires an understanding, and, on the other, appreciation of the need to nurture the inner life of the spirit as a survival strategy. Any black male who dares to care for his inner life, for his soul, is already refusing to be a victim.

It is no accident that one of the moments of heartbreak in the career of B.B. King happened at a sixties concert where he confronted a world that was turning away from the blues. A new generation of black folks wanted to dance and swing, to party and do their thing—a generation that did not want to deal with the pain of the past or of the present. King remembers: "The sixties were filled with beautiful soul because black people were more vocal about the respect we wanted and the good feeling we had about ourselves. The politics seeped into the music, and the politics were about life-affirming change." Had these politics been truly liberating they would have embraced the blues as a powerful legacy of black male redemption. Instead, King recalls: "We want to get ahead. But in pushing ahead, sometimes we resent the old forms of music. They represent a time we'd rather forget, a period of history where we suffered shame and humiliation. Makes no difference that the blues is an expression of anger against shame or humiliation. In the minds of many young blacks the blues stood for a time and place they'd outgrown." This contempt for powerful legacies of black male identity in resistance set the stage for the hip-hop generation's disdain for the emotional complexity of black male experience.

Patriarchal hip-hop ushered in a world where black males could declare that they were "keeping it real" when what they were really doing was taking the dead patriarchal protest of the black power movement and rearticulating it in forms that, though entertaining, had for the most part no transformative power, no ability to intervene on politics of domination, and turn the real lives of black men around. While the patriarchal boys in the hip-hop crew may talk about keeping it real, there has been no musical culture with black men at the forefront of its creation that has been as steeped in the politics of fantasy and denial as the more popular strands of hip-hop. The fake cool pose of "keeping it real" has really meant covering up the fact that the generations of black folks dissing the blues and engaging in modern-day shoot-outs in which patriarchal hip-hop symbolically murders blues and by extension jazz, has really been an expression of dominator culture.

Todd Boyd explains the link between the black power movement and hip-hop culture in *The New H.N.I.C.* (his title embraces the rhetoric of dominator culture—it's all about the patriarchal vision of being on top, of being the ruler, of being Mr. Big, The Man). Boyd writes:

> The Black Power movement, by contrast, was generally thwarted by the state at the mass level, but lingering tenets of this ideology have had a massive impact at the grassroots level. A conscious refusal to integrate with mainstream America now characterizes those Black people who willingly exist in their own world. Hip hop is an outgrowth of this black nationalist sentiment. . . . It is one thing to produce culture when people are legally barred from existing in the mainstream, but it is something else entirely for people to produce culture when integration appears to be an option and they choose, for whatever reasons, not to pursue it. Whereas Motown was packaged for mainstream consumption, hip hop was packaged by the sentiments of Black nationalism, and codified in the logo of the hip-hop fashion line FUBU, which means, "for us, by us."

This is the stuff of pure fantasy, since not only is hip-hop packaged for mainstream consumption, many of its primary themes—the embrace of capitalism, the support of patriarchal violence, the conservative approach to gender roles, the call to liberal individualism—all reflect the ruling values of imperialist white-supremacist capitalist patriarchy, albeit in black face. Just as the weak link in the militant black power movement was the obsession dysfunctional radical black males had with competition with white boys for patriarchal turf, hip-hop, especially gangsta rap, articulates this obsession in new forms but it's the same old song. Black men wanting to be "in charge"—in charge of the war, in charge of the woman, in charge of the world.

No wonder, then, most hip-hop culture offers black males very little "real" spiritual nourishment. Sure, it may teach them to play the dominator game and, sure, they may play all the way to wealth. But it does not teach them how to move beyond gaming to find the place of soulfulness, of being, of a cool that is about being well in your soul, being real.

10   Speaking of keeping it real, Boyd writes: "Hip hop is concerned on the other hand with being 'real,' honoring the truth of one's own convictions, while refusing to bend over to accommodate the dictates of the masses. Unlike the previous generation of people who often compromised or made do, in search of something bigger, hip-hop sees compromise as false, fake, and bogus." This version of being "real" sounds more like warmed-over

versions of white patriarchal masculinity's notion that a real man proves his manhood by remaining rigidly attached to one's position, refusing to change. It reveals the emotional immaturity that underlies much hip-hop sentiment. Ironically the mature struggles for social justice, like civil rights, that made it possible for the hip-hop generation to bop their way forward without suffering significant racist assault and repression is mocked by Boyd, who unselfconsciously states: "In the same way that civil rights spoke to the conditions back in the day, hip hop artists now speak to a populace often disillusioned by those considered overtly political in a traditional sense." Much hip-hop culture is mainstream because it is just a black minstrel show—an imitation of dominator desire, not a rearticulation, not a radical alternative. No wonder, then, that patriarchal hip-hop culture has done little to save the lives of black males and done more to teach them, as Gwendolyn Brooks's prophetic poem which used the popular vernacular phrase "we real cool" as its title, states, to embrace a vision of "we real cool" that includes the assumption that "we die soon."

Boyd's definition of cool links it to the state of being lifeless, to necrophilia: "Cool is about a detached, removed, nonchalant sense of being. An aloofness that suggests one is above it all. A pride, an arrogance even, that is at once laid back, unconcerned, perceived to be highly sexual and potentially violent." This definition of black male cool rearticulates the way unenlightened white male hipsters read black masculinity. It is a fake stereotyped notion of cool, that denies the history of the "real cool," which was not about disassociation, hardheartedness, and violence, but rather about being intensely, connected, aware, and able to judge the right action to take in a given circumstance. Boyd's commonplace version of black male cool defines it in terms that mirror the traits of sociopaths and psychopaths; it's all about disassociation. As such it is a vision of black masculinity that merely reinforces the status quo. It offers no possibilities of redemptive change or healing. It is the ultimate drug that keeps black men addicted to the status quo and in their place.

Though Boyd, and many of his cronies, like to think that calling themselves "niggas" and basking in the glory of gangsta culture, glamorizing addiction to drugs, pussy, and material things, is liberation, they personify the spritual zombiehood of today's "cool" black male. They have been bought with a price; they are not their own. And the sad fact is that they do not even know they are faking and fronting while mouthing off about keeping it real; they bring new meaning to the word *denial*. In actuality the culture

they promote is all about playing dead and loving it, or being dead
and leaving behind a legacy of death. Boyd gives expression to the
deadness that is at the core of patriarchal hip-hop's contempt for
black history and culture when he writes: "The civil rights movement was dour. It was serious, and it was ultimately heavy in the
way that it bore on the soul. Many people, black, white, and otherwise, have embraced this era while rejecting any subsequent era
as failing to live up to the standards of the one previous. . . .
America has now turned Martin Luther King Jr.'s dream into a
long weekend. In other words, civil rights has passed; get over it!"
Boyd seems to miss the point that nostalgia for the civil rights
movement is linked to the humanizing blueprints for freedom that
it offered black folks, especially black males, upholding values that
were life-enhancing, that enabled many black males to achieve
healthy esteem without embracing dominator culture.

The black power movement with its faulty embrace of gangsta
culture and violence colluded with the dominant culture in producing a cult of death that is the current ethos of black male life.
Sure, individual black men are getting their piece of the action,
making money, making sex, making war, or doing their own thing
and maybe even having a good time, but the fact remains that collectively black males today are in crisis, in a world of pain. And
yeah! For many, death is the only way out. When hip-hop culture
provides a blueprint for black male salvation we can value it as
many of us value civil rights struggle. Hip-hop culture has created
some fun subcultural playgrounds, some decent sounds and great
grooves, but it has yet to "keep it real" by interfacing with the
world beyond the subculture and mainstream commodification of
blackness in a way that deadens to truly offer black males,
young and old, blueprints for liberation, healing, a return to soul,
wholeness.

Soul healing for wounded black males necessitates a return to
the inner self. It requires that black males not only "come home"
but that they dare to make of home a place where their souls can
thrive. Mystic and spiritual teacher Howard Thurman was a black
male of the blues generation. In seeking ecstatic union with the divine he found a way to be whole. Offering a strategy of healing in
Deep Is the Hunger, Thurman tells us to bring a healing aesthetic to
where we live, to create beauty. He writes: "To bring to the place
where you live only the best and most beautiful, what a plan for
one's life! This is well within the reach of everyone. Think of using
one's memory in that way. As one lives from day to day, there are all
sorts of experiences, good, bad, beautiful, ugly, that become a part

of one's past. To develop the ability to screen one's memory so that only the excellent is retained for one's own room! All kinds of ideas pass through one's mind, about oneself, about the world, about people. Which do you keep for your own room? Think it over now, which ideas do you keep for the place where you live?" Creating beauty through art has been one of the most powerful ways individual black males have chosen to recover themselves, to declare their essential humanity. Whether it is the beauty of a Romare Bearden collage, a John Coltrane solo, or the exquisite photos of Roy DeCarava, individual black males have traditionally found a way to let their souls speak. And by that very act of speaking, of breaking silences, they resist dehumanization. John Coltrane's creates "A Love Supreme" after he chooses to do the work of recovery, turning away from the addiction that threatened to extinguish the creative spirit within him. Today's young black males seeking to find wholeness can find direction in the work and life of Coltrane, learning what not to do and what to do.

Coltrane took the broken bits and pieces of his heart and put   15 them together again. His healing required that he assume accountability for driving away the life-threatening demons that led him to self-sabotage again and again. He was not afraid to face the truth of his life. Fear of facing the truth of their lives prevents most black males from finding themselves. As long as young black males believe that fronting, wearing the mask of "cool," is the thing to do when deep down a hot rage corrupts their spirit, black men will suffer. Every black male is diminished by the wanton destruction of black masculinity that is commonplace in our nation. Although Orlando Patterson has yet to embrace fully a critique of patriarchy he is one of the few black male scholars who has dared to speak the truth about the intense loneliness most black people, especially black males, feel in this culture.

Even though popular culture has made the black male body and presence stand for the apex of "cool," it is a death-dealing coolness, not one that is life-enhancing, for black males or the folks they associate with. Young males embrace a notion of cool that is about getting pussy and getting ready to kill (or a least to make somebody think you can kill) because as an identity this one is easier to come by than the quest to know the self and to create a life of meaning. Right now in our nation not enough adult black males chart the path to healthy self-esteem for younger black males. That path requires self-acceptance, assuming accountability, letting go the politics of blame, telling the truth, and being positive. . . .

Questions for Discussion and Topics for Writing

1. In the very first paragraph of her essay, hooks writes: "Black male cool was defined by the ability to withstand the heat and remain centered." What do we generally mean by the word *cool?* List several connotations of the word. Which of them applies most directly to hooks's meaning? What does hooks mean by "centered"?

2. Moving into the body of her essay, hooks brings up blues music. What connection does she attempt to establish between the blues and the idea of "cool" that is the key theme of her piece? hooks's idea of "cool" is complex, especially when connected to personal identity. Write a summary of the section of her essay that deals with cool, the blues, self-definition, and transforming the world. (This leads up to her discussion of hip hop.)

3. According to hooks, how does hip hop deal differently with the emotional level of black male experience (differently, that is, from the blues)? In your answer, be very clear about how hooks differentiates how the blues and hip hop manage male emotions.

4. Write an essay that connects hooks's ideas about the blues in "The Coolness of Being Real" to a reading of "Sonny's Blues" by James Baldwin. Does Baldwin's story help us understand hooks's claims?

5. hooks writes: "There has been no musical culture with black men at the forefront of its creation that has been as steeped in the politics of fantasy and denial as the more popular strands of hip hop." Write an essay in which you use Michael Eric Dyson's "Gangsta Rap and American Culture" to respond to hooks's claims.

Making Connections

1. Examine lyrics by women rappers such as Jean Grae, Queen Latifah, Lil' Kim, Foxy Brown, and Bo$$. Can you find continuities among their different positions, attitudes, and rhymes? How do the lyrics of the female MCs complicate the picture of a woman's place in hip hop?

2. Compare the songs "Ether" by Nas and "Take Over" by Jay-Z. How do these songs—the words of which constitute a lyrical "battle" between the artists—use gender as the basis of their respective arguments? More specifically, how is masculinity constructed and deconstructed in each song?

3. Find the lyrics to the song "Me and Jesus the Pimp" by the Oakland-based group The Coup. How does the song use narrative to help us understand the origins of a "gangsta" version of masculinity? How do the technological metaphors (especially computers metaphors) in the song help us understand the meaning of inner-city masculinity? Is the song defending hypermasculinity? Or is it merely explaining it? Discuss.

4. Watch a music video. Describe the men and women. How do they look and act? What roles do they play? Based on your description of the video, what does it mean to be a man and what does it mean to be a woman? List the unwritten rules of gender that underlie the depictions that you see and describe.

CHAPTER 4

Growing Up Gangsta: Gangsta Rap and the Politics of Identity

It is April 29, 1992. A mostly all-white Los Angeles jury has acquitted the police officers on trial for beating Rodney King despite an evidentiary videotape that shows them bludgeoning him with nightsticks and stomping him to the ground. On the tape, an idling black-and-white spotlights King with its headlights, making an impromptu theater in the round. King, prone in the middle of the street next to his white Hyundai, stirs a little while four police officers surround him, poised to strike him as soon as he attempts to rise. South Central Los Angeles responds to the video and the acquittal with a chaotic chorus, paving the streets with broken bottles, bullet shells, fire, and blood. Stores are raided and torched; guns are fired indiscriminately into the air. Reginald Denny is dragged from his truck, beaten down, stoned with a cinderblock, and left for dead.

Ice Cube, growing up in South Central and a member of one of gangsta rap's seminal groups, NWA (Niggas With Attitude), erupts to the incident in his lyrics, revealing the volatile dynamics that led to L.A.'s extraordinary violence. On his album *Predator*, there is a tense moment when the voice of an older white woman timorously murmurs that she "thinks" that "we" hear "violence" in Ice Cube's song. On this album, coming out of South Central Los Angeles around the time of the L.A. riots, every word of her apparently simple claim trembles with meaning. Her "think" shows both a lack of urgency and a lack of certainty about what's happening; it reveals the speaker's detachment and distance, unlike the album, which announces its fealty and subtle knowledge of "what's going on." Saying "we hear" after "I think" is interesting because of its pronoun shift, which generalizes the "I" and begs the question: Who is "we?" There now appears to be an "us" and a "them." We "hear" violence rather than experience it or even see it; this suggests the safe distance the speaker has. Of course, the speaker uses the verb "hear" because she is referring directly to the music. But confusing the messenger with the message, the speaker deems the music itself violent, disregarding the conditions about which Ice Cube speaks. Coupled with a dismissive tone, "hearing violence" in the music becomes, ironically, a way of *not listening* to what is said. It is a way of condemning Ice Cube so that the speaker can continue to ignore what is happening in South Central and other low-income black and Hispanic communities in L.A. In a city notoriously spread out and segregated, remaining ignorant is easy to do. Nevertheless, the violence exists and the question remains: Who is violent and who is being harmed?

Ice Cube responds to this question in different ways with different songs, but one of the most direct reprisals to the violence of the Rodney King incident occurs in "You Ain't Gonna Take My Life." In the song, Cube addresses an imagined L.A.P.D. officer whom he aptly refers to as "Officer Kevin." The song opens with Cube calling the Officer "Mr. Dirty Harry," immediately evoking cinematic icon Clint Eastwood, his .357 Magnum revolver, and his "Make my day!" macho persona. With an air of condescension, Cube deflates the officer's fake movie image of himself as a tough-guy cop, a persona especially poignant in the streets of L.A., where Hollywood images and reality are often indistinguishable. Ice Cube then replaces this iconic image with the officer's first name. As an Irish name, "Kevin" may connote a typical white, Irish cop, but more importantly, calling the officer by his first name identifies him as an individual, undermining his authority and equalizing the power between Ice Cube and the officer.

At first, calling him "Kevin" comes off as a show of disrespect, but as the song continues, Ice Cube realigns the disequilibrium of social power to achieve parity between two individuals. What we see is that, in the midst of what appears to be mere pandering to a market hungry for images of violence, Cube weaves a more serious vision. Cube disarms Officer Kevin of any false sense of authority— an authority that becomes palpable when coupled with the officer's militaristic appearance. The cop, Cube notes, flaunts a flap-top haircut and wears spit-shined boots, all the while not giving a "fuck" about Cube's neighborhood. So, rather than looking like someone who would uphold the police motto "to protect and serve," the officer resembles a soldier ready for combat. To Ice Cube, the officer's battle-ready look reveals someone eager to bite off a piece of "nigga" ass. Cube's answer to the threat implied by the officer's appearance is retaliatory: he invites us to watch a nigga "blast a white nigga fast." While the image is violent and the language inflammatory, Ice Cube refers to himself and to the officer as "nigga," maintaining racial parity while, at the same time, equating these violent attitudes with the derogatory term *nigga*, showing them to be part and parcel of the brutality taking place in the 'hood.

Ice Cube goes on to directly relate to the officer by insisting that he, like the cop, has children, too, drastically and artfully transforming his self-imposed image as a "nigga" into his role as parent. In a sustained effort to relate to the officer, Ice Cube not only identifies himself as a parent, but also affirms a stereotypical vision of (white) American middle-class normalcy: he states he could have knocked off the cop, but knowing the cop has a wife and a dog named "Spot," Cube shows him mercy, claiming he, unlike the cop, is indeed civilized. What is interesting here is that while his language seems to reinforce common racial stereotypes, Ice Cube has "flipped the script." Because it is the perceiver—not the perceived—who constructs identity, it is the officer who is responsible for the violent and derogatory image of Ice Cube as "nigga," while it is Ice Cube who ratifies the typical vision of the white, middle-class American dream.

This reversal makes clear the implications of Ice Cube's declaration earlier in the song that while the cop hates the face of the "original" man, he must treat Cube like an "individual" man. Here Ice Cube implicitly critiques the officer's racist view of him while insisting that individual relationships trump social roles, especially when those roles enforce social inequality. By referring to himself as "original" instead of "black," he invokes the theory that all civilization began in Africa, making his face, contrary to the officer's view of him, the original image of civilized man. The pun on "original" also allows Ice Cube to somewhat self-servingly hold himself up as an "original"—an artistic nod to his individuality—but this shift in diction does more than that. By aligning being black with being civilized, Ice Cube shows that it is not South Central that is "uncivilized" and violent, but rather the attitude of the officer and the dominant culture he represents that imagines South Central in this way. Despite the critique of the officer's attitude, Ice Cube relies on a theory of human origin that also implies the commonality of the races rather than their difference. So by dispelling the negative presumptions of the officer and of people like the woman who "hears violence," Ice Cube takes the first nonviolent step toward reconciliation that is both mutual and uncompromising.

It is only the vision of the Rodney King beating that threatens Ice Cube's determined call for a real peace and respect: viewing the tape, Cube claims he was so "hot" he wanted to go out and "pop" a police officer. The images of the King beating put Ice Cube back in a defensive position as Officer Kevin is metonymically transformed into

"Mr. Nightstick." As is consistent with the rest of the song, this view of authority as violent naturally causes Cube to retaliate with an equally violent, stereotypical response. Still, Ice Cube does not repeat the violence inflicted by the cops. Instead; he directs his rage and indignation into the song, a message that condemns the incident; explains the violent, riotous response of South Central; and articulates a remedy that calls for a fundamental, dynamic change. Ultimately, it is the song that serves as the source of Cube's personal and social power.

As a means of ending violence, Ice Cube insists on there being "an understanding" that leads to acknowledgment. Although ironic, the music sends a nonviolent message by articulating the violence inherent in social dynamics in L.A. that are based on demographics rather than individual interaction. Instead of casting blame, Ice Cube attempts to erase the us/them mentality that generates hostile relations that inevitably lead to stereotypes and even deaths. A violent response is deflected into "violent" speech, a speech whose impact poignantly and powerfully reveals the conditions of the 'hood. Of course, neither the song nor Cube is naïve enough to think that the status quo will change just by writing a song about it. This struggle for equality is not easily won. Many times, Cube's response replicates the attitudes that he angrily resists. Even more, the chorus questions the possibility of a permanent reconciliation with its insistent pun on "never gonna get it." The chorus shows Cube's uncompromising stand against oppressive authority and at the same time questions whether the cop—who represents the attitudes of white dominant culture—will ever really "get it." Yet, as an articulation of what is happening, the song offers us the means and possibility of understanding and, therefore, a hope.

Gangsta Rap, the War on Drugs, and the Location of African-American Identity in Los Angeles 1988-92

ELIZABETH GRANT

Elizabeth Grant is a professional development specialist for the New-York Historical Society. She holds a Ph.D. in American Studies from the University of Birmingham, England. Her doctoral dissertation on the annual Philadelphia Greek Picnic explores race, place, and memory in the postindustrial city and reflects a broader research interest in the intersection of African-American history and culture with urban development. She has delivered papers at academic conferences on both sides of the Atlantic and has published work in the Journal of Urban History *and* The European Journal of American Culture. *The following excerpted article appeared originally in* The European Journal of American Culture *in 2002.*

---- ✦ ----

WESTSIDE: HIP HOP LA

. . . For over a decade New York City checked the flow of hip hop pouring out of struggling African-American neighbourhoods in cities such as Philadelphia, Boston and Houston. However, by 1990, Los Angeles had become the indisputable capital of the hip hop nation, a geographic dislocation accompanied by a shift in rap's basic tonal and narrative style. As in New York, LA's early hip hop scene rose out of politically and economically neglected, predominately African-American, Latino, and Chicano neighbourhoods. True to hip hop's emphasis on roots and localized identity, however, early DJs and MCs styled New York hip hop culture to musical influences and urban structures specific to LA.[1] Labelled "gangsta rap" by industry chiefs and music critics for its seeming glorification of street gang activity, LA's rap regime hypnotized the nation with tales of territorial rivalry, drug dealing and brutalizing sexual relations in the South Central boroughs of Los Angeles.

Los Angeles issued its first challenge to New York's commercial domination of the rap music industry in 1986 when Ice T released his single "'6' n tha Morning."[2] But it was NWA's 1988 album *Straight Outta Compton* that shifted the location and tone of contemporary commercial hip hop, cast the image of an angry, armed black male gang banger on the national psyche and ultimately cemented Los Angeles's place on the hip hop map. The tag "gangsta," stemming from references to the street gangs that have been active in LA's South Central and East Side communities for over thirty years, gangsta rap's violent imagery and explicit lyrics stylize LA gang culture in lyrical references to gang allegiances and drive-by shootings and in musical re-creations of Uzis, AK-47s and other street weaponry. Robin Kelley explains that this stylized gang culture generally symbolizes rhyme skills, lyrical authenticity and street knowledge rather than actual violent behaviour: "Gang bangin' itself has never been a central theme in the music. Many of the violent lyrics are not intended literally. Rather they are boasting raps in which the imagery of gang bangin' is used metaphorically to challenge competitors on the mic—an element common to all hard-core hip hop."[3]

For this first generation of gangsta rap artists, hip hop's intensifying emphasis on inner-city loyalties provided an opportunity to assert LA's takeover of the hip hop industry. According to Murray Foreman, gangsta rappers from South Central LA emphasizing gang-like territoriality, "were not only serving notice to their neighboring communities that they were in charge, but they were also serving notice to New York and the entire hip hop nation that the new sound had arrived and the balance of power . . . had tipped to the West."[4] Gang banging, then, not only symbolized hip hop's increasing territoriality, but also rooted this symbol in a West Coast, and more specifically, Los Angeles context. Moreover, West Coast artists basing their commercial identities in specific sites— Compton, Inglewood and Long Beach, for example—mapped a spatialized representation of African-American existence in LA embodied by the figure of the gangsta.

Finally, although Kelley's assessment of gangsta rap's metaphorical content is right on the money, my objective is to point out that the content and subjective position of these metaphors exist alongside political and social definitions of street gangs. By 1988, gangs had carved South Central and East LA into red and blue territories and the "phantasmagoric gangsta" had taken on a particular dynamic in the imagined ghettos of popular culture, the news media and political rhetoric.[5] Between 1988 and 1992, the "gangsta" became a dangerous weapon in the hands of political and social interests defining LA's black communities. The various ways rap artists construct this metaphorical relationship with the "gangsta" and base this identification within Los Angeles provides insight into the means by which outside political and municipal forces eventually understood and characterized South Central's African-American communities.

"IT'S TIME TO PUT COMPTON ON THE MAP": GANGSTA RAP AND THE RACIALIZATION OF LA

NWA's 1988 album *Straight Outta Compton* solidified LA's position as   5
hip hop's new commercial capital.[6] Employing the descriptive quality of rap narratives, and the visual aspects of album covers and videos in a dual objective of establishing a cohesive, gang-like identity and relating that identity to Compton, NWA shaped a racial-spatial

paradigm a generation of West Coast rap artists would emulate. As I will show, in the early years following NWA's success, Compton remained a touchstone for gangsta identity. However, as gangsta rap increased in popularity and profitability, artists adjusted NWA's Compton-based identity to accommodate gangsta rap's expanding parameters. Importantly, as these parameters expanded, the black identity of the gangsta and the relationship between this African-American identity and the city not only remained intact, but also, in fact, continued to reinforce one another.

True to Robin Kelley's analysis, NWA's representations of gang activity equate the street knowledge of the gangster with the lyrical and rhythmic skills of the gangsta rapper, an equation that requires NWA's familiarity with the urban environment of South Central LA. From the outset, NWA's gang dynamic and roots in Compton provide narrative material and the skills, knowledge and entitlement to present these narratives through music. *Straight Outta Compton's* album cover features NWA dressed almost entirely in black, their individual faces with identical stern, impassive expressions bearing down on an upward-pointed camera and projecting a cohesive gangsta identity foregrounded in the pistol Ice Cube aims into the camera. Videos feature NWA in trademark black clothing, sporting Los Angeles Kings or Raiders caps, white sneakers and gold chains. This all-black style not only resembles the monochrome style of LA's street gangs, but also focuses the viewer's eye and accentuates NWA's presence in the sweeping, panoramic shots of South Central Los Angeles composing videos such as "Straight Outta Compton" (1988), "Express Yourself" (1988), and "Alwayz into Somethin'" (1991).

The video for "Straight Outta Compton" manipulates this gang image to mark NWA's territory within Los Angeles. Using two distinct camera styles, the video counterposes NWA's perspective of Compton with that of the Los Angeles Police Department. The police perspective, represented in swift, smooth camera movements and framed by the front and side casing of a squad car windscreen, sweeps through Compton too quickly to distinguish individuals, storefronts and signs marking the streets. NWA's point of view moves at a slower pace, jerky camera movements indicating walking as the camera travels over fences and under freeway bridges into spaces inaccessible to the police in their patrol car. NWA's slower pace provides a more detailed perspective of the street signs, shop fronts and individuals indistinguishable to the police, while the group's greater mobility provides access to and knowledge of the spaces behind the street patrolled by the squad car.

The video's narrative reinforces NWA's cohesive identity and that identity's relationship to Compton. The first time we see NWA from the patrol car window, the group stands in a cluster on a street corner. Although the individual visages of NWA are indistinguishable, as the window frame of the patrol car zooms in close behind the retreating figures, it becomes clear that the group's black skin, black clothing and baseball caps identify the police target. Importantly, this identification relates directly to NWA's geographic location. Interspersed amid the LAPD's and NWA's counterposed perspectives is a series of still and action shots that focus on a black and white map of Los Angeles on which the boundaries of Compton are outlined in red. Police batons wielded by leather-gloved hands point emphatically at this sectioned area. As the video moves between the counterposed perspectives, shots of NWA on Compton's streets and images of the highlighted map, black-clad, black individuals, NWA and Compton itself become interchangeable entities. Moreover, NWA's internal relationships to one another and external ties to Compton create a semiotic formulation between the street knowledge and skills of the gangsta/ rapper and his origins in Compton that legitimatizes NWA's perspectives with the stamp of authenticity that urban, African-American perspectives in commercial hip hop warrant. Combined with lyrical references to gang allegiance ("Straight Outta Compton" opens: "Straight Outta Compton, crazy motherfucker named Ice Cube/from the gang called Niggaz with Attitude"), visual images project an exclusive, internal bond among NWA's individual members and root this bond in Compton.[7]

Early West Coast artists emulated NWA's lucrative gangsta image.[8] The video for The DOC's "It's Funky Enough" (1991) features The DOC in NWA-style black clothing, baseball hat, gold chain and white sneakers, an obvious stylistic tribute to the founders of West Coast commercial rap and a conscious confirmation of The DOC's legitimate position within the emerging gangsta rap scene, a circumstance borne out by the video's narrative. The video weaves still shots of The DOC in abandoned areas of the LA landscape with a series of scenes tracing NWA through various unconnected but recognizable areas of LA. These similar yet competing uses of the urban spaces in which NWA and The DOC are presented, and which they in turn represent, provide a critical insight into the use of the urban context in the construction of a gangsta identity. The video emphasizes NWA's knowledge of and mobility through the urban environment by actively following NWA through the recognizable LA environment. On the other hand, through a series of long frame shots of The DOC before various landmarks of the LA landscape, the video presents The DOC as an element of the urban terrain itself. While NWA's safe passage through the streets indicate their knowledge of the urban environment, their subsequent hip hop skills and powerful position on the rap scene, The DOC's location within the urban environment signifies his own rap skills, legitimates his position within West Coast hip hop and transforms the hip hop gangsta into an endemic part of the urban environment itself.

10 Furthermore, this video's representation of the urban context provides a further insight into the relationship between rap artists and the urban environments that they represent. The impressively stark presentation of LA, the noticeably vacant street landscape, combined with The DOC's apparent endemic bond to LA's streets, indicates a closed, private relationship between the gangsta and the urban environment. The gangsta and "the street" exist in a clear metaphorical relationship that replaces the actual individuals and communities forming the urban environment with the image of the gangsta rapper. Other videos uphold this gangsta-as-community metaphor, alternately presenting the rap artist as a solitary figure within the landscape, as in "It's Funky Enough" or "The DOC and the Dr" featuring Dr Dre, and placing the rap artist before crowds of individuals, for example, NWA's "Express Yourself" or Eazy-E's "Eazy-er Said than Dun" (1991).

While *Straight Outta Compton* struck the mold for the hip hop gangsta, other artists confirmed and expanded its boundaries until the gangsta came to signify not only Compton, but also black individuals and communities in Los Angeles as a whole. The role of "Compton" in this equation, however, is critical. Dr Dre explains that once NWA began selling records in 1987, Compton became a touchstone for market success and that "Compton [existed] in many ways in the music to sell records."[9] In forming a gangsta identity through a relationship with Compton, NWA transforms a specific location with a particular cultural and historical location in LA's development into a marketable element of gangsta rap. Indeed, NWA's claim to Compton might have benefited from copyright protection against eager artists such as Compton's Most Wanted (their first album *It's a Compton Thang* released in 1990). However, in the years following *Straight Outta Compton,* gangsta rap adjusted to changing structural dynamics within the rap industry, most notably the break-up of NWA and the rise of gangsta rap stars from outside Compton, and reorganized the gangsta image around a specific lifestyle based in illegal activity, fashion and, in some cases, actual gang affiliations.

The video "Alwayz into Somethin'" from NWA's 1991 album *Efil4zaggin* illustrates NWA's transformation from a cohesive, territorial gang into a network of hustling, ruthless street-wise gangstas.[10] The video, filmed almost entirely in black and white and featuring NWA in characteristic black garb, baseball hats and white sneakers, traces Eazy-E, MC Ren and Dr Dre between four locales: a car-stripping warehouse, an automobile, a prison cell and "the street." The video's narrative concentrates on the group's individual members as they move through these sites, connecting seemingly disjointed images in a collage of NWA's illegal actions; Dre steals and strips cars after escaping from prison with the help of Ren; Ren and Eazy burn property on the street; Ren brags about his murder of Ice Cube. Unlike the images of NWA I discussed above, which construct a gangsta identity through the group's internal structure and loyalty to Compton, this video shapes gang identity around criminal behaviour and relates these illegal activities to the urban environment in which they take place. Criminal activity comes to symbolize the knowledge, skills and authority of "the street" previously rooted in NWA's territorial claim to Compton.

The transformation in NWA's gangsta identity is suggestive of changes disrupting the gangsta rap industry itself. The departure of Ice Cube and Dr Dre shattered NWA's internalized hip hop gang identity. At the same time, new groups on the West Coast gangsta scene challenged NWA's claim to authenticity originally backed by NWA's spatial identification with Compton. Like NWA, rising rap artists like former NWA members Dr Dre and Ice Cube, and new stars such as Coolio incorporated specific fashion trends and visual tropes, lyrical expressions and musical styles to project the lifestyle of the hip hop gangsta. Furthermore, as rivalries split the industry along production company lines, gangsta rap artists engaged one another in the metaphorical gang banging described by Robin Kelley and challenged one another in the execution and expression of the gangsta lifestyle. By 1992, album covers, videos, films and even malt liquor advertisements had solidified the interchangeable identities of gangsta rap artists and the lifestyles they represented.

The "G" lifestyle, popularized by ex-NWA members Dr Dre and Ice Cube, replaced Compton as gangsta rap's most marketable feature.[11] Dr Dre's video "Nuthin' but a 'G' Thang" infuses Dre's musical identity with visual images of the "G" lifestyle. The video's narrative follows Dr Dre and his protégé Snoop Doggy Dog from barbecues to beach volleyball games to a packed house party as cars bounce and young people dance in perfect synchronization with

Dre's laid-back beat, connecting Dr Dre, his music and the lifestyle depicted in their identification with and of one another. More importantly for this discussion, however, as the camera cruises along the streets and freeways of South Central from Compton to Long Beach, it becomes clear that Dre's gangsta lifestyle spans the physical boundaries of Compton to project a mobile, highly accessible gangsta identity bound only by attitude, lifestyle and, ultimately, music choice.

15   If, as Dr Dre's video "Nuthin' But a 'G' Thang" illustrates, gangsta identities are both highly mobile and easily accessible through consumption of the music itself, boundaries must be drawn around the spatial context and racial identities that originally defined the gangsta. While videos and album covers convey gangsta rap's clear urban associations, lyrics make this spatial identification even more explicit by constructing the urban environment of the gangsta/rapper through the exclusion of the surrounding suburbs. In "Tales from the Darkside (Endangered Species)," Ice Cube addresses non-urban audiences directly: "You should listen to me 'cause there's more to see/Call my neighbourhood a ghetto 'cause it houses minorities/The other colour don't know you can run but not hide/These are tales from the Darkside."[12] Recognizing that by 1992 white suburban teenagers composed the majority of hip hop's commercial market (but by no means did white middle-class teens dominate rap's actual audience), Ice Cube takes up a storytelling position, indeed the position of the rap artist, to address non-black, non-urban voyeuristic outsiders about the realities and fantasies of inner-city life. Ice Cube creates a clear distinction between the geographic locations, social and racial identifications of Cube and his audiences and solidifies the urban and African-American identity of the gangsta through the explicit exclusion of his white counterpart.

Ultimately, gangsta rap embodies hip hop's urban, African-American identities in the image of the gangsta. Importantly, the black and urban identities bound in the hip hop gangsta and the racial boundaries defining Los Angeles are not isolated ideological constructs. Rather, these are symbiotic components working within the cycle of constantly engaging dominant and subversive representations of Los Angeles and its inhabitants. By 1988, the same year NWA released *Straight Outta Compton*, economic shifts, mass suburbanization and corporate gentrification of downtown Los Angeles had transformed the city into a decentred web of ethnically and economically defined neighbourhoods.[13] Within this web, the gangsta image becomes a foundation for the construction of racial, economic and political boundaries that define LA. As a basis for white and black, suburban and urban identities, the "gangsta" takes centre stage as cultural and political forces struggle for the power to define the peoples and places composing Los Angeles. Gangsta rap and its urban, African-American identities manipulate the gangsta image to project LA's black population as self-contained, cohesive, self-sufficient and empowered against police brutality and political corruption. At the same time, political rhetoric, legislation and law enforcement programs use the gangsta to implicate the black communities of South Central in increasing concerns surrounding crime and street violence. I conclude my discussion of LA's spatialized racial dynamic with a brief discussion of Los Angeles's "War on Drugs" campaign to illustrate how the urban, African-American identities projected through the gangsta imaginary were used so effectively by LA's municipal interests. I intend to show not only how the gangsta image manipulated by gangsta rap to project an empowered vision of South Central was also used to criminalize it, but also the disastrous effects of this clash between Los Angeles and its real and imagined gangstas.

REAL vs. IMAGINED: LOS ANGELES TAKES ON THE GANGSTA

LA's "War on Drugs" was part of an extensive $8 billion national anti-drug campaign launched by George Bush, Sr. in 1988, capping off nearly a century of national anti-drug campaigns in what Clarence Lusane labels the "longest war in US history."[14] Importantly, since the turn of the century, these campaigns have stigmatized drug use in widespread racial stereotypes and outright racist images.[15] Bush's "War on Drugs" incorporated racial images of drug use into already established associations of race and urban space to criminalize entire communities of inner-city minorities. Within Los Angeles, one of the urban "hot spots" targeted by Bush's $8 billion dollar incentive, the "War on Drugs" put racialized images of drug dealers and street gangs to work within LA's particular racial dynamic and targeted economically and politically isolated communities in an anti-drug, anti-gang crusade.

The disproportionate representation of minorities in the stream of drug addicts and small-time dealers herded through California's penal system during this period compels a quick examination of legal definitions of "gang" and "gang member," how the police and sheriff's departments responded to these legal definitions and how they relate to the gangsta.[16] In what Malcolm Klein describes as a reification of the "criminal street gang," section 186.22 of the California penal code defines street gangs as follows:

> . . . any organization, association, or group of three of more persons, whether formal or informal, having as one of its primary activities the commission of one or more illegal activities . . . which has a common name or common identifying sign or symbol, whose members individually or collectively engage in or have engaged in a pattern of criminal gang activity.[17]

"Group" identity, a "common name or common identifying sign or symbol" and participation in "criminal gang activity" take on a recognizable format in police operations. For example, the Gang Related Active Trafficker Suppression (GRATS) program, LA's first offensive in the modern campaign against street gangs, charged almost 300 police officers to profile suspects based on dress and hand signals. Similarly, the Street Terrorism and Prevention (STEP) Act of 1988 calls for the indictment of "any person who actively participates in a criminal street gang," effectively turning gang membership into a felony.[18] Initiatives like GRATS and STEP not only fuse individuals into one collective enemy, the "street gang," but also reveal an inherent elasticity in California's formal definition of street gangs that eventually allowed for an extension of these legal parameters around social groups, families and entire communities. It is in this extension that the gangsta imaginary becomes most useful.

In *City of Quartz*, Mike Davis explains that as the fervour surrounding street gangs and drugs mounted, LA's municipal, legislative and judicial bodies created anti-gang and anti-drug programs that criminalized "successive strata of the [South Central] community: 'gang members', then 'gang parents', followed by whole 'gang families', 'gang neighborhoods', and perhaps even a 'gang generation.'"[19] Compiling popular associations between gangs and drugs with the racial and spatial identifications attached to both drugs *and* street gangs, LA's "War on Drugs" campaign targeted the gangsta and the black communities of South Central represented by the gangsta imaginary effectively to "criminalize gang members and their families as a class."[20] The racial and spatial identities of the gangsta located these gang members and their families in South Central and ultimately turned the "War on Drugs" into a battle for control of both the ideological power structures and the physical spaces of South Central.

20   In a notorious public statement defending the LAPD's tactics in the "War on Drugs," Chief Daryl Gates captures the militaristic

quality incorporated into programs like Operation Safe Streets or Operation HAMMER and in political rhetoric comparing gang activity with guerrilla warfare: "This is war . . . We want to get the message out to the cowards out there, and that's what they are, rotten little cowards—we want the message to go out that we're going to come and get them".[21] A Los Angeles police captain describes his department's line of attack, "We do sweeps. We spend a day looking through their rooms, their houses. Those that we find in violation go to jail. Those that don't . . . are left with the thought that we're coming back. We'll announce when—when we knock on the door. Our attitude is that they are special."[22] The clear spatial imagery articulated in statements proclaiming police intentions to "come and get" gangs, to enter their neighborhoods, homes and bedrooms and to herd offenders into squad cars, police vans and gang-tracking databases is put into practice in initiatives targeting specific communities and geographic regions of South Central.

In 1989, Chief Daryl Gates authorized the narcotics division of the LAPD to establish a "narcotic enforcement zone" of police barricades and checkpoints around a 27-block area of Pico-Union. The following month, the LAPD extended these barricades through South Central, creating "strategic hamlets" for law enforcement deployment throughout the region. One such campaign targeted Central Avenue, the backbone of African-American historical and cultural development in Los Angeles, in an attempt to curtail the socializing and gathering considered instrumental in gang formation and drug dealing. Similarly, Operation Knockdown, protected under the STEP Act, bulldozed entire housing districts and apartment complexes thought to harbour drug-dealing gangs, turning the legal campaign against gangs and drugs into a physical assault on the urban terrain itself. Knockdown blurred any distinction between its gang target and the physical spaces and communities these gangs represented.[23] Overall, community barricading, extensive crime sweeps and technologically advanced surveillance systems criminalized entire communities and physical regions of South Central Los Angeles in an effort to contain and eradicate an illusive adversary, the urban black gangster.

Almost ten years after the 1992 uprisings, criticism of the Los Angeles Police and Justice Departments seems abundant and perhaps long overdue. Nine years after protests erupted at the crossroads of Normandy and Florence, the elite Ramparts Division of the CRASH unit is under investigation and the LAPD faces millions of dollars in litigation and settlement fees for incidents of police brutality, civil rights violation and homicide. At the height of the Reagan/Bush "War on Drugs" campaign, however, LA's finest set the standard for anti-gang and anti-drug forces across the US. In television shows and news reports, the LAPD represented the force of law in a battle against urban chaos. Rife with racist stereotypes and classist fears, the ideological warfare between imagined gangstas and the fantastic LAPD carved deep trenches across Los Angeles and divided the city into recognizable regions characterized by class, race and ethnicity. As the LAPD acted on paranoia surrounding racial and class differences, the thin line between the image of a gang-controlled Compton and the actual streets of South Central disappeared. The real/imagined relationships between gangs and law enforcement agencies reveal how the racial and spatial identifications of the gangsta imaginary function in the formation of African-American racial identity within Los Angeles. Between 1988 and 1992, unrestrained gang and police activity engaged on concrete and fantastic planes, and ultimately shaped "Compton" in the image of a cop-hating, gun-toting, blue/red wearing, drug-dealing African-American male gang member. The massive explosion of pent-up frustration following the Rodney King verdict in 1992 perhaps only points to the deep impact of this gangsta image on the south central communities and individuals "Compton" initially represented.

Notes

1. On West Coast rap and gangsta rap, see: Brian Cross, *It's Not About a Salary . . .: Rap, Race and Resistance in Los Angeles* (London: Verso, 1993); Robin D.G. Kelley "Kickin' Reality, Kickin' Ballistics." In Perkins, pp. 117–58; Kelley, *Yo' Mama's Disfunktional!: Fighting the Culture Wars in Urban America* (Boston: Beacon Press, 1997).

2. "6'n the Morning." *Rhyme Pays*, Sire Records, 1987.

3. Kelley (1996), p. 123; Kelley (1997), pp. 38–40.

4. Foreman, p. 81.

5. Mike Davis explains that the dramas surrounding LA's bloody gang wars formulated in the "phantasmagoric gangsta" of the public imagination: "[T]he contemporary gang scare has become an imaginary class relationship, a terrain of pseudo-knowledge and fantasy projection. But as long as the actual violence was more or less contained to the ghetto, the gang wars were also a voyeuristic titillation to white suburbanites devouring lurid imagery in their newspapers or on television", Davis (1992), p. 270.

6. *Straight Outta Compton* (Priority, 1988).

7. "Straight Outta Compton" from *Straight Outta Compton*.

8. See, for example, "The DOC," *No One Can Do It Better* (Ruthless, 1989). "Compton's Most Wanted." *It's a Compton Thang* (EMI, 1990): *Straight Chekn'em* (Epic, 1991).

9. Dr Dre, quoted in Cross, p. 198.

10. *Efile4zaggin* (Priority, 1991).

11. Ice Cube, *Amerikkka's Most Wanted* (Priority, 1990); *Death Certificate* (Priority, 1991); *The Predator* (Priority, 1992); Dr Dre, *The Chronic* (Death Row, 1992).

12. This boundary gains even more explicit geographic and racial distinction in *Amerikkka's Most Wanted's* title track: "Word, who the fuck has heard?/It's time to make a trip to the suburbs. Let 'em see a nigga invasion/Point blank for the Caucusion." Ice Cube, "Tales from the Darkside (Endangered Species)", and "Amerikka's Most Wanted." *Amerikkka's Most Wanted* (Priority Records, 1990). Dr Dre confirms Ice Cube's construction of a spatial and racial boundary around the gangsta identity when he raps about the 1992 Los Angeles uprisings: "You see when niggas get together, they get mad 'cause they can't fade us/Like my niggas from south central Los Angeles/They find they can't handle us/Bloods, Crips on the same squad/With Ese's thumpin', nigga it's time to stop and mob". "The Day the Niggaz Took Over." *The Chronic* (Priority Records, 1992).

13. On Los Angeles, see Davis (1992) and *Ecology of Fear: Los Angeles and the Imagination of Disaster* (New York: Vintage Books, 1998); Allen J. Scott and Edward W. Soja (eds.), *The City: Los Angeles and Urban Theory at the End of the Twentieth Century* (Berkeley: University of California Press, 1996). pp. 336–64: Kelley (1996); Edward W. Soja, *Thirdspace: Journeys to Los Angeles and Other Real and Imagined Places* (Cambridge. MA: Blackwell Publishers, 1996); David Relff, *Los Angeles: Capital of the Third World* (London: Orion Books, 1991).

14. Clarence Lusane, *Pipe Dream Blues: Racism and the War on Drugs* (Boston: South End Press, 1991). p. 68. On Reagan, Bush and the "War on Drugs," see: Michael Omi and Howard Winant, *Racial Formation in the United States, From the 1960s to the 1990s* (New York: Routledge, 1991). pp. 138–40; Jimmie L. Reeves and Richard Campbell, *Cracked Coverage: Television News, the Anti-Cocaine Crusade, and the Regan Legacy* (London: Duke University Press, 1994); Jesse Daniels, *White Lies: Race, Class, Gender, and Sexuality in White Supremacist Discourse* (New York: Routledge, 1997). pp. 71–100. On associations between gangs and drugs, see Richard Cervantes (ed.), *Substance Abuse and Gang Violence* (Newbury Park: Sage Publications, 1992).

15. On the history of the US's War on Drugs and its racial aspects, see Timothy A. Hickman, "Drugs and Race in American Culture: Orientalism in the Turn-of-the-Century Discourse of Narcotic Addiction," *American Studies.* 41:1 (2000). pp. 71–92.

16. Since the 1980s, Los Angeles's African-American prison population has tripled. By 1990, 1,860 blacks were imprisoned for every 100,000, compared to just 289 whites. Robin Kelley points out that these figures exist despite a higher proportion of crack abuse in white as compared to black communities. See: Kelley (1997), pp. 99-100: Lusane, pp. 33–34: Reeves and Campbell, p. 44.

17. Klein, p. 28. On LA gang culture see: Malcolm Klein, *The American Street Gang: Its Nature, Prevalence, and Control* (Oxford: Oxford University Press, 1995); Mike Davis, *City of Quartz: Excavating the Future in Los Angeles* (New York: Random House, 1992), pp. 299-302; Susan Anderson, "A City Called Heaven: Black Enchantment and Despair in Los Angeles." Scott and Soja, pp. 336–64; Kelley (1996), p. 131.

18. *Los Angels Times,* quoted in Davis (1992), p. 272. Davis explains that the first GRATS offensive "on the flimsy 'probable cause' of red shoelaces or high-five handshakes . . . mounted nine sweeps. Impounded five hundred cars and made nearly fifteen hundred arrests." Davis (1992), pp. 280–83. See also Klein, pp. 178–82.

19. Davis (1992), p. 284

20. *Ibid.* (1992), p. 278.

21. Gates quoted in Davis (1992), p. 268.

22. Unidentified police chief quoted in Klein, p. 161.

23. For more on the implications of police barricading in Los Angeles, see Davis (1992), pp. 257–58, 277. For details on community barricading, including contemporary reactions to these campaigns, see: Jesse Katz, "Gang Sweeps Earn Low Marks." *Los Angeles Times,* 18 June 1990; Dean E. Murphy, "Barricades, Police Visits Give Hope to Crime Plagued Neighborhood," *Los Angeles Times,* 22 June 1991.

Questions for Discussion and Topics for Writing

1. An interesting element of Grant's article on gangsta rap is her use of video for the NWA album *Straight Outta Compton.* Reread this section of her essay. Write a summary of the two paragraphs about the video and point out how Grant uses it to support her argument. What key points does she make here?

2. Take question #1's analysis further by looking at Grant's reading of DOC's video, *It's Funky Enough.* What relationship does Grant see existing between the rapper and her or his environment? Why is this significant to her? (Note: Grant's use of videos to support her argument is an excellent example of how to use pop culture's texts to support an argument in an essay.)

3. How does Grant's interpretation of gangsta rap videos feed into the latter stages of her argument in this essay? Write a paragraph explaining how this interpretive section of the essay relates to the end of the essay (where she discusses, in particular, the notorious doings of the LAPD in the early 90s).

4. Use Grant's discussion of NWA to lead into an analysis of lyrics by this same group. Write a paper that extends Grant's analysis to written texts by this group.

Gangsta Rap and American Culture

MICHAEL ERIC DYSON

Michael Eric Dyson is Avalon Professor in the Humanities at the University of Pennsylvania. Dyson's research focuses on race, religion, popular culture, and contemporary crises faced by the African-American community. An acclaimed author and renowned public intellectual, Dyson has written many books, including Holler If You Hear Me: Searching for Tupac Shakur, Between God and Gangsta Rap, *and* Making Malcolm: The Myth and Meaning of Malcolm X. *His most recent book is* Come Hell or High Water: Hurricane Katrina *and the* Color of Disaster. *The piece that follows is an excerpt from Dyson's 1997 work,* Between God and Gangsta Rap.

———————————— ✦ ————————————

The recent attacks on the entertainment industry, especially gangsta rap, by Senator Bob Dole, former Education Secretary William Bennett, and political activist C. Delores Tucker, reveal the fury that popular culture can evoke in a wide range of commentators. As a thirty-five-year-old father of a sixteen-year-old son and as a professor and ordained Baptist minister who grew up in Detroit's treacherous inner city, I too am disturbed by many elements of gangsta rap. But I'm equally anguished by the way many critics have used its artists as scapegoats. How can we avoid the pitfall of unfairly attacking black youth for problems that bewitched our culture long before they gained prominence? First, we should understand what forces drove the emergence of rap. Second, we should place the debate about gangsta rap in the context of a much older debate about "negative" and "positive" black images. Finally, we should acknowledge that gangsta rap crudely exposes harmful beliefs and practices that are often maintained with deceptive civility in much of mainstream society, including many black communities.

If the fifteen-year evolution of hip-hop teaches us anything, it's that history is made in unexpected ways by unexpected people with unexpected results. Rap is now safe from the perils of quick extinction predicted at its humble start. But its birth in the bitter belly of the '70s proved to be a Rosetta stone of black popular culture. Afros, "blunts," funk music, and carnal eruptions define a "back-in-the-day" hip-hop aesthetic. In reality, the severe '70s busted the economic boom of the '60s. The fallout was felt in restructured automobile industries and collapsed steel mills. It was extended in exported employment to foreign markets. Closer to home, there was the depletion of social services to reverse the material ruin of black life. Later, public spaces for black recreation were gutted by Reaganomics or violently transformed by lethal drug economies.

Hip-hop was born in these bleak conditions. Hip-hoppers joined pleasure and rage while turning the details of their difficult lives into craft and capital. This is the world hip-hop would come to "represent": privileged persons speaking for less visible or vocal peers. At their best, rappers shape the tortuous twists of urban fate into lyrical elegies. They represent lives swallowed by too little love or opportunity. They represent themselves and their peers with aggrandizing anthems that boast of their ingenuity and luck in surviving. The art of "representin'" that is much ballyhooed in hip-hop is the witness of those left to tell the afflicted's story.

As rap expands its vision and influence, its unfavorable origins and its relentless quest to represent black youth are both a consolation and challenge to hip-hoppers. They remind rappers that history is not merely the stuff of imperial dreams from above. It isn't just the sanitizing myths of those with political power. Representing history is within reach of those who seize the opportunity to speak for themselves, to represent their own interests at all costs. Even rap's largest controversies are about representation. Hip-hop's attitudes toward women and gays continually jolt in the unvarnished malevolence they reveal. The sharp responses to rap's misogyny and homophobia signify its central role in battles over the cultural representation of other beleaguered groups. This is particularly true of gangsta rap.

5   While gangsta rap takes the heat for a range of social maladies from urban violence to sexual misconduct, the roots of our racial misery remain buried beneath moralizing discourse that is confused and sometimes dishonest. There's no doubt that gangsta rap is often sexist and that it reflects a vicious misogyny that has seized our nation with frightening intensity. It is doubly wounding for black women who are already beset by attacks from outside their communities to feel the thrust of musical daggers to their dignity from within. How painful it is for black women, many of whom have fought valiantly for black pride, to hear the dissonant chord of disdain carried in the angry epithet "bitch."

The link between the vulgar rhetorical traditions expressed in gangsta rap and the economic exploitation that dominates the marketplace is real. The circulation of brutal images of black men as sexual outlaws and black females as "'ho's" in many gangsta rap narratives mirrors ancient stereotypes of black sexual identity. Male and female bodies are turned into commodities. Black sexual desire is stripped of redemptive uses in relationships of great affection or love.

Gangsta rappers, however, don't merely respond to the values and visions of the marketplace; they help shape them as well. The ethic of consumption that pervades our culture certainly supports the rapacious materialism shot through the narratives of gangsta rap. Such an ethic, however, does not exhaust the literal or metaphoric purposes of material wealth in gangsta culture. The imagined and real uses of money to help one's friends, family, and neighborhood occupies a prominent spot in gangsta rap lyrics and lifestyles.

Equally troubling is the glamorization of violence and the romanticization of the culture of guns that pervades gangsta rap. The recent legal troubles of Tupac Shakur, Dr. Dre, Snoop Doggy Dogg, and other gangsta rappers chastens any defense of the genre based on simplistic claims that these artists are merely performing roles that are divorced from real life. Too often for gangsta rappers, life does indeed imitate and inform art.

But gangsta rappers aren't *simply* caving in to the pressure of racial stereotyping and its economic rewards in a music industry hungry to exploit their artistic imaginations. According to this view, gangsta rappers are easily manipulated pawns in a chess game of material dominance where their consciences are sold to the highest bidder. Or else gangsta rappers are viewed as the black face of white desire to distort the beauty of black life. Some critics even suggest that white record executives discourage the production of "positive rap" and reinforce the desire for lewd expressions packaged as cultural and racial authenticity.

But such views are flawed. The street between black artists and record companies runs both ways. Even though black artists are often ripe for the picking—and thus susceptible to exploitation by white and black record labels—many of them are quite sophisticated about the politics of cultural representation. Many gangsta rappers helped to create the genre's artistic rules. Further, they have figured out how to financially exploit sincere and sensational interest in "ghetto life." Gangsta rap is no less legitimate because many "gangstas" turn out to be middle-class blacks faking home boy roots. This fact simply focuses attention on the genre's essential constructedness, its literal artifice. Much of gangsta rap makes voyeuristic whites and naive blacks think they're getting a slice of authentic ghetto life when in reality they're being served colorful exaggerations. That doesn't mean, however, that the best of gangsta rappers don't provide compelling portraits of real social and economic suffering.

Critics of gangsta rap often ignore how hip-hop has been developed without the assistance of a majority of black communities. Even "positive" or "nation-conscious" rap was initially spurned by those now calling for its revival in the face of gangsta rap's ascendancy. Long before white record executives sought to exploit transgressive sexual behavior among blacks, many of us failed to lend support to politically motivated rap. For instance, when political rap group Public Enemy was at its artistic and popular height, most of the critics of gangsta rap didn't insist on the group's prominence in black cultural politics. Instead, Public Enemy and other conscientious rappers were often viewed as controversial figures whose inflammatory racial rhetoric was cause for caution or alarm. In this light, the hue and cry directed against gangsta rap by the new defenders of "legitimate" hip-hop rings false.

Also, many critics of gangsta rap seek to curtail its artistic freedom to transgress boundaries defined by racial or sexual taboo. That's because the burden of representation falls heavily on what may be termed the race artist in a far different manner than the one I've described above. The race artist stands in for black communities. She represents millions of blacks by substituting or sacrificing her desires and visions for the perceived desires and visions of the masses. Even when the race artist manages to maintain relative independence of vision, his or her work is overlaid with, and interpreted within, the social and political aspirations of blacks as a whole. Why? Because of the appalling lack of redeeming or nonstereotypical representations of black life that are permitted expression in our culture.

This situation makes it difficult for blacks to affirm the value of nontraditional or transgressive artistic expressions. Instead of viewing such cultural products through critical eyes—seeing the good and the bad, the productive and destructive aspects of such art—many blacks tend to simply dismiss such work with hypercritical disdain. A suffocating standard of "legitimate" art is thus produced by the limited public availability of complex black art. Either art is seen as redemptive because it uplifts black culture and shatters stereotypical thinking about blacks, or it is seen as bad because it reinforces negative perceptions of black culture.

That is too narrow a measure for the brilliance and variety of black art and cultural imagination. Black folk should surely pay attention to how black art is perceived in our culture. We must be mindful of the social conditions that shape perceptions of our cultural expressions and that stimulate the flourishing of one kind of art versus another. (After all, die-hard hip-hop fans have long criticized how gangsta rap is eagerly embraced by white record companies while "roots" hip-hop is grossly underfinanced.)

But black culture is too broad and intricate—its artistic mani-   15
festations too unpredictable and challenging—for us to be *obsessed* with how white folk view our culture through the lens of our art. And black life is too differentiated by class, sexual identity, gender, region, and nationality to fixate on "negative" or "positive" representations of black culture. Black culture is good and bad, uplifting and depressing, edifying and stifling. All of these features should be represented in our art, should find resonant voicing in the diverse tongues of black cultural expressions.

Gangsta rappers are not the first to face the grueling double standards imposed on black artists. Throughout African-American history, creative personalities have sought to escape or enliven the role of race artist with varying degrees of success. The sharp machismo with which many gangsta rappers reject this office grates on the nerves of many traditionalists. Many critics argue that since gangsta rap is often the only means by which many white Americans come into contact with black life, its pornographic representations and brutal stereotypes of black culture are especially harmful. The understandable but lamentable response of many critics is to condemn gangsta rap out of hand. They aim to suppress gangsta rap's troubling expressions rather than critically engage its artists and the provocative issues they address. Or the critics of gangsta rap use it for narrow political ends that fail to enlighten or better our common moral lives.

Tossing a moralizing *j'accuse* at the entertainment industry may have boosted Bob Dole's standing in the polls over the short term. It did little, however, to clarify or correct the problems to which he has drawn dramatic attention. I'm in favor of changing the moral climate of our nation. I just don't believe that attacking movies, music, and their makers is very helpful. Besides, right-wing talk radio hosts wreak more havoc than a slew of violent films. They're the ones terrorist Timothy McVeigh was inspired by as he planned to bomb the Federal Building in Oklahoma City.

A far more crucial task lies in getting at what's wrong with our culture and what it needs to get right. Nailing the obvious is easy. That's why Dole, along with William Bennett and C. Delores Tucker, goes after popular culture, especially gangsta rap. And the recent attempts of figures like Tucker and Dionne Warwick, as well as national and local lawmakers, to censor gangsta rap or to outlaw its sale to minors are surely misguided. When I testified before the U.S. Senate's Subcommittee on Juvenile Justice, as well as the Pennsylvania House of Representatives, I tried to make this point while acknowledging the need to responsibly confront gangsta rap's problems. Censorship of gangsta rap cannot begin to solve the problems of poor black youth. Nor will it effectively curtail their consumption of music that is already circulated through dubbed tapes and without the benefit of significant airplay.

A crucial distinction needs to be made between censorship of gangsta rap and edifying expressions of civic responsibility and community conscientiousness. The former seeks to prevent the sale of vulgar music that offends mainstream moral sensibilities by suppressing the First Amendment. The latter, however, is a more difficult but rewarding task. It seeks to oppose the expression of misogynistic and sexist sentiments in hip-hop culture through protest and pamphleteering, through community activism, and through boycotts and consciousness raising.

20   What Dole, Bennett, and Tucker shrink from helping us understand—and what all effective public moralists must address—is why this issue now? Dole's answer is that the loss of family values is caused by the moral corruption of popular culture, and therefore we should hold rap artists, Hollywood moguls, and record executives responsible for our moral chaos. It's hard to argue with Dole on the surface, but a gentle scratch reveals that both his analysis and answer are flawed.

Too often, "family values" is a code for a narrow view of how families work, who gets to count as a legitimate domestic unit, and consequently, what values are crucial to their livelihood. Research has shown that nostalgia for the family of the past, when father knew best, ignores the widespread problems of those times, including child abuse and misogyny. Romantic portrayals of the family on television and the big screen, anchored by the myth of the Benevolent Patriarch, hindered our culture from coming to grips with its ugly domestic problems.

To be sure, there have been severe assaults on American families and their values, but they have not come mainly from Hollywood, but from Washington with the dismantling of the Great Society. Cruel cuts in social programs for the neediest, an upward redistribution of wealth to the rich, and an unprincipled conservative political campaign to demonize poor black mothers and their children have left latter-day D. W. Griffiths in the dust. Many of gangsta rap's most vocal black critics (such as Tucker) fail to see how the alliances they forge with conservative white politicians such as Bennett and Dole are plagued with problems.

Bennett and Dole have put up roadblocks to many legislative and political measures that would enhance the fortunes of the black poor they now claim in part to speak for. Their outcry resounds as crocodile tears from the corridors of power paved by bad faith.

Moreover, many of the same conservative politicians who support the attack on gangsta rap also attack black women (from Lani Guinier to welfare mothers), affirmative action, and the redrawing of voting districts to achieve parity for black voters. The war on gangsta rap diverts attention away from the more substantive threat posed to women and blacks by many conservative politicians. Gangsta rap's critics are keenly aware of the harmful effects that genre's misogyny can have on black teens. Irionically, such critics appear oblivious to how their rhetoric of absolute opposition to gangsta rap has been used to justify political attacks on poor black teens.

That doesn't mean that gratuitous violence and virulent misogyny should not be opposed. They must be identified and destroyed. I am wholly sympathetic, for instance, to sharp criticism of gangsta rap's ruinous sexism and homophobia, though neither Dole, Bennett, nor Tucker have made much of the latter plague. "Fags" and "dykes" are prominent in the genre's vocabulary of rage. Critics' failure to make this an issue only reinforces the inferior, invisible status of gay men and lesbians in mainstream and black cultural institutions. Homophobia is a vicious emotion and practice that links mainstream middle-class and black institutions to the vulgar expressions of gangsta rap. There seems to be an implicit agreement between gangsta rappers and political elites that gays, lesbians, and bisexuals basically deserve what they get.

But before we discard the genre, we should understand that gangsta rap often reaches higher than its ugliest, lowest common denominator. Misogyny, violence, materialism, and sexual transgression are not its exclusive domain. At its best, this music draws attention to complex dimensions of ghetto life ignored by many Americans. Of all the genres of hip-hop—from socially conscious rap to black nationalist expressions, from pop to hardcore—gangsta rap has most aggressively narrated the pains and possibilities, the fantasies and fears, of poor black urban youth gangsta rap is situated in the violent climes of postindustrial Los Angeles and its bordering cities. It draws its metaphoric capital in part from the mix of myth and murder that gave the Western frontier a dangerous appeal a century ago.

Gangsta rap is largely an indictment of mainstream and bourgeois black institutions by young people who do not find conventional methods of addressing personal and social calamity useful. The leaders of those institutions often castigate the excessive and romanticized violence of this music without trying to understand what precipitated its rise in the first place. In so doing, they drive a greater wedge between themselves and the youth they so desperately want to help.

If Americans really want to strike at the heart of sexism and misogyny in our communities, shouldn't we take a closer look at one crucial source of these blights: religious institutions, including the synagogue, the temple, and the church? For instance, the central institution of black culture, the black church, which has given hope and inspiration to millions of blacks, has also given us an embarrassing legacy of sexism and misogyny. Despite the great good it has achieved through a heroic tradition of emancipatory leadership, the black church continues to practice and justify *ecclesiastical apartheid.* More than 70 percent of black church members are female, yet they are generally excluded from the church's central station of power, the pulpit. And rarely are the few ordained female ministers elected pastors.

Yet black leaders, many of them ministers, excoriate rappers for their verbal sexual misconduct. It is difficult to listen to civil rights veterans deplore the hostile depiction of women in gangsta rap without mentioning the vicious sexism of the movements for racial liberation of the 1960s. And of course the problem persists in many civil rights organizations today.

Attacking figures like Snoop Doggy Dogg or Tupac Shakur— or the companies that record or distribute them—is an easy out. It allows scapegoating without sophisticated moral analysis and action. While these young black males become whipping boys for sexism and misogyny, the places in our culture where these ancient traditions are nurtured and rationalized—including religious and educational institutions and the nuclear family—remain immune to forceful and just criticism.

30   Corporate capitalism, mindless materialism, and pop culture have surely helped unravel the moral fabric of our society. But the moral condition of our nation is equally affected by political policies that harm the vulnerable and poor. It would behoove Senator Dole to examine the glass house of politics he abides in before he decides to throw stones again. If he really wants to do something about violence, he should change his mind about the ban on assault weapons he seeks to repeal. That may not be as sexy or self-serving as attacking pop culture, but it might help save lives.

Gangsta rap's greatest "sin" may be that it tells the truth about practices and beliefs that rappers hold in common with the mainstream and with black elites. This music has embarrassed mainstream society and black bourgeois culture. It has forced us to confront the demands of racial representation that plague and provoke black artists. It has also exposed our polite sexism and our disregard for gay men and lesbians. We should not continue to blame gangsta rap for ills that existed long before hip-hop uttered its first syllable. Indeed, gangsta rap's in-your-face style may do more to force our nation to confront crucial social problems than countless sermons or political speeches.

Questions for Discussion and Topics for Writing

1. Look at the introduction to Dyson's essay. What rhetorical strategies does he use to set up his piece? Can you identify his essay's argument? If so, how does he set up this argument? List the main claims his essay makes.
2. Dyson writes: "The link between the vulgar rhetorical traditions expressed in gangsta rap and the economic exploitation that dominates the marketplace is real." Read the paragraph for which this quote is the topic sentence, and read the paragraph that immediately follows. Write a summary of the content of the two paragraphs. Follow your summary with an analysis of Dyson's style of argumentation. How is the section you have analyzed typical of Dyson's argumentative style in the essay as a whole?
3. Toward the middle of his essay, Dyson introduces the term *race artist*. Read through this section of his essay carefully (the paragraph in which the term occurs, and the two or three paragraphs that follow). What special burdens are faced by African-American artists? What standards are imposed upon them that are not faced by artists of other races? How do racially based critical standards affect our perception of black-produced art?
4. Much of Dyson's essay is directed against conservative politicians and cultural critics who, he suggests, fail to perceive the breadth and depth of issues that gangsta rap at its best deals with. Write an essay in which you choose an album by a gangsta rapper or group (Ice Cube, NWA, Snoop Dog, Tupac Shakur, etc.), and use it to test some of Dyson's claims.
5. Dyson's essay invokes debates about gangsta rap that were particularly intense in the middle of the 1990s. He brings up figures such as Bob Dole and C. Delores Tucker. Research one or both of these figures in relation to what they had to say about gangsta rap. Write a paper that lays out explicitly the nature of their criticism. What were the exact terms of their criticism? Is Dyson fair in his representation of their views?

Should Ice Cube's Voice Be Chilled?

JON PARELES

Jon Pareles is chief pop music critic for The New York Times, *having assumed this position after the legendary Robert Palmer vacated it in the late 1980s. Pareles previously served as staff writer for* Crawdaddy!, Rolling Stone, *and* The Village Voice. *The following piece appeared in* The New York Times *on December 8, 1991.*

———————————— ✦ ————————————

Ice Cube must be pleased about the reception for *Death Certificate*. In the last month, the album of angry raps zoomed up to No. 2 on Billboard's album chart and brought denunciations from groups that believe Ice Cube's virulent diatribes are racist: proof that he's not only popular but important.

Welcome to the bitterly contested zone of hate speech, which can lead to disciplinary action on some college campuses, arrest in some states and, now, a best-selling album that some people want to squelch. In the past, rockers who slipped into bigotry accused their accusers of nit-picking a line or two. Ice Cube's devotes long stretches of his album to knee-jerk racial and class prejudices.

Hate speech is hard to define but disturbing and threatening to many of its targets, and it has become a major battleground in constitutional law. On Wednesday, the United States Supreme Court heard arguments over whether a St. Paul law against cross-burning violates the First Amendment.

Death Certificate offers more complex (and sometimes contradictory) messages than a cross-burning, but it's not subtle. Ice Cube knows who he hates, and his raps bluntly insult and threaten violence against homosexuals, women, whites who exploit blacks, whites who covet black women, blacks who date white women, Korean shopkeepers, rappers who cross over to pop, the Los Angeles chief of police, self-destructive ghetto blacks and more.

5   The album is divided into "the death side"—purportedly ironic gangster raps about gunplay and sex—and "the life side," which reduces politics to grudge matches, often defined on racial lines. On the life side, Ice Cube is serious. Clearly influenced by the Rev. Louis Farrakhan's Nation of Islam, which he endorses in liner notes, Ice Cube favors black separatism, although he doesn't want his black nation to include homosexuals ("true niggers ain't gay") or yuppies. In his opposition to miscegenation, he probably has a

lot in common with the pre-campaign David Duke and his notions of racial purity.

The Simon Wiesenthal Center, a Jewish human-rights group, urged four major record-store chains to stop selling the album, calling it a "cultural Molotov cocktail." The center had previously protested songs by Public Enemy, Guns 'n' Roses and Madonna, but has not called for an album's withdrawal.

It singled out "No Vaseline," a put down of Ice Cube's former group, N.W.A. The main metaphor is a homophobic one, and at one point Ice Cube envisions hanging and burning N.W.A.'s Eazy-E. The center cited Ice Cube's references to the group's manager as a Jew and his suggestion that N.W.A. "put a bullet in his temple/ You can't be the nigga for life crew with a white Jew telling you what to do." (N.W.A.'s current album is called *Efil4zaggin*, intended to be read backward.)

The center also cited "Black Korea," in which Ice Cube rails against "Oriental one-penny countin' " shopkeepers who "follow me up and down your market." The song threatens a "nationwide boycott" and continues: "Pay respect to the black fist or we'll burn your store right down." The Korean-American Coalition has also condemned that rap. The British album will delete "No Vaseline" and "Black Korea," although the album will still include inflammatory material.

In a rare editorial about an album's contents, Billboard magazine described *Death Certificate* as "the rankest sort of racism and hatemongering." The editorial specifically rejected the Wiesenthal Center's request for removal of the album, but concluded, "Each of us must decide whether or not Ice Cube's record is fit to sell or purchase."

A response by James Bernard, senior editor at the rap maga-   10
zine *The Source*, said Billboard's conclusion favored censorship because the magazine's editors "are too dainty and thin-skinned to hear the anger and rage and frustration that many people are forced to deal with every day."

The rage and frustration are real; so is the demagoguery that would exploit them, and the stupidity of some who are enraged. Ice Cube has decided that his people have been bullied too long, and that the appropriate reaction, as it would be in a gang war, is to identify the enemy and perpetrate vengeance. It's an ugly, simplistic reaction, an escalation rather than a solution. If Ice Cube were running for political office, seeking the power to realize his fantasies, he'd most likely be defeated as decisively as David Duke was.

By not only replying to Ice Cube's ideas but urging that he be silenced, the Wiesenthal Center handed him a tactical bonanza. Now he has opposition, white and Jewish to boot, that's out to muzzle him, proving that even paranoids have real enemies. The issue becomes not whether Ice Cube's raps are worth heeding, but whether they can be heard at all. When Jesse Helms and George Bush win elections with racially divisive commercials, Ice Cube's supporters can easily charge that the censorship is selective. As for hype, many rappers and rockers would give up their drum machines to be perceived as "a cultural Molotov cocktail."

Why are people buying *Death Certificate?* Most, I suspect, are not endorsing its racism; they're savoring the action-movie thrills of Ice Cube's dirty words, his machismo, his gift for violent imagery and his general anger—N.W.A.'s formula. While Ice Cube has said that album is addressed to black listeners, and others don't matter, it's unlikely that *Death Certificate* reached No. 2 solely through sales to blacks; whites are buying it, too, and are probably not persuaded to see themselves as "the devil."

This year, N.W.A., Guns 'n' Roses, Metallica and Skid Row have all hit No. 1 because, doctrines aside, they're mad as hell and ready to profit from it. The recession has left young people un- and underemployed, disillusioned and seething. Some will fall under the sway of political demagogues, some will join gangs; Ice Cube didn't invent us- vs.-them thinking. A far larger audience, however, will just play loud music.

15   None of Ice Cube's ideas—some half-baked, some arguable and some pernicious—will surprise anyone who is aware of the racial rhetoric of American cities. Ice Cube is not the most responsible voice; someone who calls himself "the nigga you love to hate" doesn't pretend to be. Ugly as some of his thinking is, however, he has a right to be heard by those who are curious about his message—and, then, to be challenged for his prejudices.

Questions for Discussion and Topics for Writing

1. Pareles equates Ice Cube with white separatists like David Duke. Is this a fair comparison? Besides the fact that Duke is white and Cube is black, are there any differences between them that might critique this comparison?
2. What evidence does Pareles provide for his claim that Ice Cube's response to systematic racism is an "ugly simplistic reaction"? Do you agree? Why or why not?
3. After reading Pareles, do you agree that "Ice Cube has a right to be heard?" Are you surprised that Pareles ends his article this way? Ultimately, is there any speech that should be censored? If so, can you give some examples? What is the price for deeming some speech unspeakable?

4. Find a newspaper article that discusses a hip hop album. Then, listen to the album or read the lyrics to several of the songs. Compare what you hear on the album to what you read in the article. Then construct an argument in response to the article. Do you agree with its assessment? Disagree? Both? Explain your view using quotations from both the album and the article to support your claims.

Gangsta Culture

BELL HOOKS

bell hooks is Distinguished Professor of English at City College in New York. One of the leading scholars and public intellectuals of her generation, hooks has written dozens of articles and books on the intersecting issues of race, feminism, and politics. Her published works include Ain't I a Woman? Black Women and Feminism, Feminist Theory from Margin to Center, Talking Back: Thinking Feminist, Thinking Black, *and* Teaching to Transgress: Education as the Practice of Freedom. *The following piece is taken from* We Real Cool: Black Men and Masculinity *(2004).*

◆

. . . Young beautiful brilliant black power male militants were the first black leftists to loudly call out the evils of capitalism. And during that call they unmasked wage slavery, naming it for what it was. Yet at the end of the day a black man needed money to live. If he was not going to get it working for the man, it could come from hustling his own people. Black power militants, having learned from Dr. King and Malcolm X how to call out the truth of capitalist-based materialism, identified it as gangsta culture. Patriarchal manhood was the theory and gangsta culture was its ultimate practice. No wonder then that black males of all ages living the protestant work ethic, submitting in the racist white world, envy the lowdown hustlers in the black communities who are not slaves to white power. As one young gang member put it, "working was considered weak."

Black men of all classes have come to see the market-driven capitalist society we are living in as a modern Babylon without rules, without any meaningful structure of law and order as a world where "gangsta culture" is the norm. Powerful patriarchal players (mostly white but now and then men of color) in mainstream corporate or high-paying government jobs do their own version of the gangsta culture game; they just do not get caught or when they do they know how to play so they do not end up in jail for life or on death row. This is the big stage most black male hustlers want to perform on, but they rarely get a chance because they lack the educational preparation needed. Or their lust for easy money that comes quick and fast does them in: soul murder by greed. In his book *The Envy of the World: On Being a Black Man in America*, Ellis Cose deliberately downplays the impact of racially based exploitation on black men's lives. To make his point that black men, and not systems of domination (which he suggests they should be able to transcend with the right values), are the problem, he must exclude any discussion of work, of joblessness.

Cose comes close to a discussion of work when he writes about young black male investment in gangsta culture but he never really highlights black male thinking about jobs and careers. When discussing the lure of the "street" he makes the important point that the street often seduces bright young males attracting them to a life of hustling, of selling drugs. Cose contends: "The lure of drug money for young inner-city boys is so strong because it offers such huge rewards to those who otherwise would have very little." He quotes a former drug dealer who puts it this way: "I came from poverty and I wanted nice things and money and everything. . . . I quit high school and . . . I just got caught up. . . . It was like, 'I'm eighteen. I want my money now.'" The grandiose sense of entitlement to money that this black male felt is part of the seduction package of patriarchal masculinity.

Every day black males face a culture that tells them that they can never really achieve enough money or power to set them free from racist white tyranny in the work world. Mass media schools the young in the values of patriarchal masculinity. On mass media screens today, whether television or movies, mainstream work is usually portrayed as irrelevant, money is god, and the outlaw guy who breaks the rules prevails. Contrary to the notion that black males are lured by the streets, mass media in patriarchal culture has already prepared them to seek themselves in the streets, to find their manhood in the streets, by the time they are six years old. Propaganda works best when the male mind is young and not yet schooled in the art of critical thinking. Few studies examine the link between black male fascination with gangsta culture and early childhood consumption of unchecked television and movies that glamorize brute patriarchal maleness. A biased imperialist white-supremacist patriarchal mass media teaches young black males that the street will be their only home. And it lets mainstream black males know that they are just an arrest away from being on the street. This media teaches young black males that the patriarchal man is a predator, that only the strong and the violent survive.

This is what the young black power males believed. It is why so many of them are dead. Gangsta culture is the essence of patriarchal masculinity. Popular culture tells young black males that only the predator will survive. Cleaver explains the message in *Soul on Ice:* "In a culture that secretly subscribes to the piratical ethic of 'every man for himself'—the social Darwinism of 'survival of the fittest' being far from dead, manifesting itself in our ratrace political system of competing parties, in our dog-eat-dog economic system of profit and loss, and in our adversary system of justice where truth is secondary to the skill and connections of the advocate—the logical culmination of this ethic, on a person-to-person level, is that the weak are seen as the natural and just prey of the strong." This is the ethic lots of boys in our society learn from mass media, but black boys, way too many of them fatherless, take it to heart.

Prisons in our nation are full of intelligent capable black men who could have accomplished their goals of making money in a responsible legitimate way but who commit crimes for small amounts of money because they cannot delay gratification. Locked down, utterly disenfranchised, black men in prison are in a place where critical reflection and education for critical consciousness could occur (as was the case for Malcolm X), but more often than not it is a place where patriarchal maleness is reinforced. Gangsta culture is even more glamorized in our nation's prisons because they are the modern jungle where only the strong survive. This is the epitome of the dog-eat-dog Darwinian universe Cleaver describes. Movies represent the caged black male as strong and powerful (this is the ultimate false consciousness) and yet these images are part of the propaganda that seduce and entice black male audiences of all classes. Black boys from privileged classes learn from this same media to envy the manhood of those who relish their roles as predators, who are eager to kill and be killed in their quest to get the money, to get on top.

In his memoir *The Ice Opinion*, rapper and actor Ice T talks about the lure of crime as a way to make easy money. Describing crime as "like any other job" he calls attention to the fact that most young black men have no problem with committing crimes if it gets them money. He makes the point that it is not only money that attracts black males to criminal activity, that "there's definitely something sexy about crime" because "it takes a lot of courage to fuck the system." There is rarely anything sexy about paid labor. Often black males choose crime to avoid the hierarchy in the work-force that places them on the bottom. As Ice T explains: "Crime is an equal-opportunity employer. It never discriminates. Anybody can enter the field. You don't need a college education. You don't need a G.E.D. You don't have to be any special color. You don't need white people to like you. You're self-employed. As a result, criminals are very independent people. They don't like to take or-ders. That's why they get into this business. There are no applica-tions to fill out, no special dress codes. . . . There's a degree of freedom in being a criminal." Of course Ice T's cool description of crime seems rather pathetic when stacked against the large num-ber of black males who are incarcerated, many of them for life, for "easy money" crimes that gained them less than a hundred dollars. The fantasy of easy money is pushed in popular culture by movies. It is pushed by state-supported lotteries. And part of the seduction is making individuals, especially men, feel that they deserve money they have not earned.

Of course there are lots of black males out in the world making money by legitimate and illegitimate means and they are still trapped in the pain of patriarchal masculinity. Unlike the world of responsible legitimate work, which, when not exploitative, can be humanizing, the world of money making, of greed, always dehu-manizes. Hence the reality that black males who have "made it" in the mainstream often see their lives as empty and meaningless. They may be as nihilistic as their disenfranchised underclass poor black brothers. Both may turn to addiction as a way to ease the pain.

Very few black men of any class in this nation feel they are do-ing work they find meaningful, work that gives them a sense of purpose. Although there are more black male academics than ever before in our nation, even among the highest paid there is a lack of job satisfaction. Work satisfies black males more when it is not perceived to be the location of patriarchal manhood but rather when it is the site of meaningful social interaction as well as fulfilling labor. There has been a resurgence of black-owned busi-nesses in the nineties precisely because many black male entre-preneurs find that racism abounds in work arenas to such a grave extent that even jobs they liked were still made unbearably stress-ful. Owning one's own business and being the boss has allowed individual black men to find dignity in labor.

10   Hedonistic materialist consumerism with its overemphasis on having money to waste has been a central cause of the

demoralization among working men of all races. Responsible middle-class black men who embody all that is best about the Protestant work ethic find that work satisfies best when it is not placed at the center of one's evaluation of manhood or selfhood but rather when it is seen simply as one aspect of a holistic life. At times an individual black male may be somewhat dissatisfied with his job and yet still feel it is worthwhile to endure this dissatisfaction because of the substantive ways he uses his wages to create a more meaningful life. This holds true for working black men across class. Throughout my life, I have been inspired by the example of my father. Working within a racist system where he was often treated disrespectfully by unenlightened white people, he still managed to have standards of excellence that governed his job performance. He, along with my mom, taught all his children the importance of commitment to work and giving your best at any job.

Despite these lessons our brother K. has been, throughout his life, lured by easy money. Lucky, in that his attempts to participate in gangsta culture happened early enough in his life to push him in other directions in midlife, he is still struggling to find a career path that will provide greater satisfaction for the soul. Like so many black males in our culture, he wants to make lots of money. Though he has a responsible well-paying job, his ability to be proud of where he is and what he has accomplished is often diminished by fantasies of having more. When he focuses his energies on doing more, rather than having more, his life satisfaction increases.

During the periods of his life when he was unemployed K. did spend his time working on self-development. Many black males in our culture face joblessness at some point in their lives. For some unemployment may be their lot for months, for others years. Patriarchal masculinity, which says that if a man is not a worker he is nothing, assaults the self-esteem of any man who absorbs this thinking. Often black males reject this way of thinking about work. This rejection is a positive gesture, but they often do not replace this rejection of the patriarchal norm with a constructive alternative.

Given the state of work in our nation, a future where widespread joblessness, downsizing, and reduction in wages is becoming more normal, all men, and black men in particular, are in need of alternative visions of work. Throughout their history in the United States decolonized black men have found those alternatives. Significantly, they see unemployment as time to nurture creativity and self-awareness. Not making money opened the space for them to rethink investment in materialism; it changed their perspectives. They engaged in a paradigm shift. Martin Luther King, Jr., in his critique of materialism, describes this shift as a "revolution of values." King invited black men and all men to "work within the framework of democracy to bring about a better distribution of wealth" using "powerful economic resources to eliminate poverty from the earth." Enlightened individual black men who make no money or not enough money have learned to turn away from the marketplace and turn toward being—finding out who they are, what they feel, and what they want out of life within and beyond the world of money. Even though they have not chosen "leisure" time, they have managed to use it productively. In his 1966 anti-war speech at Berkeley, Stokely Carmichael offered this utopian vision: "The society we seek to build among black people is not a capitalistic one. It is a society in which the spirit of community and of humanistic love prevail." Imagine the revolution of values and actions that would occur if black men were collectively committed to creating love and building community.

Until a progressive vision of productive unemployment can be shared with black men collectively, intervening on the patriarchal assumption that equates unemployment with loss of value as well as challenging the materialist assumption that you are what you can buy, most black men (like many of their white counterparts among the poor and disenfranchised) will continue to confront a work world and a culture of joblessness that demoralizes and dehumanizes the spirit. Black male material survival will be ensured only as they turn away from fantasies of wealth and the notion that money will solve all problems and make everything better, and turn toward the reality of sharing resources, reconceptualizing work, and using leisure for the practice of self-actualization.

Questions for Discussion and Topics for Writing

1. In what ways does gangsta culture serve as the vehicle for patriarchal manhood? How is this equation related to work?

2. Early in the essay, hooks quotes Ice T, who considers crime as "like any other job." How does this statement become ironic in the context of hooks's argument? In what ways does the criminal desire to achieve "a degree of freedom" from the workforce make work the central aspect of one's identity?

3. How does work offer a palliative to destructive patriarchal manhood? How does it shift from a paradigm of "doing more, rather than having more"? Do you agree with hooks's estimation of what she argues is "best about the Protestant work ethic"?

4. In the penultimate paragraph, hooks describes an "alternative vision of work" that sees "unemployment as a time to nurture creativity and self-awareness." Alternatively, in the last paragraph, hooks turns her attention to the current patriarchal vision that prefers "fantasies of wealth." How does hip hop participate in both of these visions? In what ways does hip hop validate Stokely Carmichael's utopian vision of "society in which the spirit of community and of humanistic love prevail"? In what ways does hip hop perpetuate "the materialist assumption that you are what you can buy"?

5. In an essay, describe in detail what it means for you to be either a man or a woman. Then explore the ways that this identity is both liberating and limiting. By considering the social rules of your gender role, are there alternative ways of expressing your male or female identity? Use insights from hooks to support your answers.

Making Connections

1. Stagolee, a historical figure and folk hero, is considered by many critics to be a prototype of the contemporary gangsta rapper persona. Use the Internet or other research sources to gather information about Stagolee. How does this character help connect hip hop culture—in particular gangsta rap—to African-American cultural traditions?

2. Who was C. Delores Tucker? How did this African-American Civil Rights leader find herself embroiled in controversies involving gangsta rap and its supposed ill effects on the status of blacks in contemporary American society? Locate newspaper articles detailing Tucker's involvement in this culture war. What were the terms of her criticism of gangsta rap? How did she personalize her attacks? How did rap music respond to her, especially leading rappers like Tupac Shakur?

3. Watch the video footage of the Rodney King beating that occurred in Los Angeles on March 3, 1991. Describe what you see in a short, detailed, written summary. Now, write an essay in which you discuss how your experience of the video might affect the way you listen to and interpret gangsta rap. How might the King beating help us understand the anti-social stance of gangsta rap, particularly gangsta rap's hostility toward law enforcement (as exemplified in expressions such as "fuck tha police")?

4. Research the rapper Bo$$. Write a short summary of her life and career. How did her career come to an end? What was the role of the *Wall Street Journal* in her demise as a rapper? Write a paper in which you discuss the issue of authenticity as it applies to a gangsta rapper's public image. To what extent is this image "real" or manufactured? Why is realism or "keeping it real" so vital to a gangsta rapper's persona? To what extent is keeping it real—in the context of a commodified culture like hip hop—ever really possible?

CHAPTER 5

Mapping Rap: East Coast, West Coast, Third Coast, and Beyond

*Communities are to be distinguished, not by their falsity/
genuineness, but by the style in which they are imagined.*
—BENEDICT ANDERSON, *Imagined Communities*

At its imagined roots, America is a place of discovery, invention, and exile. This has been palpably embedded in the way the map of America has been drawn and redrawn. As a decidedly American music, hip hop is also about discovery, invention, and exile. With graffiti, hip hop reclaims and redesigns public space; with specific styles of dress; it unmoors cultural boundaries from specific locales. Moreover, early D-Js like Africa Bambataa, Kool Herc, and Grandmaster Flash carved up the contours of the Bronx into separate territories. From gangsta rap emerged the conception of the 'hood that conceived of the contours of nation in terms of east, west, and third coasts. Recently, many rappers assert that, as Ice Cube put it, "every 'hood's the same," making the idea of territorial borders portable. At all times and in all places, hip hop has been powerfully used to help re-imagine the boundaries, and even its history—to know and declare "Where you're from"—is understood in spatial terms.

Such declarations of loyalty to specific locales or shout-outs seem to begin and end nearly every song. To some, the apparent ubiquity of these pronouncements may start to sound redundant like verbal tropes without much consequence other than to start or wrap up lyrics. However, considered in the context of reimagining a community, shout-outs reveal a potent political and social force. For example, Jay-Z is famous for giving shout-outs to the Marcy

Projects (a housing development in Brooklyn) during his concerts. For Jay-Z fans, the Marcy Projects is an informal capital, part of their topography even if they are listening in D.C., Detroit, or California and have never lived in or been to the Projects.

On the hip hop compilation album *No More Prisons*, there are shout-outs to all those living in prisons. The lines of community are redrawn and extended to contain the matrix of prisons which, in very real ways, affect the communities to which they are tied. With a disproportionate number of young black men in prison, those who are locked up are felt in their absence, and it is the purpose of the song to reinstate their presence in the largely African-American communities to which they remain tied. By acknowledging the ways in which the prison system is an integral part of the "ghetto" and by drawing attention to a social crisis existing in lower-income urban communities that are otherwise marginalized and ignored by mainstream America, hip hop becomes a way of acknowledging and reclaiming those who have been dispossessed and exiled.

But it is not just shout-outs that redefine space. Within hip hop, there seem to be endless ways to reimagine and redraw the map. In the song "I'm an African," Dead Prez makes the geography of America subsidiary to Africa, claiming, "It's not about where you stay, it's about the motherland." Recalling the philosophy of Marcus Garvey and dovetailing on similar protestations by earlier rap groups such as Public Enemy, Dead Prez rejects any direct identification with America, reminding listeners that the history of Africans in America is one of forced migration and enslavement. In the song, the states of America are not united by their political relationship to one another but by virtue of the fact that in every state there exist the descendents of the African Diaspora. Even more, Dead Prez personifies Africa as "momma" while making personal identity a matter of country by insisting "I'm an African." This chiasmus reminds listeners how much personal identity is linked to the ways one chooses to delineate community and, by extension, nation. By redefining their relationship to both Africa and America and by reuniting disparate communities by redefining the borders of the United States, Dead Prez ingeniously shows the ways in which the political, social, and personal become intertwined and require imaginative responses.

Of course, reimagining place as a means of reclaiming personal and social identity did not begin with hip hop. It is ever-present in African-American music. Take just one earlier example—Ella Fitzgerald's famous song "Take the A Train." If it were not so famous, the song would be considered strange for devoting its lyrics to giving directions. Why would the listener who knew Fitzgerald's music need directions to Harlem? The song is thus directed toward the listener who is somehow an outsider and not part of Fitzgerald's immediate community. Most likely, the song is directly addressed to the white, upper-class socialite, the *flaneur* who liked to "slum" in Harlem. Thus, the song serves as a protest against racist attitudes that at once enforce and exploit ghettoization, revealing how such a system maintains a racial underclass even while recognizing its profound cultural production.

This same type of invitation to and revision of place continues in hip hop with songs like Gang Starr's "The Place Where We Dwell." As with "Take the A Train," the song gives directions, in this case, to Brooklyn. As with "Take the A Train," "The Place Where We Dwell" is also an occasion to acknowledge a place with a rich, black cultural heritage. Like "Take the A Train," the song is an invitation, but the invitation is clearly double-edged, using invitation as a means of representation by maintaining a clear distinction between insider and outsider. While the outsider is invited in, the invitation makes clear that Brooklyn isn't necessarily a safe place to be an outsider. In an incisive twist to the idea of America welcoming immigrants with open arms at the same time that it marginalizes them, Gang Starr at once invites the outsider in and then slams the door. In this case, however, the visitor is imagined as a participant in the dominant culture while the rapper represents the socially marginalized. As the word *dwell* in the title reminds us by suggesting impermanence and transience, the song, like Dead Prez's, subtly recalls the uprootedness of African American beginnings. So here, those historically dispossessed become empowered while those usually in power become the tourists and the strangers, suddenly discovering that they, too, are exiles.

These few examples begin to suggest ways in which hip hop redraws the lines of community and reenvisions both the local and the national. By breaking down easy distinctions between here and there, us and them, hip hop—now an international phenomenon—reimagines the global as well. While it is possible to argue that in going global hip hop is inadvertently participating in America's colonizing impulses, hip hop seems to distinguish itself by activating the latent powers and particularities of local cultures rather than merely imposing itself and making a place over in its own image. By representing where it's at, exactly when, and particularly whom, hip hop has gone from redrawing the lines of New York's five boroughs to revising the borders of a nation, to reimagining the contours of the globe.

'Represent': Race, Space, and Place in Rap Music[1]

Murray Forman

Murray Forman is Assistant Professor of Communication Studies at Northeastern University. Forman's main research interests are the social uses of popular music and the critical analysis of media industries, cultural production, and communication. Forman's published works include The 'Hood Comes First: Race, Space, and Place in Rap *and* Hip-Hop and That's the Joint!: The Hip-Hop Studies Reader, *co-edited with Mark Anthony Neal. This selection comes from* Popular Music, *January 2001.*

———————— ✦ ————————

. . . Describing the early stages of rap music's emergence within the hip hop culture for an MTV "Rap-umentary", Grandmaster Flash, one of the core DJs of the early scene, recalls the spatial distribution of sound systems and crews in metropolitan New York:

> We had territories. It was like, Kool Herc had the west side. Bam had Bronx River. DJ Breakout had way uptown past Gun Hill. Myself, my area was like 138th Street, Cypress Avenue, up to Gun Hill, so that we all had our territories and we all had to respect each other.

The documentary's images embellish Flash's commentary, displaying a computer generated map of the Bronx with coloured sections demarcating each DJ's territory as it is mentioned, graphically separating the enclaves that comprise the main area of operations for the competing sound systems.

This emphasis on territoriality involves more than just a geographical arrangement of cultural workers and the regionalism of cultural practices. It illuminates a particular relationship to space or, more accurately, a relationship to particular places. As Flash conveys it, the sound systems that formed the backbone of the burgeoning hip hop scene were identified by their audiences and followers according to the overlapping influences of personae and turf. The territories were tentatively claimed through the ongoing cultural practices that occurred within their bounds and were reinforced by the circulation of those who recognized and accepted their perimeters. It is not at all insignificant that most of the dominant historical narratives pertaining to the emergence of hip hop (i.e., Hager 1984; Toop 1984) identify a transition from gang-oriented affiliations (formed around protection of turf) to music and break dance affiliations that maintained and, in some cases, intensified the important structuring systems of territoriality.

Flash's reference to the importance of "respect" is not primarily addressing a respect for the skills or character of his competitors (although, elsewhere (George 1993) he acknowledges this as well). Rather, his notion of respect is related to the geographies that he maps; it is based on the existence of circumscribed domains of authority and dominance that have been established among the various DJs. These geographies are inhabited and bestowed with value; they are understood as lived places and localized sites of significance, as well as being understood within the market logic that includes a product (the music in its various live or recorded forms) and a consumer base (various audience formations). The proprietary discourse also implies, therefore, that even in its infancy hip hop cartography was to some extent shaped by a refined capitalist logic and the existence of distinct market regions. Without sacrificing the basic geographic components of territory, possession and group identity that play such an important role among gang-oriented activities, the representation of New York's urban spaces was substantially revised as hip hop developed.

Clearly, however, the geographical boundaries that Flash describes and which are visually mapped in the documentary were never firm or immovable. They were cultural boundaries that were continually open to negotiation and renegotiation by those who inhabited their terrains and who circulated throughout the city's boroughs. As the main form of musical expression within the hip hop culture, the early DJ sound systems featured a series of practices that linked the music to other mobile practices, such as graffiti art and "tagging." Together, these overlapping practices and methods of constructing place-based identities, and of inscribing and enunciating individual and collective presence, created the bonds upon which affiliations were forged within specific social geographies. Hip hop's distinct practices introduced new forms of expression that were contextually linked to conditions in a city comprised of an amalgamation of neighbourhoods and boroughs with their own highly particularised social norms and cultural nuances.

HIP HOP, SPACE AND PLACE

Rap music takes the city and its multiple spaces as the foundation of its cultural production. In the music and lyrics, the city is an

audible presence, explicitly cited and digitally sampled in the reproduction of the aural textures of the urban environment. Since
its inception in the mid-to-late 1970s, hip hop culture has always
maintained fiercely defended local ties and an in-built element of
competition waged through hip hop's cultural forms of rap, break-
dancing and graffiti. This competition has traditionally been
staged within geographical boundaries that demarcate turf and
territory among various crews, cliques, and posses, extending and
altering the spatial alliances that had previously cohered under
other organisational structures, including but not exclusive to
gangs. Today, a more pronounced level of spatial awareness is one
of the key factors distinguishing rap and hip hop culture from the
many other cultural and subcultural youth formations currently
vying for attention.

Throughout its historical evolution, it is evident that there has
been a gradually escalating urgency with which minority youth
use rap in the deployment of discourses of urban locality or
"place," with the trend accelerating noticeably since 1987–88.
With the discursive shift from the spatial abstractions framed by
the notion of "the ghetto" to the more localised and specific discursive construct of the "hood" occurring in 1987–88 (roughly cor-
responding with the rise and impact of rappers on the U.S. West
Coast), there has been an enhanced emphasis on the powerful ties
to place that both anchor rap acts to their immediate environments and set them apart from other environments and other
hoods as well as from other rap acts and their crews which inhabit
similarly demarcated spaces.

Commenting in 1988 on rap's "nationwide" expansions beyond
New York's boroughs, Nelson George writes, "Rap and its Hip Hop
musical underpinning is now the national youth music of black
America . . . rap's gone national and is in the process of going regional" (George 1992, p. 80). George was right, as rap was rising out
of the regions and acts were emerging from the South (Miami-
based 2 Live Crew or Houston's The Geto Boys), the Northwest
(Seattle's Sir Mix-A-Lot and Kid Sensation), the San Francisco Bay
area (Digital Underground, Tupac, Too Short), Los Angeles (Ice T,
N.W.A.) and elsewhere. Indeed, the significance of the east-west
split within U.S. rap cannot be overstated since it has led to several
intense confrontations between artists representing each region
and is arguably the single most divisive factor within U.S. hip hop
to date. Until the mid-1990s, artists associated with cities in the
Midwest or southern states often felt obligated to align themselves
with either East or West, or else they attempted to sidestep the issue

deftly without alienating audiences and deriding either coast. In the past several years, however, Houston, Atlanta and New Orleans have risen as important rap production centers and have consequently emerged as powerful forces in their own right.

Today, the emphasis is on place, and groups explicitly advertise their home environments with names such as Compton's Most Wanted, Detroit's Most Wanted, the Fifth Ward Boyz, and South Central Cartel, or else they structure their home territory into titles and lyrics, constructing a new internally meaningful hip hop cartography. The explosion of localized production centers and regionally influential producers and artists has drastically altered the hip hop map and production crews have sprung up throughout North America. These producers have also demonstrated a growing tendency to incorporate themselves as localized businesses (often buying or starting companies unrelated to the music industry in their local neighbourhoods, such as auto customizing and repair shops) and to employ friends, family members and members of their wider neighbourhoods. Extending Nelson George's observation, it now seems possible to say that rap, having gone regional, is in the process of going local. . . .

HOMEBOYS AND PRODUCTION POSSES

Greg Tate suggests that, "every successful rap group is a black fraternal organization, a posse" (1992, p. 134). On the same theme, Tricia Rose writes that "rappers' emphasis on posses and neighbourhoods has brought the ghetto back into the public consciousness" (1994, p. 11). For Public Enemy's Chuck D, posse formations are a necessary response to the fragmentive effects of capitalism: "the only way that you exist within that mould is that you have to put together a 'posse', or a team to be able to penetrate that structure, that block, that strong as steel structure that no individual can break" (Eure and Spady 1991, p. 330). As each of these commentators suggests, the posse is the fundamental social unit binding a rap act and its production crew together, creating a collective identity that is rooted in place and within which the creative process unfolds. It is not rare for an entire label to be defined along posse lines with the musical talent, the producers and various peripheral associates bonding under the label's banner.

With collective identities being evident as a nascent reference throughout rap's history in group names like The Sugarhill Gang, Doug E. Fresh and the Get Fresh Crew, X-Clan, or the 2 Live Crew, the term "posse" was later unambiguously adopted by rap artists such as California's South Central Posse or Orlando's DJ Magic Mike, whose crew records under the name "the Royal Posse". In virtually all cases, recording acts align themselves within a relatively coherent posse structure, sharing labels and producers, appearing on each other's recording and touring together.

The term *posse* is defined as a "strong force or company" (*Concise Oxford Dictionary*, 1985) and for many North Americans it summons notions of lawlessness and frontier justice that were standard thematic elements of Hollywood westerns in the 1940s and 1950s. This is, in fact, the basis of the term as it is applied within rap circles, although its current significance is related more precisely to the ways in which the Jamaican posse culture has over the years adapted the expressive terminology and gangster imagery of the cinema to its own cultural systems. In her illuminating research on the sinister complexities of the Jamaican posse underworld, Laurie Gunst (1995) explains how the posse system grew under the specific economic, political, and cultural conditions of mid-1970s Jamaica, evolving into a stratified and violent gang culture that gained strength through the marijuana, cocaine and crack trade. As she explains, the Jamaican posse system has, since 1980, been transplanted to virtually every major North American city.

The Jamaican posse expansion is important in this context as it coincides almost precisely with the emergence of rap and hip hop in New York's devastated uptown ghetto environments. This connection is strengthened when rap's hybrid origins that were forged in the convergence of Jamaican sound systems and South Bronx funk are considered. The concept of the posse has, through various social mechanisms and discursive overlays, been traced upon many of rap's themes, images, and postures that take the forms of the pimp, hustler, gambler and gangster in the music's various subgenres that evolved after 1987. Rap has also been influenced by the gangland models provided by the New York mafia and Asian Triad gangs.

Since roughly 1987 hip hop culture has also been influenced by alliances associated with West Coast gang systems. Numerous rap album covers and videos feature artists and their posses representing their gang, their regional affiliations or their local 'hood with elaborate hand gestures. The practice escalated to such an extent that, in an effort to dilute the surging territorial aggression, Black Entertainment Television (BET) passed a rule forbidding explicitly gang-related hand signs on its popular video programmes.

"THE 'HOOD TOOK ME UNDER": HOME, TURF AND IDENTITY

It is necessary to recognise that the home territory of a rapper or rap group is a testing ground, a place to hone skills and to gain a local reputation. This is accurately portrayed in the 1992 Ernest Dickerson film *Juice* where the expression "local" is attributed to the young DJ Q in one instance suggesting community ties and home alliances whereas, in another context, it is summoned as a pejorative term that reflects a lack of success and an inability to mobilise his career beyond the homefront. In interviews and on recordings most rappers refer to their early days, citing the time spent with their "home boys", writing raps, perfecting their turntable skills, and taking the stage at parties and local clubs or dances (Cross 1993). Their perspective emerges from within the highly localised conditions that they know and the places they inhabit.

As a site of affiliation and circulation, the 'hood provides a setting for particular group interactions which are influential in rap music's evolution. In rap, there is a widespread sense that an act cannot succeed without first gaining approval and support from the crew and the 'hood. Successful acts are expected to maintain connections to the 'hood and to "keep it real" thematically, rapping about situations, scenes and sites that comprise the lived experience of the 'hood. At issue is the complex question of authenticity as rap posses continually strive to reaffirm their connections to the 'hood in an attempt to mitigate the negative accusations that they have sold out in the event of commercial or crossover success. Charisse Jones has noted a dilemma confronting successful rap artists who suddenly have the economic means to "get over" and leave the 'hood. As she writes in the *New York Times* (24 September 1995, p. 43), contemporary artists such as Snoop Dogg or Ice T are often criticised for rapping about ghetto poverty and gang aggression while living in posh suburban mansions.

Those who stay in the 'hood generally do so to be closer to friends and family, closer to the posse. While a common rationale for staying in the 'hood is familiarity and family bonds, in numerous cases artists also justify their decisions to stay along a creative rationale, suggesting that the 'hood provides the social contexts and raw resources for their lyrics. Others leave with some regret, suggesting that the 'hood may constitute "home" but its various tensions and stresses make it an entirely undesirable place to live (this is even more frequent among rappers with children to support and nurture); there is no romanticising real poverty or real danger.

The 'hood is, however, regularly constructed within the discursive frame of the "home," and the dual process of "turning the 'hood out" or "representing" (which involves creating a broader profile for the home territory and its inhabitants while showing respect for the nurture it provides) is now a required practice among hard-core rap acts. The posse is always explicitly acknowledged and individual members are greeted on disk and in live concerts with standard "shout-outs" that frequently cite the streets and localities from which they hail. This continual reference to the important value of social relations based in the 'hood refutes the damning images of an oppressed and joyless underclass that are so prevalent in the media and contemporary social analyses. Rap may frequently portray the nation's gritty urban underside, but its creators also communicate the importance of places and the people that build community within them. In this interpretation, there is an insistent emphasis on support, nurture and community that coexists with the grim representations that generally cohere in the images and discourses of ghetto life.

As in all other popular music forms, "paying dues" is also part of the process of embarking on a rap music career, and the local networks of support and encouragement, from in-group affiliations to local club and music scenes, are exceedingly important factors in an act's professional development. One way that this is facilitated is through the posse alliances and local connections that form around studios and producers. For example, in describing the production house once headed by DJ Mark, The 45 King, the rap artist Fab 5 Freddy recalls that "he had this posse called the Flavor Unit out there in New Jersey . . . He has like a Hip Hop training room out there, an incredible environment where even if you weren't good when you came in, you'd get good just being around there" (Nelson and Gonzales 1991, p. xiii).[2] This pattern is replicated in numerous instances and is also exemplified by the production/posse structure of Rap-A-Lot Records in Houston (home to acts such as the Geto Boys, Scarface, Big Mike, Caine, and The Fifth Ward Boyz) where the company was forced to relocate its offices because "artists were always kicking it there with their posses like it was a club" (*Rap Sheet*, October 1992, p. 18). By coming up through the crew, young promising artists learn the ropes, acquire lessons in craft and showmanship, attain stage or studio experience and exposure and, quite frequently, win record deals based on their apprenticeships and posse connections.

20   Few rap scholars (Tricia Rose and Brian Cross being notable exceptions) have paid attention to these formative stages and the

slow processes of developing MC and DJ skills. There is, in fact, a
trajectory to an artist's development that is seldom accounted for.
In practice, artists' lyrics and rhythms must achieve success on the
home front first, where the flow, subject matter, style and image
must resonate meaningfully among those who share common
bonds to place, to the posse and to the 'hood. In this sense, when
rappers refer to the "local flavour", they are identifying the detailed inflections that respond to and reinforce the significance of
the music's particular sites of origin and which might be recog-
nised by others elsewhere as being unique, interesting and, ultimately, marketable.

THE SPATIALISATION OF PRODUCTION STYLES

The posse structures that privilege place and the 'hood can be seen
as influential elements in the evolution of new rap artists as well
as relevant forces in the emergence of new, regionally definable
sounds and discourses about space and place. For example, critics
and rappers alike acknowledge the unique qualities of the West
Coast G-funk sound which defined a production style that
emerged with Dr Dre's work on the *Deep Cover* soundtrack and the
release of his 1992 classic *The Chronic* (Death Row/Interscope),
and arguably reached its apex with the 1994 release of Warren G's
Regulate . . . G Funk Era (Violator/Rush Associated Labels). Other
local artists in this period, such as the Boo Yaa Tribe, Above the
Law, Compton's Most Wanted, and DJ Quick, also prominently
featured variations on the G-funk sound and reinforced its influence in the industry as an identifiable West Coast subgenre.
G-funk makes ample use of standard funk grooves by artists including George Clinton, Bootsy Collins, Gap Band, or the late
Roger Troutman, and is characterized as being "laid-back" and
sparse, featuring slow beats and longer sample loops. While it was
regarded as a regionally distinct sound, it was also often related
specifically to Dr Dre's production style and was comparatively
categorized by its difference from the more cacophonous East
Coast jams (recognisable in the early work of the Bomb Squad, the
production crew of the rap act Public Enemy). As Brian Cross
(1993) notes, however, the impact of the G-funk style among California rap acts is also related to the extended influence of late
1970s funk music in the Southwest that was a consequence of limited access to independently produced and distributed rap product
in the early 1980s, delaying rap's geographic expansion from New
York to the Los Angeles area.

Explaining the Bomb Squad's production processes following the release of Public Enemy's *Fear of a Black Planet* (1990, Def Jam), Chuck D describes his production posse's familiarity with various regional styles and tastes and their attempts to integrate the differences into the album's tracks. As he states:

> Rap has different feels and different vibes in different parts of the country. For example, people in New York City don't drive very often, so New York used to be about walking around with your radio. But that doesn't really exist anymore. It became un-fashionable because some people were losing their *lives* over them, and also people don't want to carry them, so now it's more like "Hey, I've got my Walkman". For that reason, there's a treble type of thing going on; they're not getting much of the bass. So rap music in New York City is a headphone type of thing, whereas in Long Island or Philadelphia . . . it's more of a bass type thing. (Dery 1990, p. 90)

These regional distinctions between the "beats" are borne out in the example of the Miami production houses of Luther Campbell or Orlando's Magic Mike. In Florida (and to some extent, Georgia) the focus is on the bass–Florida "booty bass" or "booty boom" as it has been termed–which offers a deeper, "phatter", and almost subsonic vibration that stands out as a regionally distinct and authored style.[3] Within US rap culture, artists and fans alike reflect an acute awareness that people in different parts of the country produce and enjoy regional variations on the genre; they experience rap differently, structuring it into their social patterns according to the norms that prevail in a given urban environment. Thus, the regional taste patterns in South Florida are partially influenced by the central phenomenon of car mobility and the practice of stacking multiple 10- or 15-inch bass speakers and powerful subwoofers into car trunks and truck beds.

Add to these stylistic distinctions the discursive differences within rap from the various regions (i.e., the aforementioned Gangsta Rap from the West Coast crews, the chilling, cold-blooded imagery from Houston's "Bloody Nickle" crews on Rap-A-Lot Records, or the "pimp, playa and hustla" themes that are standard among Oakland and San Francisco cliques), the localized posse variations in vocal style and slang, or the site-specific references in rap lyrics to cities, 'hoods, and crews, and a general catalogue of differences in form and content becomes clearly audible. What these elements indicate is that, while the rap posse provides a structured identity for its members, it can also provide a referential value to the production qualities and the sound of the musical product with which it is associated.

Endnotes

[1]Glossary of Terms

Gangsta Rap: popularized in 1987–88 by Los Angeles-based artists such as Niggaz With Attitude (N.W.A) and Ice T, this rap subgenre is renowned for its uncompromising lyrical depictions of gang culture, gun violence, antiauthoritarian attitudes, drug distribution and use, prostitution, etc. The frequent expressions of racist attitudes, homophobia, sexism, misogyny, and anti-social aggression are often criticized with progressive social movements and among mainstream commentators, making the artists who are most clearly associated with the subgenre pariahs of a sort.

homeboys/boyz: once used as a term to delineate the differences between urban and rural blacks in the U.S., the term "homeboy" has undergone a transition and today refers primarily to one's immediate circle of male family, friends and neighbourhood acquaintances who inhabit a generally common social space (although it can also be used more expansively as an endearing term when referring to those of common affinity who inhabit other places and spaces). The term *homegirls* is also used in this manner.

hood: an abbreviation of "neighbourhood." The term was amplified and widely disseminated within rap's hip hop vernacular, especially after 1988. It refers primarily to urban ghetto regions and other local sites of significance.

Message Rap: a subgenre of rap that overly and explicitly engages with political and cultural themes relating to race, economics, social justice, history, etc. Message Rap often isolates actual situations or events, elevating them for analysis or criticism in rap's public media forum. KRS-1 and Public Enemey are among the artists most commonly associated with this subgenre.

pimp, playa, hustla: these forms are symbolically linked to the icons of ghetto success portrayed in 1970s "blaxploitation" films, a distinct films, genre that included films such as Shaft, Superfly, The Mack, Cleopatra Jones and Coffy. Featuring black directors and lead actors, these films were commonly set in the ghetto neighbourhoods of U.S. cities and portrayed a highly stylized image of 1970s street life accompanied by well-known r&b soundtracks. The pimps, playas and hustlas of these films were commonly involved with the illegal financial practicies of prostitution, gambling, extortion, etc., but in hip hop and rap the meanings of these terms are altered and refer to the control and domination of rap and the capacity to generate wealth in new music business contexts.

possee, crew, clique: these are generally (but not exclusively) male fraternal organizations that display pronounced spatial allegiances and have a membership that is bound together by shared affinities. The terms can be used interchangeably.

representing: employing multiple communicative modes and cultural practices to define and articulate individual or posse identities, spatial locales grounded in the 'hood, and other aspects of individual and collective significance.

shout-outs: originating with the traditional Jamaican sound systems, this is the practice whereby the DJ or MC literally call out the names of friends and crew members, or the names of streets and neighbourhoods through which they circulate, in an expression of appreciation and respect. Shout-outs can be heard in both live concert performances and on recorded tracks.

subwoofer: powerful bass speakers that are designed to provide maximum clarity of low frequency tones and a visceral rumbling effect without compromising the quality of the overall sound reproduction.

tagging: the practice of using markers or spray paint to write one's name on public property. Tags are small and rapidly deployed and should not be confused with larger, more complicated and multi-coloured graffiti.

toaster: an early Jamaican concedent of the contemporary rapper, the toaster accompanied the DJ's rhythm tracks by "chatting" on the microphone. Classic artists displaying the toaster vocal style who emerged on the Jamaican music scene between 1968 and 1971 are U-Roy, Big Youth, and I-Roy.

turf: urban geographical space that is claimed on behalf of a gang or other cohesive group as a possession to be policed and defended against real or perceived intruders.

turning the "hood out": similar to representing', this involves the specific articulation and announcement of one's proximate geographical locale and the individuals and features which constitute it and define its distinct character.

²The Flavor Unit posse at the time included such Rap notables as Queen Latifah, Monie Love, Apache, Lakim Shabazz, and Naughty By Nature who, perhaps more than the rest, explicitly refer to their origins as New Jersey rappers hailing from 118th Street, "Illtown", in East Orange. After internal restructuring, the posse's most bankable star, Queen Latifah, emerged as the executive head of Flavor Unit Management.

³For a detailed examination of the Florida "bass" phenomenon, see the special feature of *The Source*, March 1994.

References

Chambers, Iain. 1985. *Urban Rhythms: Pop Music and Popular Culture* (London)

Cross, Brian. 1993. *It's Not About a Salary: Rap, Race, and Resistance in Los Angeles* (London)

Dery, Mark. 1990. "Public enemy: Confrontion", *Keyboard*, September

Eure, Joseph and Spady, James. (eds) 1991. *Nation Conscious Rap* (New York)

Garofalo, Reebee. 1997. *Rockin' Out: Popular Music in the USA* (Boston)

George, Nelson. 1992. *Buppies, B-Boys, Baps and Bohos: Notes on Post-Soul Black Culture* (New York) 1993. "Hip-hop's founding fathers speak the truth", *The Source*, November

Gilroy, Paul. 1992. "It's a family affair", in *Black Popular Culture*, (ed) Gina Dent (Seattle)

Gunst, Laurie. 1995. *Born Fi Dend: A Journey Through the Jamaican Posse Underworld* (New York)

Hager, Steve. 1984. *Hip Hop: The Illustrated History of Break Dancing, Rap Music, and Graffiti* (New York)

Jones, Charisse. 1995. "Still hangin in the 'hood: rappers who stay say their strength is from the streets", *The New York Times*, 24 September, pp. 43–6

Keith, Michael and Pile, Steve. (eds) 1993. *Place and the Politics of Identity* (New York)

Lipsitz, George. 1990. *Time Passages: Collective Memory and American Popular Culture* (Minneapolis)

Nelson, Havelock and Gonzales, Michael. 1991. *Bring the Noise: A Guide to Rap Music and Hip Hop Culture* (New York)

Pike, Jeff. 1990. "At long last, Seattle is suddenly hot", *Billboard*, 18 August, pp. 30–4

Rap Pages. 1991. "The world according to Ice-T", October, pp. 54–67

Rap Sheet. 1992. "The bloody 5: a day in the hood", October, pp. 18–26

Robins, Kevin. 1991. "Tradition and translation: national culture in its global context", in *Enterprise and Heritage: Crosscurrents of National Culture*, eds John Corner and Sylvia Harvey (New York)

Rose, Tricia. 1994. *Black Noise: Rap Music and Black Culture in Contemporary America* (Hanover)

Samuels, David. 1991. "The rap on rap", *The New Republic*, 11 November

Shocked, Michelle and Bull, Bart. 1992. "LA riots: cartoons vs. reality", *Billboard*, 20 June, p. 6

The Source. 1994. Special Issue: Miami Bass, March

Tate, Greg. 1992. "Posses in effect: Ice-T", in *Flyboy in the Buttermilk: Essays on Contemporary America* (New York)

Toop, David. 1984. *The Rap Attack: African Live to New York Hip Hop* (Boston) 1991. *Rap Attack: African Rap to Global Hip-Hop* (New York)

Ward, Brian. 1998. *Just My Soul Responding: Rhythm and Blues, Black Consciousness, and Race Relations* (Berkeley)

Questions for Discussion and Topics for Writing

1. A key characteristic of scholarly writing and research is a desire to create new knowledge. This motivation is generally articulated early in the work, often in the introduction. How does Forman articulate the purpose of his essay? How does he hope to add new knowledge to the study of hip hop culture? Where has previous criticism fallen short in his view?

2. How was "place" crucial to the origins of hip hop? Put differently, how was place crucial to the way the origins of hip hop were imagined? How is the notion of "respect" bound up in these early definitions of hip hop and rap music?

3. What is a "posse"? How is this a place-based conception? What connotations does the term *posse* carry? What connection does Forman find between American hip hop and Jamaican posses?

4. An intriguing element of Forman's argument is his discussion of "Jamaican posse culture." We normally do not associate a posse with Jamaica. We tend to link it to American westerns, television programs and movies associated with cowboy adventures, six-guns, and the American conquest of the West and Native American cultures and territories. Research the idea of the posse, and trace it in relation to both its traditional American West manifestations and to its later incorporation into Jamaican culture. Write an essay that follows the migration of the term *posse*, being sure to make connections between different phases of its journey through cultural history.

5. Apply Forman's spatial analysis to rap lyrics written by regionally distinct artists (South vs. West, for example). Be sure to note features that are both endemic to hip hop itself and those that reflect regional competition.

Reaching Toward Hip-Hop's Homeland

AYANNA PARRIS

Ayanna Parris graduated from Vassar College in 2006 with a degree in African Studies. She is currently working with Nomadic Wax, promoting African rap to American audiences. Her contribution to this volume is an excerpt from her undergraduate thesis Nyumbani Ni Nyumbani: Tanzanian Rap and the Globalization of Black Identity. *She plans to return to Tanzania to expand her research into the dynamic Tanzanian hip hop scene.*

◆

> *"Tumerudi msingi. Inabidi kurudi* 'da Bronx" "We've taken it back to the foundation. You gotta return to da Bronx."
> —John Chacalito, Aang Serian Studios

> *"Nyumbani ni nyumbani hata kama hushakaani"* "Home is home even if you don't stay there anymore."
> —Wanaume Family, "Nyumbani"

Anyone who knows anything about hip-hop will locate the foundation in the South Bronx (the South South Bronx). Heads in Tanzania are no exception. When I first traveled to the East African country, I saw it firsthand. On a ferry ride from Dar-es-Salaam to Zanzibar, I distracted myself from seasickness by watching two young Tanzanian men in front of a blue screen rapping over heavily synthesized beats. Their imitation of American rappers tickled me. They bobbed their heads and gesticulated as if pointing to the invisible words that were coming out of their mouths. They even had the gangsta scowl that I now associate with *Source* and *XXL* covers. I did not understand a word of the Swahili they were speaking, but I laughed at the beautiful bootleg-ness of the spectacle.

When I returned years later as a student at the University of Dar-es-Salaam, I found Tanzanian hip-hop to be a lot less bootleg and far more beautiful than I could have imagined from that initial sample. Hip-hop has grown tremendously since those first days in the Bronx. It has evolved into the powerful force that is global hip-hop consisting of several local hip-hop communities and cultures. The tension between the local and global hip-hop is clear in the expressions and imaginings of community present in the Tanzanian scene. In my conversations with the participants of this community, both producers and consumers of Tanzanian hip-hop, I found that while my hip-hop had gone global, Tanzanian hip-hop remained distinctly local. What I found was clearly related to everything I know about hip-hop, but it was not mere imitation. The way that I was embraced, as black American, as the perceived owner of the foundation, signaled a connection in the making. Tanzania was reaching towards a cultural homeland.

Tanzanian hip-hop is perhaps better contextualized within Tanzanian cultural expression than in the somewhat overwhelming phenomenon of global hip-hop. Rapper Balozi Dola, whose name appropriately means ambassador, explains that his hip-hop is ruled by a different value system. Hip-hop culture in Dar-es-Salaam is limited to clothing and rap music. Turntabling, breakdancing and graffiti never took root. Dola claims, "Tanzanians don't go out there and do crazy stuff. They are really respectful people. If you do that everybody would say 'Hey what's wrong with him. He's a Tanzanian, why is he doing that?'" ("De-Plow-Matz"). While the disparity between Tanzanian and American hip-hop cultures is certainly a result of different values, but there are other important contributing factors. Turntable practices, for example, are nearly impossible without access to specific technological resources. And in the case of graffiti, both values and context alienate Tanzanians from the expression. Graffiti developed in New York City largely as a way to announce the presence of marginalized identities that were contained to specific places. In Tanzania, hip-hoppers firmly establish themselves as authentically Tanzanian and thus their access to public space is rarely questioned (a notable exception is found in women's experiences).

Graffiti is not completely foreign to Tanzania. In Zanzaibar's Stone Town, the letters CUF, the acronym for Tanzania's second most popular political party the Civic United Front, are drawn in white chalk on many of the town's old walls. But for the most part, the expression is contained to the private spaces of people's homes, small concert venues and notebooks. At Wanaume Family concerts, they have begun a practice of bringing out a cardboard wall in order to showcase the graffiti talents of the members. One Wanaume fan and self-proclaimed hip-hop activist, told me that this is a tribute to the founding fathers of hip-hop. Abbas Maunda, a former member of Kwanza Unit and leader of the rap crew High Class Underground Souls attempts to make sense of similar practices within Tanzanian hip-hop, stating, "We can live the same hip-hop, but in an African way" ("Kwanza Unit"). The persistent presence of black American symbols in Tanzanian hip-hop is attributable to cultural obsession with the origins of the form, what Imani Perry calls hip-hop's "nostalgic sensibility" (Perry 56). Over the course of hip-hop becoming a Tanzanian phenomenon, the music and symbols of American hip-hop have continued to flow into Tanzania. And even while its violence, abusive language and sexual irresponsibility are loudly condemned, and even with the existence of a unique Tanzanian hip-hop iconography, black American style, language, and identities are often embraced.

5   Although the histories of the Bronx and Dar-es-Salaam are not one, young Tanzanians imagine themselves as part of one global hip-hop community. In doing so, they create a link between these histories. Stuart Hall's concept of articulation provides a framework for understanding how a relationship can be desired, built and maintained between dissimilar groups. "An articulation is thus the form of the connection that can make a unity of two different elements, under certain conditions. It is a linkage which is not necessary, determined, absolute and essential for all time" (qtd. in Kelley, "Unfinished Migrations" 19). In the theatres of global politics and economy, and in many aspects of global culture, the small country is barely visible. Denied access to more privileged manifestations of globality, Tanzania forges a connection with the black American homeland of hip-hop, providing a way to relate to at least one global discourse. And in the face of the many narratives that name globalization as little more than a force that threatens local cultures, communities and traditions, this identification serves to help young Tanzanians embrace some aspects of globalization.

Members of the Tanzanian hip-hop community follow contemporary American rap and style. Artists are influenced not only by the foundational American rappers, but also on contemporary stars and underground recording artists. The prolific producer P-Funk is constantly aware of obscure American artists, and is rumored to push copies of bootlegged CDs and hip-hop magazines on to the rappers that he works with. Any music shop or stand holds a combination of local and global artists. II Proud is stacked beside 2Pac. A Gangstas With Matatizo flyer posted next to a G-Unit poster. The juxtaposition speaks to the desire of Tanzanian hip-hop fans to elevate their local stars to the global status of American artists.

Identification with black America is often expressed through direct imitation. The first hip-hop expressions in Tanzania in the mid-1980s were rap battles judged by the performers' likeness to American rappers. Although this imitation occurred in the context of economic liberalization, this kind of relationship to foreign culture was not new. The Mganda dance, of the Matengo people in Southern Tanzania, provides an important precedent. The competitive *ngoma* is performed by men dressed in an imitation of the British costume—white shorts, white shirt, dark tie, white knee-high socks and black shoes. Stephen Hill explains,

> Mganda is a linear men's dance that borrows heavily from colonial military brass band practice in costumes, instruments, movement styles, and hierarchies of command and control. The ensemble accompanying mganda features a military style bass drum, two side drums—local reproductions of snare drums— and the dancers, called askari, or "soldier," play kazoos in imitation of trumpets. Paralleling reasons for beni's immense popularity between the Wars, Matengo men found mganda attractive because it represented, in their own terms, "modernity." Their attraction centered on mganda's flashy, European style costumes, military inspired administrative hierarchies, rationalized competition, and general European associations, which they saw as *kisasa*, or "modern/of the present" and representing *ustaarabu*, or "civilization" (Hill 35).

He explains that dance, which has been performed for over five decades, is judged in terms of the performance's ability to capture modernity. Through imitation, the Matengo create a way to claim ownership over it. Mganda fuses flattering representations of Europeanness with derisive ones, situating the performance itself (a Matengo creation) as the true measure of civilization.

The narratives of grandeur present in some of the more popular Tanzanian rap reveal this tendency. The imitation is at times, thinly veiled ridicule of American rap. The tone in which The Belics rhyme about an extravagant house party, or Professor Jay brags about his collection of luxury cars has made some begin to refer to these and similar narratives as "rap katuni," literally cartoon rap. More often, however, it is a reflection of a yearning for community with American counterparts. Despite its growing internality, Tanzanian hip-hop continues to find pleasure in imitating and adapting American hip-hop culture.

10 This trend is most clear in Tanzanian hip-hop fashions. Although there have been efforts to localize Tanzanian hip-hop style, most notably with the 120 clothing line, most hip-hoppers copy American styles. Second-hand clothing, or *mitumba*, imported from Western nations provides access to hip-hop gear. At Manzese, one of the larger *mitumba* markets in Dar-es-Salaam, one can find Nikes, baggy jeans, and T-shirts from so-called hip-hop brands (i.e., Fubu, Sean Jean, Ecko). Rapper A.Y. often wears a white T-shirt wrapped around his head, a style popular in New York City. In the video for *"Nampenda Yeye,"* Mike T is wearing a G-Unit T-shirt. Similarly, wave-caps and do-rags have become stylish in some circles despite the fact that the braided and close-cut hairstyles that they were created to maintain are not popular among Tanzanian men. In equatorial Dar-es-Salaam, down coats and Timberland boots now have a market. Knowing the worth of these images, *mitumba* vendors often increase the price of certain styles. Unlike in the Mganda dance, however, the American hip-hop costume is only intimated. While some music videos will show artists in the flyest of hip-hop gear from head to toe, more often there are only a few signifiers of American hip-hop—a New York Yankees cap, a large (fake) diamond earring, a Roc-A-Wear sweater. Those symbols are mixed with local ones—Tanzanian flags and colors, beads and textiles.

In addition, the Swahili-speaking hip-hop community as well has adopted some American hip-hop language. The word *freshi* has gained such widespread use that it is used in national advertisements (*"Ni poa, Ni freshi, Ni yako"* It's cool, it's fresh, it's yours is the slogan for SM cigarettes). The word *ghetto* has been transformed into the Swahili slang *geto*. Despite the originally exploitative use of the word, Tanzanians signify on American hip-hop's already signified meaning. The word is commonly used in reference to an individual's personal space or room and indicates proud ownership of that space. (Juma Nature's usage more closely resembles the American hip-hop meaning when he uses *kigetogeto* to describe hip-hop language and knowledge.) Signs for barbershops, copy centers, locksmiths and markets that are written in English are often written in black vernacular English (Ali B's Cutz, for example, which also showcases pictures of famous black American men such as Will Smith, 50 Cent and Tupac as models of different haircuts). Several English words are even familiar to those with no other exposure to the language—*bling* and *jiggy* have enjoyed especially widespread use.

More striking is the adoption of a certain hip-hop identity endemic to America. When I saw the word "nigga" etched into a desk in my University of Dar-es-Salaam lecture hall, I was at first angered. But after those first few seconds in which my heart had already started racing, I remembered where I was and was immediately confused and thought, *what does the word even mean over here?* Perry explains that "nigga" has become a very public word through hip-hop (142). Black expressive cultures of the West have long provided a voice for an often-silenced community and the commodification of black popular culture has brought the margins to the center. Although this shift opens public space up to black culture, it does little to challenge its social marginality, as Stuart Hall writes, "what replaces invisibility is a kind of carefully regulated, segregated visibility" (Hall 23). In that space, in but not of the mainstream, American rap is necessarily a response to white hegemony. Tricia Rose writes:

> A large and significant element in rap's discursive territory is engaged in symbolic and ideological warfare with institutions and groups that symbolically, ideologically, and materially oppress African Americans. In the way, rap music is a contemporary stage for the theater of the powerless (Rose 100–101).

As hip-hop globalizes the scope and context of this warfare is changing, but the contours of the conflict are the same. In both the Unites States and Tanzania, hip-hop provides a space for black subjectivity. And despite the fact that hip-hop arrives in Tanzania on the wings of American cultural imperialism, Tanzanians appreciate the space that it opens for blackness in global culture.

Several rap artists and crews use the word to describe themselves—Nigger Pure, Niggaz With Power (N.W.P.), Proud Niggaz, Nigga One, and Nigga Jay (who has since graduated to Professor Jay). The stepchild of the notoriously inflammatory racial slur "nigger," "nigga" and its widespread use in American rap has been widely condemned within the music, by music critics, and overwhelmingly by black advocates of respectable (read:

bourgeois) race representations. Robin Kelley defends the use of
the word, explaining,

> To comprehend the politics of ghettocentricity, we must under-
> stand the myriad ways in which the most ghettocentric segments
> of the West Coast hip-hop community have employed the term
> 'Nigga.' Gangsta rappers, in particular, are struggling to ascribe
> new, potentially empowering meanings to the word. Indeed, the
> increasingly common practice of spelling the word N-i-g-g-a sug-
> gests a revisioning. [. . .] 2Pac (Tupac Shakur) insists on his 1991
> album 2Pacalypse Now that "Nigga" stands for "Never Ignorant,
> Getting Goals Accomplished." More common, however, is the use
> of "Nigga" to describe a condition rather than a skin color or cul-
> ture. Above all, "Nigga" speaks to a collective identity shaped by
> class consciousness, the character of inner-city space, police re-
> pression, poverty, and the constant threat of intraracial violence
> fed by a dying economy. Part of NWA's "Niggaz4Life" on
> *Efilzaggin*, for instance, uses "Nigga" almost as a synonym for
> "oppressed" (Kelley, "Kickin Reality, Kickin' Ballistics" 137).

15   The nostalgia that Perry identifies in American rap is present
in Tanzanian rap as well, compelling artists and fans to continu-
ously reinforce their cultural roots, both real and imagined, in
America, even as the form comes into itself as uniquely Tanzanian.
     The relation to the "nigga," and black American identity in
general, may be a way for Tanzanian hip-hop heads to claim allegiance to a globally articulated marginal identity. While American
hip-hop's narratives of luxury provide a glimpse of foreign privilege, the nigga grounds hip-hop in social marginality. Kelley explains that he is defined not only by blackness but also by its
associated lack. Individuals with little knowledge of the specifici-
ties of American racism that created both niggers and niggas recognize this condition. While many global identities have been
proven inaccessible to Tanzanians because they are defined
through their privilege, the nigga is accessible because of its marginality (and desirable because of its ability to find pleasure in that
space).
     The accessibility of this identity is based on the idea of a com-
monality grounded in racial identity. Professor Jay remarks, "In
that time [1989] I liked to listen to rap like Public Enemy. They really attracted me to rapping because I saw the way black men liked
the music and the way they searched for their own voice" (qtd. in
Perullo 95). When I spent time in Tanzania, it took a while for me

to realize that the call "Nigga!" from a stranger was one of recognition, and often celebration, of my black American identity. As Kelley explains, nigga identity signifies oppression, but it also, especially in the eyes of Tanzanian hip-hop heads, represents resistance. It becomes a space for young black Tanzanian subjectivity. In young Tanzanian men calling themselves niggas we see the aspiration for a connection with black Americans.

Although articulation is a communication that takes place across difference, it is not always imagined as such. In this case, the connection is naturalized with claims of collective racial identity. As one university student and self-proclaimed hip-hop head explained: .

STUDENT:	Wanasema 'I'm African, 'I'm African' kwa ajili wananifanana kwa hivyo tunafanana, si ndio? Mbona sijiiti 'nigga'? Kwa sababu gani? Miye nigga. Sisi sote tuna ngozi nyeusi, wote tuna shida.
AP:	Matatizo tofauti?
STUDENT:	Kidogokidogo tu
STUDENT:	They say 'I'm African' because they look like me, so we're the same. So why don't I call myself 'nigga'? Why? I'm a nigga. We both have black skin, both have problems.
AP:	Aren't the problems different?
STUDENT:	Only a little bit

The degree to which black American and black Tanzanian problems are similar is not of concern here. What this student's comments highlight is the degree to which race is utilized to describe a common condition.

Appadurai uses the term "culturalism" to describe "the conscious mobilization of cultural differences in the service of larger national or transnational politics" (Appadurai 15). As with Hall's articulation, the concept highlights the potential for relationships forged across difference. Appadurai, however, inserts the work of the imagination into the discussion. As my classmate and I continued our conversation, we considered the vast differences between black America and black Africa, but focused on the similarities. It became clear that despite difference, we imagined similarity as the grounds for identification.

The articulation of a connection between Tanzanian and American hip-hop communities is not experienced as the forging 20 a new relationship. It is imagined as the natural course of events given the racial and cultural similarity of the two groups. Calling oneself a nigga contributes to the naturalization of this connection. Along with the other forms of identification, it blurs the boundary between Tanzanian and American hip-hop communities. Hall writes, "The unity formed by this combination or articulation is always, necessarily, a 'complex structure,' a structure in which things are related, as much in their differences as through their similarities" (Hall, "Race, Articulation, and Societies" 39). The established fact that these are distinct communities (and that even as the articulation is made, Tanzanians know this) forces the question why, I paraphrase Hall, if these groups do not form one identity, if neither group can be said to be defined by the other, if we are not reducible to each other or even developed by the same conditions or contradictions, is this relationship so compelling? ("Race, Articulation, and Societies" 38). What stands to be gained and lost with this particular articulation of unity?

Balozi Dola has described the condition of contemporary Tanzanian youth as an identity crisis. The fear that Tanzanian culture will be lost, abandoned, or stolen is a postcolonial concern often addressed with the construction and maintenance of Tanzanian national culture. Since independence, Tanzania has used cultural production to legitimize itself, often overvaluing the so-called traditional because the dominant global narratives about cultural and economic development locate modernity in the West. Black Americans, who are "in but not of the West" (Gilroy 3), provide an example of modern black identities that do not require erasure of the racial/cultural self.

What stands to be gained in the building of a bridge between Tanzanian and American hip-hop communities is the opportunity to experience black modernity. Through rap music and hip-hop culture, Tanzanians work to reconcile Africa with modernity (much in the same way that black Americans mediate blackness with America). The dominant discourse on modernity and modernization has been slow to include black people and cultures on equal ground. New discourses of modernity are necessary if blackness is to occupy a space within it. In *The Black Atlantic*, Paul Gilroy argues for an understanding that includes the enslaved and colonized while unveiling the horror and violence of the systems that create those conditions. In theorizing such a modernity, he challenges the myth of the grand narratives on which modernity is said to be based.

There are vast differences between Tanzanian and American hip-hop communities as each operates within national structures.

Gilroy's black Atlantic framework, an international network meant to incorporate Europe, Africa, and the New World, offers a way to understand these articulations of collectivity. He contends that black Atlantic identity exists because in the disparate locations there is a desire to transcend the "constraints of the nation state" (19). Coming together, in reality or in the imaginary, on the grounds of racial identity and celebrating it while highlighting the immense diversity within is a new way to live racial identification and community. Gilroy, frustrated with the limiting and unproductive options of black essentialism and black pluralism, has named the arts, specifically music, as the space where new ideas can be articulated. In hip-hop and other black cultural spaces "[l]ines between self and other are blurred and special forms of pleasure are created as a result of the meetings and conversations that are established between one fractured, incomplete, and unfinished racial self and others" (79). The Tanzanian identification with black America and its articulation across disparate black identities allows us to theorize about blackness in new ways. While postmodern discourses are shifting away from the idea of the essential black subject (and reactionary hypermodern discourses insist on the existence of a black soul), hip-hop provides a space for both meaning and diversity. We find in the place of the essential black subject, unfinished identities (Gilroy), new ethnicities (Hall), radical black subjectivities (hooks). And in the construction of these fresh visions of blackness, there is great potential for new relationships across the diverse spectrum of African and Afro-diasporic experience.

Works Cited

Appadurai, Arjun. *Modernity at Large: Cultural Dimensions of Globalization.* Minneapolis: University of Minnesota Press, 1996.

Gilroy, Paul. *The Black Atlantic: Modernity and Double Consciousness.* Cambridge: Harvard University Press, 1993.

Hall, Stuart. "New Ethnicities." *Black British Cultural Studies.* Ed. Houston Baker et al. Chicago: University of Chicago, 1996. 79–96.

———. "Race, Articulation, and Societies Structured in Dominance." *Black British Cultural Studies.* Ed. Houston Baker et al. Chicago: University of Chicago, 1996. 6–30.

———. "What Is This 'Black' in Black Popular Culture?" *Black Popular Culture.* Ed. Michele Dent. Seattle: Bay Press, 1992. 21–33.

Hill, Steven. "Death of Mganda?: Continuity and Transformation in Matengo Music." *Africa Today* 48 (2001): 27–41.

hooks, bell. *Yearning.* Boston: South End Press, 1990.

Kelley, Robin D. G. "Kickin' Reality, Kickin' Ballistics: Gangsta Rap and Postindustrial Los Angeles." *Droppin' Science: Critical Essays on Rap Music and Hip-Hop Culture*. Ed. William Eric Perkins. Philadelpia: Temple University Press, 1996. 117–158.

Kwanza Unit. 10 March 2006.
http://www.musikmuseet.se/mmm/africa/ku.html

Patterson, Tiffany Ruby and Robin D. G. Kelley. "Unfinished Migrations: Reflections on the African Diaspora and the Making of the Modern World." *African Studies Review* 43 (2000): 11–45.

Perry, Imani. *Prophets of the Hood: Politics and Poetics in Hip-Hop*. Durham: Duke University Press, 2004.

Perullo, Alex. "Hooligans and Heroes: Youth Identity and Hip-Hop in Dar-es-Salaam, Tanzania." *Africa Today* 51 (2005): 75–102.

Rose, Tricia. *Black Noise: Rap Music and Black Culture in Contemporary America*. Middletown, CT: Wesleyan University Press, 1994.

De-Plow-Matz. 10 March 2006.
http://www.musikmuseet.se/mmm/africa/dipl.html

Questions for Discussion and Topics for Writing

1. Tanzanian hip hop is a result of globalization of black American culture. How does the identification with black style, language, and identity allow Tanzanian youth to participate in global identities? In what ways can the global reinforce the local?

2. Parris discusses how imitation is an expression of Tanzanian culture. How do Tanzanian "heads" use imitation of hip hop to express their own culture? Do you think this type of imitation is similar to the types of "imitation" one finds in hip hop like sampling and signifyin'?

3. What does Parris say is to be gained by making the connection between American and Tanzanian hip hop? How does race function in making this connection? Does such a function change your sense of what race is?

4. Use "Reaching Toward Hip-Hop's Homeland" as a model for a research paper. Explore the use of hip hop in a country other than America. Then relate it to aspects of American hip hop. How does international hip hop use or exploit American hip hop? How does it relate to hip hop's acknowledged origins in the South Bronx in particular and the United States in general?

New Orleans Hip Hop Is the Home of Gangsta Gumbo

KELEFA SANNEH

Kelefa Sanneh is a pop music critic for The New York Times. *His articles have appeared in* The Village Voice, The Boston Phoenix, *and*

The Source. *Sanneh also serves as a contributing editor to* Transition Magazine, *based at Harvard and edited by Henry Louis Gates and Kwame Appiah. The following article appeared in* The New York Times *on April 23, 2006.*

————————— ✦ —————————

For thousands of people—we'll probably never know exactly how many—Hurricane Katrina was the end. But for listeners across the country, that not-quite-natural disaster also marked the beginning of a party that hasn't ended yet. Ever since those awful days last year, the country has been celebrating the rich musical heritage of New Orleans.

There was a blitz of benefit concerts, including "From the Big Apple to the Big Easy," a pair of shows held simultaneously at Madison Square Garden and Radio City Music Hall last September. A New Orleans jam session closed the show at the Grammy Awards in February. There have been scads of well-intentioned compilations, including *Our New Orleans: A Benefit Album for the Gulf Coast* (Nonesuch), *Hurricane Relief: Come Together Now* (Concord) and *Higher Ground Hurricane Relief Benefit Concert* (Blue Note), a live album recorded at the Jazz at Lincoln Center Benefit. At the Rock and Roll Hall of Fame induction ceremony last month, a video segment paid tribute to New Orleans music through the years, from Louis Armstrong to the Neville Brothers; there was also the inevitable New Orleans jam session.

But one thing all these tributes have in common is that they all ignored the thrilling—and wildly popular—sound of New Orleans hip-hop, the music that has been the city's true soundtrack through the last few decades.

Rap music remains by far New Orleans's most popular musical export. Lil Wayne, Master P, Juvenile, Mannie Fresh, B. G., Mystikal and many other pioneers have sold millions of albums, and they have helped make their city an indispensable part of the hip-hop world. Unlike all the other musicians celebrated at post-Katrina tributes, these ones still show up on the pop charts, often near the top. (Juvenile's most recent album made its debut at No. 1, last month.) Yet when tourists and journalists descend upon the city next weekend, for the New Orleans Jazz and Heritage Festival, they'll find only one local rapper on the schedule: Juvenile, who is to appear on the Congo Square Louisiana Rebirth Stage at 6 p.m. Saturday.

Maybe New Orleans rappers don't mind being left out. No doubt most of them prefer popularity—and its rewards—to respect. But why should they have to choose?

Hip-hop was long considered unfit for polite society. And yet the extraordinary snubbing of New Orleans hip-hop comes at a time when the genre is gaining institutional validation. The Smithsonian Institution's National Museum of American History recently announced plans for a hip-hop exhibit. The Rock and Roll Hall of Fame and Museum exhibited "Roots, Rhyme and Rage: The Hip-Hop Story" in 1999. Colleges and universities around the country are offering conferences and courses devoted to hip-hop history. At the same time that hip-hop is being written out of the history of New Orleans, it's being written into the history of America. Could that possibly be a coincidence?

The story of New Orleans hip-hop begins in earnest with what is known as bounce music: festive beats, exuberant chants, simple lyrics that ruled local nightclubs and breezeway parties in the late 1980's and early 90's. The future hip-hop star Juvenile got his start in the bounce-music scene. But like many New Orleans musicians before him, Juvenile found out that having a citywide hit wasn't quite the same as having a nationwide hit.

By the mid-90's, Southern hip-hop was starting to explode, and so some New Orleans entrepreneurs figured out ways to go national. Master P, a world-class hustler and less-than-world-class rapper from the city's rough Calliope projects, founded a label called No Limit, and used it to popularize a distinctively New Orleans-ish form of hard-boiled hip-hop. For a time Master P was one of pop music's most successful moguls. (He made the cover of *Fortune*, and he never let anyone forget it.)

Master P's crosstown rivals were the Williams brothers, proprietors of Cash Money Records, which eventually replaced No Limit as the city's dominant brand name. Cash Money signed up the hometown hero Juvenile (who was raised in the Magnolia projects), as well as the city's greatest hip-hop producer, Mannie Fresh. Working with a great group of rappers including Lil Wayne and B. G., Fresh perfected an exuberant electronic sound; he did as much as anyone to pull the musical legacy of New Orleans into the 21st century. You could hear brass bands in the synthesizers, drum lines in the rattling beats, Mardi Gras Indians in the sing-song lyrics. (If you're wondering where to start, try Juvenile's head-spinning 1998 blockbuster, "400 Degreez," which has sold 4.7 million copies.)

10   Like most musical stories, this one doesn't really have a happy ending—or any ending at all. Master P's empire dissolved, which explains why you might recently have seen him on *Dancing With the Stars*. Mystikal, one of the city's best and weirdest rappers, split with No Limit in 2000, and he's currently serving a jail sentence for

sexual battery and tax evasion. Juvenile, B. G. and Mannie Fresh have all left Cash Money, though Lil Wayne remains.

Then came Katrina. Not all of the city's stars were living in New Orleans when the storm hit, but all lost houses or cars or—at the very least—a hometown. Lil Wayne moved his mother to Miami; Mannie Fresh set up shop in Los Angeles; B. G. is living in Detroit.

But the music never stopped. Juvenile's *Reality Check* (UTP/-Atlantic), released last month, was the fastest-selling CD of his career; for the defiant first single, "Get Ya Hustle On," he filmed a video in the devastated Lower Ninth Ward. B. G. recently released a strong new album, *The Heart of tha Streetz Vol. 2 (I Am What I Am)* (Koch); it was strong enough, in fact, to earn him a new record contract with Atlantic. In "Move Around," the album's first single, Mannie Fresh sings (sort of) the cheerful refrain: "I'm from the ghetto, homey/ I was raised on bread and baloney/ You can't come around here, 'cause you're phony."

And then there's Lil Wayne, who last fall released *Tha Carter 2* (Cash Money/Universal), perhaps the finest album of his career (it has sold about 900,000 copies so far). In his slick lyrics and raspy voice, you can hear a city's swagger and desperation:

> All I have in this world is a pistol and a promise
> A fistful of dollars
> A list full of problems
> I'll address 'em like P.O. Boxes
> Yeah, I'm from New Orleans, the Creole cockpit
> We so out of it
> Zero tolerance
> Gangsta gumbo—I'll serve 'em a pot of it

All right, so this isn't the stuff that feel-good tributes are made of. Despite the topical video, "Get Ya Hustle On" is a mishmash of political commentary and drug-dealer rhymes. (The song included the well-known couplet, "Everybody tryna get that check from FEMA/ So he can go and score him some co-ca-een-uh.") And much of the music portrays New Orleans as a place full of violence and decadence: expensive teeth, cheap women, "choppers" (machine guns) everywhere. If you're trying to celebrate the old, festive, tourist-friendly New Orleans, maybe these aren't the locals you want.

Furthermore, much of the post-Katrina effort has focused on "saving" and "preserving" the city's musical heritage. Clearly top-selling rappers don't need charity. In fact, many have been quietly helping, through gifts to fellow residents and hip-hop charities like David Banner's Heal the Hood Foundation.

But it's worth remembering that many New Orleans hip-hop pioneers—from DJ Jimi to the influential group U.N.L.V.—aren't exactly millionaires. And for that matter, many rappers aren't nearly as rich as they claim. In any case, glowing recollections aren't the only way to pay tribute to the city. The story of Katrina is in large part a story of poverty and neglect; it's no coincidence that many of the rappers come from the same neighborhoods that still haven't been cleaned up. Surely the lyrics to a Juvenile song aren't nearly as shocking as those images most of us saw on television.

The language of preservationism sometimes conceals its own biases. If all the dying traditions are valuable, does that also mean all the valuable traditions are dying? If a genre doesn't need saving, does that also mean it's not worth saving? If New Orleans rappers seem less lovable than, say, Mardi Gras Indians or veteran soul singers, might it be because they're less needy? Cultural philanthropy is drawn to musical pioneers—especially African-American ones—who are old, poor and humble. What do you do when the pioneers are young, rich and cocky instead?

Believe it or not, that question brings us back to the Smithsonian, which has come to praise hip-hop. Or to bury it. Or both. The genre is over 30 years old by now, and while its early stars now seem unimpeachable (does anyone have a bad word to say about Grandmaster Flash or Run-DMC?), its current stars seem more impeachable than ever. From 50 Cent to Young Jeezy to, well, Juvenile, hip-hop might be even more controversial now than it was in the 80's; hip-hop culture has been blamed for everything from lousy schools to sexism to the riots in France. In a weird way, that might help account for the newfound respectability of the old school. To an older listener who's aghast at crack rap, the relatively innocent rhymes of Run-DMC don't seem so bad. If the new generation didn't seem so harmful, its predecessors might not seem harmless enough for the national archives.

Maybe the New Orleans hip-hop scene—"gangsta gumbo"— just hasn't been around long enough to make the history books. But that will change, as the rappers start seeming less like harbingers of an ominous future and more like relics of a colorful past. New Orleans hip-hop will endure not just because the music is so thrilling, but also because the rappers vividly evoke a city that is, for worse and (let's not forget) for better, never going to be the same.

20   After all, long before his name was affixed to an airport, Louis Armstrong, too, seemed manifestly unfit for polite society. Back when he recorded "Muggles," an ode to marijuana, he was a symbol of the so-called "jazz intoxication" that was corrupting an earlier generation the way hip-hop is corrupting this one.

A quarter-century from now, when the social problems that Juvenile and others so discomfitingly rap about have become one more strand of the city's official history, they may find themselves honored in just the kinds of musical tributes and cultural museums that currently shut them out. By then, their careers will probably have cooled off. They'll be less influential, less popular, less controversial; not coincidentally, they'll have a less visceral connection to the youth of New Orleans. And finally, their music—and maybe also their recording studios, their custom jewelry, their promotional posters—will seem to be worth saving. Perhaps, like so many other pop-music traditions, "gangsta gumbo" is a dish best preserved cold.

Questions for Discussion and Topics for Writing

1. What factors account for New Orleans hip hop being left out of the post-Katrina effort to preserve New Orleans music? In the end, is being left out a good or a bad thing? Are there ways that being left out is a sign of hip hop's vitality while preservation is a death knell?

2. How do you reconcile hip hop's controversial music that makes it unfit for polite society with charities like David Banner's Heal the Hood Foundation? What does this say about hip hop's role in the New Orleans community? What does this say about perceptions of hip hop as a whole?

3. Sanneh talks about the biases of "the language of preservationism" by offering a series of pointed questions. Offer some provisional responses to one or more of these questions. Then argue whether or not "the language of preservationism" ultimately helps or hurts hip hop.

4. Sanneh makes an allusion to Shakespeare's *Julius Caesar* when he argues that the Smithsonian "has come to praise hip hop. Or to bury it. Or both." First, what do you think Sanneh means by this? After paraphrasing his argument, look up the allusion. The phrase is part of Marc Antony's funeral speech for Julius Caesar. What is the rhetorical effect of this speech? What does Marc Antony intend and what is the end result? Does this allusion relate to hip hop in any way? Does understanding this allusion add or complicate Sanneh's argument? Use the allusion to speculate on the role of hip hop in post-Katrina New Orleans.

Hip Hop Stole My Black Boy
Kiese Laymon

Kiese Laymon was born in Jackson, Mississippi, and attended Mill-saps College, Jackson State University before finally earning his B.A.

from Oberlin College. He completed his M.F.A at Indiana University in 2001, and is currently Assistant Professor of English, Africana Studies, and Creative Writing at Vassar College. His debut novel, My Name Is City, *is about a nineteen-year-old black youth who buries himself in a hole for six days during which he remembers and rewrites a frightening week of his ten-year-old youth that ends in murder, rebirth, and mystery. His novel will be published in 2007. Laymon's debut book of essays,* At My Age, *will be published in spring 2008. The following piece was written for the present volume.*

---- ✦ ----

In 1998, I stood in the basement bathroom of Mudd Library at Oberlin College and asked myself, "Quick, Kie, what in the hell is a cipher?" It was a question I couldn't ask out loud, as I was speaking of the word, not *Tha Cypher,* a magazine that Rich Santiago, from the Bronx, and David Jacobs, from Manhattan, were creating outside the bathroom. The word "cipher," I remembered, initially crept up on me in a much smaller Central Mississippi bathroom in 1992.

Fifteen minutes into our lunch period, seven of us descended into what we called the B-boy bathroom. B-boy for us neither meant Breaker Boy, Bad Boy nor Bronx Boy; it meant Black Boy. There, B. Dazzle, who was the little brother of god-emcee Kamikaze of the group Crooked Lettaz, chaired a lyrical demolition of Stacy "King Slender" Hill.

I slouched between two urinals, hands cupped over mouth, providing a weak beat box while B. Dazzle went on and on about how "I build bombs like MacGyver so Southern niggas need to get wiser/ Or puff some dank to get higher before approaching my Cipher." Every black boy in the bathroom caught a vibe from his lyrics, or at least we acted like we did, *in spite* of the fact that we were the Southern niggas who needed to get wiser and *because* we were the Southern niggas who ironically felt wiser, realer just by listening to B. Dazzle. The six of us, including the just dissed King Slender, bobbed our heads and pumped our fists like we knew what everything in his rhyme, including his "cipher," really meant.

You had to be a B-boy to enter our space. No Black girls, Asians or white folks stepped foot in the B-boy bathroom when we rocked it, except for "K. Parry," a theatric Rocky Balboa type. Parry tried to Eminem his way into our space with some sharp wit and dramatic vocal bombast. The large thespian wobbled his way into the bathroom in some stone-washed cut offs and penny loafers. He proceeded to spit a monologue that didn't even rhyme before getting sliced up by the previously demolished "King Slender" who said something like, ". . . I'm Clubber Lang, white nigga, not Stacy Hill/In the nigga version of the movie, it's Rocky B. who gets killed." He ended it by saying, "Live on, Apollo Creed." Classic.

Black girls couldn't be a real part of our space either because 5 getting caught in the opposite sex's bathroom got you suspended for a week. We cracked open the door of the bathroom just enough so they could hear. And what they heard, probably more than our actual rhymes, were our responses to our rhymes. As the beat box-accompanied boasts, confessionals, and critiques moved from between urinals and stalls out the door of the bathroom into the hallway, the Black girls, white folks, Asians and wack niggas could only consume and interrogate the sound, not the creative culture or experience from whence that sound sprang. Our cipher was off limits to them, B. Dazzle said. And quiet as it was kept, we wanted it that way. We wanted the Black girls, especially, to need to hear what we were up to from a distance, but we refused to conceive them as our primary audience.

The Black girls in the hall were positioned in the same way we were positioned as Southern eavesdroppers of New York Hip-Hop. Some would get close as they could to the crack of the door, but they could never come all the way in. We understood that the seven Southern Black boys in that space were private, mysterious and desired by folk who didn't really know how or why we did what we did. That belief made us feel more powerful, possessed, closer to real Hip-Hop and strangely closer to New York.

Within that B-boy room, all of us knew that Hip-Hop credibility had little to do with the quality of your boast, intensity of your critique, or the passion of your confessional. Really, it was all rooted in your Hip-Hop aesthetic. And that aesthetic seemed to be rooted in geography. Hip-Hop and New York became unspoken adjectives in small spaces like this, and one's worth in the B-boy room was based almost solely on how Hip-Hop or New York the other six listeners thought you and your style were.

Though I had a decent bit of Hip-Hop credibility for spending summers in upstate New York visiting my father (to most Black Mississippians, New York State meant New York City), my rhyme style was too deliberate, dirty, local, filled with too many "or" words that were pronounced with a long "o" to be considered authentic New York. "Now I need no mic," I would rap, "just a slow ass tempo/Step to me wrong and motherfucka, you in fo'/a beat down that'll go down in your history books/Come try and fuck with Kie, Get yo ego took." That was the favorite of my four lyrical styles. And the other three styles, though dope in their own way, sounded remarkably close to that one. In the B-boy bathroom my rhymes swayed the crowd, but the movement started and stopped in between those two Central Mississippi urinals. B. Dazzle, on the other hand, moved the crowd to different states, figuratively and literally, and his character was as desired and enigmatic as his rhymes.

The myth was that B. Dazzle and his older brother, Kamikaze, spent summers not in Poughkeepsie, Rochester, Albany or Syracuse, but at a cousin's project in the South Bronx. The myth allowed us to slavishly follow when B. Dazzle chided us to use the term "Hip-Hop" instead of rap and cipher instead of rap circle. "Hip-Hop is more lyrical, more New York, nigga," he told me. He said it was universal, real, filled with brothers in ciphers dropping knowledge, breaking, deejaying, graffiti writing, showing and proving, while rap music, on the ashy Black hand side, was artistically inferior, country-sounding and local. The myth of B. Dazzle's Hip-Hop origins explained why we all knew he would fulfill his dream of becoming a god emcee. Henry James didn't have to tell us that geography was fate. Shit, we knew that. The six of us had similar dreams of being divine emcees, too, though we knew geography wouldn't allow it. Plus, our mamas and grandparents had other plans, and they made sure we became multiple dreamers who actualized boring dreams like becoming managers, counterfeiters, computer engineers, sergeants, pimps and college professors.

10   As much as parts of us tried not to be, we were country Black boys with little to no experience with real New York Hip-Hop except Yo! MTV Raps and Rap City or when the Freshfest came to the Coliseum or KRS-ONE came to Jackson State Univeristy. And by Mississippi standards, the seven of us weren't even that country because we were from the city of Jackson. We were disciples of the Holy Trinity of Emcees at the time—KRS, Kane and Rakim—and we passed notes in class arguing who was the best. But as Hip-Hop moved from the boroughs to Compton in late 80's and early 90's, daring West Coast soldiers, West Coast sensibilities and West-of-us-rappers seemed more in line with our reality. While we felt like we were eavesdropping on many of the New York rappers and madly in love with what we heard, Scarface, Ice Cube and MC Ren seemed to conceive us as members of their cipher and they seemed to like us back. One moved through their local culture with West Coast Southern twang, proud to be black and psychologically afflicted, in long cars with windows down, not enclosed subway trains. We found their local fantasy of shooting cops, white folks, busters, and rival gang members with sawed off shotguns more

appealing than metaphorically shooting wack emcees who lacked adequate Afrocentricity or literally shooting some nigga named Don G. mafioso style.

This isn't to say that the deep Southern cupboard was completely bare. The 2 Live Crew guided us into puberty with the finest lyrical pornography and infectious hooks to come out of any state, but we didn't think of them as deeply Southern. And the emcees who we did think of as deeply Southern like MC Thick from New Orleans (who was influenced by NWA's repping of Compton, which was influenced by KRS-ONE's repping of the South Bronx) repped tiny Marrero, Louisiana in his minor regional hit, "Marerro." MC Thick rapped about specific Southern locale, but there was little extremely Southern-sounding about his boasts.

MC Thick was passable to B. Dazzle because he didn't sound or rap deeply Southern. Though we appreciated MC Thick, adored Cube, Scarface and MC Ren, we still reserved our deep love for New York. While the six of us reveled in being Black boys who loved New York Hip-Hop, B. Dazzle, through his lyrics, clothes, sensibility and utterances of "ciphers" reveled in being New York Hip-Hop. And being New York Hip-Hop trumped being a Black Boy who loved New York Hip-Hop in 1992. Common Sense rapped in 1994 about faithfully loving HER. We could and couldn't relate, because while the last thing on earth we admitted to wanting to be was a woman or a gay man, our love interest, nonetheless was a he, a HIM. HE was New York Hip-Hop, and around our way, his Holy local apostle was a gap-toothed brother with skills and chappy lips named B. Dazzle. The booming acoustics of the B-boy bathroom and the B-boy imagination were his mecca and since this was before the advent of player-hation, we couldn't hate. All we could do is not let on that we loved him as much as we did, and try hard as hell to be down.

That was then.

Rewind, or fast forward back to my standing in an Oberlin College bathroom in 1998. While Rich Santiago and D. Jakes were in the A-level of the library trying to find titles for their new Hip-Hop magazine, Rich looked at me and said, "Yo Kie, what about *Tha Cypher*. And I was on some, "Yeah man. That's it." Now, exactly why I thought *Tha Cypher* was it, is where the story gets a bit shameful and confusing. At the time, when I heard "cipher," I didn't think of a tight circle of brothers taking turns boasting, critiquing, and confessing themselves into the world over a beat box. The word *cipher* reminded me solely of B. Dazzle and my faulty obsession. It sounded industrial, sleek, New York, like if the magazine could speak, through gapped fronts, it would say "I am Hip-Hop, son. Y'ah mean? What!"

15   And I guessed that's what Rich and them wanted in a magazine. But honestly, I understood a few hours later that I might have been be too country, too dirty, too much of a Black boy—might have smelled too many boiling chitlins, said "fenda" too many times, got my ass waxed by too many switches off the Chinaberry tree, comfortably ridden in too many pine-combed cabs of pick-up trucks—to thoroughly understand what a cipher was in 92 or 98. When I said "cipher" over and over again in that bathroom with all its jaggedly dangling connotations, it sounded fake, forced, clean. Was our Black boy Central Mississippi space just another cipher? The more I said the word, the more I felt like Puffy's verse in *Benjamins*, Michael Jackson's chin, Vanilla Ice's fade, Soul Train post Don Cornelius and OJ's alibi. I felt like a something, not a somebody, with forced style and suspect substance, a something that would go to all lengths to never acknowledge its dirtiness, a something that created pleasure in being the opposite of a Mississippi Black boy.

Don't get me wrong! In college, like lots of Southern Black boys, I could bring the ever fake and flexible "Word" "N'am sayin'?" or "Yo, son" where need be. But stripped of verbal signifiers of Hip-Hop, I was left kinda naked. I became what I was running from in that Mississippi B-boy bathroom in 1992, the opposite of NYC B-boy. I was an unrefined, red eyed, dirty, Mississippi Black boy looking for both acceptance and something to resist anywhere I could find it. In 1992, it was B. Dazzle and in 1998 at Oberlin, it was *Tha Cypher*. Both times, the "it" I really wanted to accept, resist and love was New York Hip-Hop. But to love and resist New York Hip-Hop, I had to believe Hip-Hop and New York were ends in themselves that had little to do with Black Southern me.

And this is where it's gets tricky because by 1998 the South had begun to accept itself, accept its dirtiness. Or at least it had begun to define itself (which is less meaningful and lasting than acceptance) as "Dirty," a word that was just as resistive and reactive as it was descriptive and offensive. When Goodie Mob asked the question on classic *Soul Food*, "What you niggas know about the Dirty South?" New York Hip-Hop's honest answer should have been, "Yo, not a gotdamn thing, son. And we ain't really trying to know either. What!"

The South, dismissed as culturally slow, meaningless and less hip (hop) than the Northeast was on the verge of bursting through bicoastal ciphers and placing itself smack dab in the middle. And this came about precisely when Southern rappers embraced the dirty offensive part of the "Dirty" South. 1998 was the year that the Calio Projects of New Orleans met Hip-Hop. Everything Master P and No Limit put out went Gold and Platinum. All over the country, people claimed to be "Bout It." UGK, underground Southern glory at its rawest, was about to show Jay Z and the country how to Big Pimp. Outkast was a few years removed from driving a Southernplayeristic Cadillac from Atlanta to space and back with *ATLiens* and they were about to redefine sonic chemistry with *Aquemini*. Far from crunk, but also far from the clean bounce of Kriss Kross, Goodie Mob released a follow up to critically acclaimed *Soul Food* that pronounced they were *Still Standing*.

Inside the library, Djakes and Rich were busy trying to create a magazine that mimicked New York Hip-Hop ciphers, but in the town of Oberlin, Ohio and surrounding cities like Cleveland, Detroit and St. Louis, folk were listening and loving how Southern Black boys were redefining Hip-Hop ciphers and sound. Folk in these other cities watched these Southern artists learn what artists west of the deep South learned ten years earlier and Midwest artists like Bone learned four years earlier: they understood that interrogation and imitation of New York Hip-Hop artistry and aesthetics was fruitless without innovatively applying what one had interrogated and imitated to one's local culture, one's place. This understanding was at the core of the success of NWA, Bone, and eventually Outkast.

In 1998, if one really listened, one could hear thousands of Southern Black boys opting to keep it real (local) by unapologetically ordering the chaos of their country lives through a country lens with little regard to whether it was going to be accepted by real New York Hip-Hop. Blasphemous as it sounds, New York Hip-Hop started to seem boring by early 1998. Tupac and the Dogg Pound had already given us a scathing critique of New York Hip-Hop as being created in tinny vacuums through language and culture that was barely alive. True or not, one got the sense that the lyrics of most New Yorkish emcees, minus Nas, Biggie, Jay Z and Lauryn Hill (and they were borrowing a lot from the artistry of NWA, Ice Cube, Scarface and Snoop) were filled with cloned clauses and corny hooks sustained by pacemakers. There was lots of programmed "Damn, son" in the writing of the bars, but no tight-loose-fleshed-out soul-stirring "Hmmm. Uh Oh!" in the execution of the songs.

New York Hip-Hop, in 98, seemed to be on the verge of needing a newer version of Kane, KRS, and Rakim, or it needed old ass

20

Dr. Kervorkian to put it out of its misery. Dr. K came with a little more melanin than expected, donning a fist full of fried fish, less breath control, a sweaty forehead, a dapper ass Afro and amazing hunger. As great a moment as this was for the South, was there anyone who thought that Southern Hip-Hop would move beyond the heights reached in 1998? How could it?

That was then.

Rewind or fast-forward to 2006. I'm standing in the bathroom of Vassar College, a college 65 miles north of New York City, asking myself, "What am I doing? Do I love Hip-Hop?" During the last year, I sold a Hip-Hop inspired novel called *CITOYEN* and taught two courses on Hip-Hop and Critical Citizenship. Many of my students are New York'bred lovers of Hip-Hop. Yesterday, I noticed that six of my kids had on those white Lance Armstrong–style wrist bands that say "I Love Hip-Hop." Their love for Hip-Hop, interestingly, doesn't know what to do with Southern Hip-Hop. They don't love the South or Southern Hip-Hop, and they're sure that most Southern artists haven't, as Albert Murray said of Black Southern writers in 1989, stylized their Southern worlds into significance.[1] Significance here means lyrically digestable, aesthetically acceptable terms for "real lovers" of New York Hip-Hop. And they're unsure of what it means that three major Hip-Hop publications have Southern artists on their cover (T1 is on *XXL*, the whole Houston crew is on the cover of *The Source* and Lil Wayne is on the cover of *Vibe*).

They're equally unsure how to deal with the fact that the South now sells millions more albums and gets way more spins than any other region in the country. So many of my students, like many other so-called purists, dismiss Southern Hip-Hop as ignorant, catchy, pop, hollow, shameful. Most of my students know, and want me to believe, that in addition to white suburbia's uncritical devouring of the music minus culture and the countless emcees pandering to the Black girl audience in the hallway and corporate America's glossy detailing of Hip-Hop, the music is dying because Three-Six Mafia won an Oscar, Trina shows her booty, repetitive-ass Mike Jones went platinum and Li'l Jon can't rap. But it's not just the so-called purists.

25   "A lot of the music that comes out of the South is kind of simplified," said bastion of Hip-Hop purity, 50 Cent to mtv.com. ". . .But when they don't take the time to make it the highest quality possible, it hurts the actual hip-hop. . ." Lord have mercy. The irony of this statement is manifold. It's not simply that 50—like a

less skilled Snoop—has made millions ingeniously marketing his version of infectious hooks and Southern-sounding simplicity, and is now critiquing the South. Nor is it that 50 is coming out as actually caring about Hip-Hop, something that he, like Hova, often calls "this rap shit" or "the game." What's really strange is that 50 is acknowledging that Southern emcees and Southern sound now have the power to damage the New York Black Boy cipher. The South, to quote Mr. Andre 3000, definitely has something to say and people outside the bathroom, on the other side of the building, outside the building, way over in New York are intensely listening. But what are they hearing? Does contrast create depth everywhere but in the deep South? Outkast, the funkiest, downright most consistently innovative and deft defying, meaningful musical group of my lifetime comes from the deep South. And so does Bow Wow, a young brother who has a nice crib and platinum plaques, but whose artistry is, well, not so deft defying. Depth. 50's notion of the South as simplified is depth-deficient and leads to Outkast being exceptionalized as the jewel of the South, not the jewel of Hip-Hop. Similarly, even on the cover of one of the magazines mentioned earlier, T.I. is called the "Jay Z of the South?" One wonders if any group from New York will ever be referred to as the Outkast of New York? The Luda of the Northeast? The Scarface of Brooklyn?

Hip-Hop, if we really understand 50, is a complex NYC B-boy cipher. Others can enter the cipher by invitation only. The unrefined, simple Southern Black boys pushing their way into the cipher are weakening and diluting its power, authenticity, and essence (unless the Southern B-boys have NYC B-boy aesthetic) by refusing to love only the NYC part. Within Hip-Hop, it's been acceptable to love the NYC part of that NYC Black boy cipher forever, but we could never actively love, accept, or articulate the Black boy part, a part that is not necessarily NYC. This refusal to love and accept has led to a devaluing of the South and really, it has exacerbated the notion that Hip-Hop was an end in and of itself. Hypermasculine Black boys across the country have loved hypermasculine Black boys through Hip-Hop since Sugar Hill took it national in 1979. But we couldn't admit or voice that affection for Black boys because only gay boys, Black girls, strange white folk and others are supposed to love Black boys. And if culture taught us anything, we learned long before Hip-Hop that we must never share the loves of gay boys, Black girls, strange white folks and others unless it's a material love. Every Black boy emcee and Black boy lover of Hip-Hop knows this.

Why else would so many Black boy emcees and appreciators of Hip-Hop, post Common's classic, still define the music and culture as "SHE" or "HER" while Americans like Bill O'Reilly, David Stern, Shelby Steele, John McWhorter, and Anne Coulter hide their hollow love, hate and suspicion of "HE" (Black boys) under the guise of a love, hate and suspicion of Hip-Hop?

Strangely, I understood all of this 14 years ago in that Central Mississippi B-boy bathroom. I also understood that loving HIM wasn't enough. Isolated from caring Black girls in the hallway and a destructive white gaze in my Central Mississippi world, I longed for Hip-Hop and loved the NYC B-boy through the likes of Kane, KRS, Rakim and B. Dazzle. But even in that safe space, in longing for Hip-Hop and loving B. Dazzle, I couldn't fully love myself, Black girls, or the culture that created Black boys, Black girls and Hip-Hop. The raggedy clinking of this essay should not contradict the fact that we Southern Black boys owe NYC B-boys an almost unpayable debt. They gave us means to boast, critique and confess ourselves into a peculiar existence. And really, they let us love them. For that, I will always respect New York ciphers and sounds. But that doesn't negate my fears; it feeds them.

It's taken fourteen years for me to understand why my uttering the word cipher still frightens me. The cipher reminds me of the me who, even as I write this, longs for a cool New York B-boy writerly mask or acceptance from all the New York B-boys who might read this essay. The cipher reminds me of the fear that what I have created, boasted, confessed, and critiqued into existence will never ever be significant without a stylization that accommodates New York B-boy writerly sensibilities. It reminds me that Hip-Hop was definitely fathered in the South Bronx by Kool Herc and years earlier, its spirit was born in Sorrow Songs and Jazz. But my utterance of the cipher neglects the Black Boys, Invisible Men, Native Sons and Blues People who grandfolked Hip-Hop into existence. And just like its grandfolks, while painfully brilliant, innovative and inspiring at times, Hip-Hop hasn't come close to meaningfully loving, accepting, and disagreeing with Black girls; it's kept them in the hallway. It hasn't come close to faithfully disarming and laughing at white gazes. Nor has it even come close to gracefully mediating the schizophrenic relationship with the "nigger" and the "nigga." And it probably never will.

But if it can't do these things, or we can't do these things through Hip-Hop, in proclaiming a love for Hip-Hop, from what are we running? In and out of B-boy ciphers, we're asking a music and a so-called culture to do the real work of the self, the soul and Black Southerners. And we, Black Southerners, through life, love, and labor are the generators and architects of American music, narrative, language, capital, and morality. Take away all those stolen West African girls and boys forced to find an oral culture to express, resist and signify in the South and we have no rich American idiom. Erase Nigger Jim from our literary imagination and we have no American story of conflicted movement, place, and moral conundrum. Remove Black Southern survival of Slavery and Jim Crow and you have no Aunt Jemima, Uncle Tom, John Henry, Martin King, Condeleeza Rice, Colin Powell and Oprah Winfrey hoisted as the moral centers of our fractured American institutions of literature, activism, politics, and television. Eliminate the Great Migration of Southern Black girls and boys, you have no Los Angeles, Chicago, Detroit, Indianapolis, Cleveland, or New York City. Expunge the Sorrow Songs, Gospel and Blues of the deep South and we have no Rock and Roll, R&B or Funk. Even today, if one whitens out the tired determined eyes of the survivors of Hurricane Katrina, we have no contemporary visual that blatantly exposes our leadership as devaluing the lives of Southern Black boys and girls.

When Outkast won the *The Source* "Best New Artist" award 30
over 10 years ago at the Apollo, New York booed. Andre 3000 addressed the booing of "them closed minded folks" with the defiant utterance that "the South got something to say." Up until this very point, I've agreed Andre to death and hoped to God he was right. I now know that he was and he wasn't. The South not only has something to say to New York Hip-Hop, it's been saying it for years, decades, centuries. As Hip-Hop has grown way bigger than New York, New York B-boy ciphers now have to listen. I don't know if what emcees in Mississippi are saying today is monumentally simpler, deeper or wacker than what's coming out of the mouth of New York emcees. Nor do I have any idea what contemporary Central Mississippi sayings and ciphers are like without massive adoration for New York B-boys. I do, 14 years and 4540 words later, know one thing: without the historic and contemporary sayings and doings of Southern Black boys and girls, Hip-Hop would be pallid as the white piece of paper on the next page of this book and as hollow as the center of the next cipher. Shh . . . shh . . . listen. Go ahead and listen hard.

Yeah, you know it, too. And "that's all I got to say" about that. Classic.

Notes

1. Murray, Albert. "Regional Particulars and Universal Statement in Southern Writing." *Callaloo.* 0.38 (1989): 3–6.

Questions for Discussion and Topics for Writing

1. Laymon refers to the word *cipher* many times in his essay. Look up the term. Be sure to look it up in conjunction with hip hop. Note the definition, and then write a paragraph explaining the term's significance to Laymon's essay, especially in his anecdotes from 1992.

2. Laymon's essay is especially relevant to a chapter on mapping rap because of his frequent references to the East Coast and to the South. What tensions does Laymon identify between East Coast hip hop and the southern United States? How does this tension impact his developing identity?

3. How does Laymon divide his essay? What are its central parts? Write a short essay analyzing how the three parts of this paper work. Do the parts interrelate? If so, how?

4. Where, ultimately, does Laymon situate Southern culture with respect to the rest of American culture and civilization? What relationship does he see, culturally, between the South and the rest of the United States? How does this section of the essay relate to key tensions in the essay as a whole?

5. Murray, Albert. "Regional Particulars and Universal Statement in Southern Writing." *Callaloo.* 0.38 (1989): 3–6.

Making Connections

1. A key theme in Chapter Five's readings involves a dialectic between notions of "local" and "global" in both regional and international manifestations of hip hop. Using the Internet or your library's research databases, look into hip hop's appearance and growth in a nontraditional site (nontraditional meaning not the East or West Coasts of the United States). Places to examine would include: African countries, such as Tanzania or South Africa; any European countries (French gangsta rap, especially in the *banlieues* of Paris, for example); or any other nation or region that is interesting to you. Having located sources, pay particular attention to that country's or region's articulation of its relationship to American hip hop. Is American hip hop a hegemonic force in such areas? Or is this relationship more complex, more of a local appropriation of the global phenomenon?

2. Another crucial thread running through this chapter's readings has to do with the relationship between America's hip hop coasts: East, West, and "Third" (America's Gulf region). Research the regional dimensions of American hip hop. You might begin by focusing on one region such as the Third Coast, or southern hip hop (sometimes called the Dirty South). Having located sources on the Dirty South, for example, what do you discover about how this southern manifestation of hip hop culture constitutes itself differently from other regions? How does southern hip hop articulate its differences? How do such self-descriptions point to tensions between regions, be they artistic or political? You might particularly look at the highly creative and productive hip hop scene in Houston and compare it to the equally rich offerings in the Bay area of California (Oakland and San Franciso).

3. One way of imagining hip hop is that it creates unofficial "geographies." In other words, hip hop has a way of creating and mapping spaces that transgress or transcend official political demarcations (such as boundaries between cities and states). A good example of this is the way early hip hop artists set up territories within the Bronx, creating unofficial artistic spheres of influence within officially constituted spaces. Another such unofficial mapping involves hip hop's embrace of prison populations. As part of a project investigating hip hop's geographies, undertake some research into hip hop's connection to prisons. How does hip hop imagine its relationship to prison and to incarcerated populations? Do you see signs of an extended community? Is prison an extension of the 'hood? How does this change our idea of place or redefine our idea of community?

4. When one considers the related concepts of hip hop and place, one is often drawn to the notion of origins. For example, many people call the Bronx the birthplace of hip hop. As part of a project looking into the idea of geography and cultural origins, examine the roots of hip hop in New York in the late 1970s and compare them to the birth of gangsta rap in the late 1980s (and to gangsta rap's explosive growth in the early 1990s). Do you see any parallels in the social conditions of New York and Los Angeles? How did hip hop artists respond differently to the conditions they found in their respective regions?

CREDITS

Crenshaw, Kimberle, "Beyond Racism and Misogyny: Black Feminism and 2 Live Crew." From *Boston Review* 16, No. 6 (1991): 6--33. Reprinted by permission of the author.

Dyson, Michael Eric, "Gangsta Rap and American Culture," From *Between God and Gangsta Rap: Bearing Witness to Black Culture* by Michael Eric Dyson. Copyright © 1996 by Michael Eric Dyson. Reproduced with permission of Oxford University Press.

Flores, Juan, "Puerto Rican and Proud, Boyee!: Rap, Roots, and Amnesia," From *Microphone Fiends: Youth Music and Youth Culture*, edited by Andrew Ross and Tricia Rose, New York: Routledge Press, pp. 89–98. Copyright © 1994 by Routledge Publishing Inc. Used by permission of Routledge Publishing Inc. via Copyright Clearance Center.

Forman, Murray, "'Represent': Race, Space, and Place in Rap Music." From *Popular Music*, (2000), 19:65–90. Reprinted with permission of Cambridge University Press.

Frere-Jones, Sasha, "Ghost's World," From *The New Yorker*, March 20, 2006. Used by permission of the author.

Grant, Elizabeth, "Gangsta Rap, the War on Drugs, and the Location of African-American Identity in Los Angeles 1988–92," From *European Journal of American Culture*, April 2002 (vol. 21, issue 1), pp. 4–15. Used by permission of the author and The European Journal of American Culture.

hooks, bell, "Gangsta Culture," From *We Real Cool: Black Men and Masculinity* by bell hooks. Copyright © 2004 by Gloria Watkins. Reproduced with permission of Routledge Publishing, Inc. via Copyright Clearance Center.